W9-DHH-981

# RUNNING
# YOUR OWN SHOW

# Wiley Series on Small Business Management
### Rick Stephan Hayes, Editor

# RUNNING YOUR OWN SHOW

## Mastering the Basics of Small Business

**Richard T. Curtin**

A Ronald Press Publication
**JOHN WILEY & SONS**
New York   Chichester   Brisbane   Toronto   Singapore

Copyright © 1982 by John Wiley & Sons, Inc.

All rights reserved. Published simultaneously in Canada.

Reproduction or translation of any part of this work
beyond that permitted by Sections 107 or 108 of the
1976 United States Copyright Act without the permission
of the copyright owner is unlawful. Requests for
permission or further information should be addressed to
the Permissions Department, John Wiley & Sons, Inc.

This publication is designed to provide accurate and
authoritative information in regard to the subject
matter covered. It is sold with the understanding that
the publisher is not engaged in rendering legal, accounting,
or other professional service. If legal advice or other
expert assistance is required, the services of a competent
professional person should be sought. *From a Declaration
of Principles jointly adopted by a Committee of the
American Bar Association and a Committee of Publishers.*

*Library of Congress Cataloging in Publication Data:*

Curtin, Richard T., 1941-
  Running your own show.

  (Wiley series on small business management,
ISSN 0271-6054)
  "A Ronald Press publication."
  Includes index.
  1. Small business—Management. 2. Self-
employed.  I. Title.  II. Series.

HD62.7.C87      658'.022      81-14746
ISBN 0-471-86074-3          AACR2

Printed in the United States of America

10  9  8  7  6  5  4  3  2  1

# PREFACE

Anyone can be an employee. There are thousands of jobs offered daily. But for many, it is not enough to be an employee. They want more from their efforts than a salary.

There are many rewards for those who act out their dreams and eventually become owners of their own businesses. There is status from the beginning, there is usually more money, and there is definitely more freedom.

But the rewards do not come all at once. There may be less money in the beginning, and it may take weeks or months before the money is as plentiful as earned while being an employee. There is freedom, but if this freedom is abused, it means the failure of the business. It will be necessary to work harder in your own business than it was as someone's employee, and this necessity for hard work means that the new freedom is illusory, at least in the beginning.

If you focus only on the rewards, you will likely become discouraged by reality. But, if you begin your adventure with an awareness of the problems, with the eventual rewards in perspective, you will not regret becoming a businessperson.

RICHARD T. CURTIN

*November 1981*

# CONTENTS

# RUNNING
# YOUR OWN SHOW

# 1

# NOT AN EASY DECISION

## WHY DO THIS?

Every year thousands of people quit their jobs and go into business for themselves. There are over 10 million sole proprietorships, one million partnerships, and almost 2 million corporations in the United States. Most of these businesses began with someone tossing and turning nights; examining alternatives until they could no longer concentrate on anything else; seeking advise and support from friends and relatives; and finally, filled with self-doubt, taking the big step. Someone planning on making the same move should start by examining what they hope to accomplish—what motivates them.

Many people who leave a secure job and invest their life's savings in a business do so without having a clear idea why they're doing it. Confusion as to the motivation can cause the wrong business decisions to be made and increase the chance of failure in an already high-risk undertaking.

Take Freddy's experience: When Freddy Fastrack, a bachelor, quit his job at the bank, he had been working 37½ hours per week. Since he wasn't closely supervised, he often took two hours for lunch, and if things weren't too busy at his desk he would surreptitiously study the stock market listings in the Wall Street Journal instead of asking for more work. Freddy thought of himself as a good employee, but he did chafe at the impersonality and the discipline (having to be at work by 8:30 A.M., wearing a tie, needing permission to leave early) and felt that a person of his talents was undoubtedly underpaid and a real money-maker for his employer. He quit his job and bought a car wash, telling his friends he was tired of the low pay and he was going to make more money.

To an outsider, Freddy hasn't improved his status by leaving the bank.

1

He has to work much harder to pay his bills. The car wash he bought requires that he show up every morning at 5:30 A.M. to be ready for the 6:00 rush. He's often at the car wash until 8:00 in the evening. The first six months Freddy was at the car wash seven days a week, but now his helper covers Monday, the slow day, so Freddy can have a six-day week. Instead of a weekly take home check of $187.50 plus fringe benefits, Freddy's average profit is $300 a week out of which he makes payments on the money he borrowed to buy the business, his social security taxes, estimated taxes in lieu of withholding taxes, workman's compensation insurance premiums, unemployment insurance premiums, and health, disability, and life insurance premiums, leaving between $150 and $160 to live on. Freddy has studied the car wash business enough to know that, while his income will increase, it will not increase at a dramatic pace and that he would have made more money with less effort if he had stayed at the bank.

Still, Freddy's a happy man and wouldn't go back to the bank even if they doubled his salary. Freddy thought he left the bank only to make more money, but he's found that other things are more important to him—the freedom to dress and act as he pleases, to set his own hours (longer or not), and the status of owning his own business are what keep Freddy happy.

What motivates you? Do you want the freedom to come and go during the day? The right to decide what you'll do each day? The power to tell a prospective customer that you don't want his business? The right to discharge a subordinate without asking permission? The excitement of "doing your own thing"? Something to relieve boredom and to add zest to your life? The pleasure of managing all the fruits of your efforts? The satisfaction of telling other people what to do—of being the boss? The status of owning the company?

The most common error people make when they go into business is to assume that they want to make a lot of money and that they are prepared to do whatever is necessary to achieve that goal. Not so. Very few people are motivated entirely by money.

How about you? Most people would like to have more money, but few are willing to do what is necessary to acquire it. If you are unsure how important money is to you, examine what you do with the money you now have. The only way to accumulate money so it can work for you is to spend less than you earn. Do you save regularly? Do you spend most of your money on necessities and save the rest, or do you spend all you earn? If you haven't felt strongly enough about money in the past to save regularly, it is unlikely that you can use money to keep yourself motivated to build a business of your own.

Sometimes people hope to solve personal problems by buying a business and changing careers. No one I know of has ever solved personal problems this way. Sometimes a change will mask the problems, causing them to reappear in a different form. Darrel Dum had been fighting with his wife when he purchased the photography studio, but exhaustion from the long hours and the excitement of the new endeavor resulted in a halt to their fighting for a few months. When the initial excitement wore off, the problems reappeared, but instead of fighting over Darrel's temper or his refusal to go out evenings, they fought over the long hours he spent working or the fact that he always seemed preoccupied when he was home. Darrel would have been better advised to resolve his marital problems before becoming a businessman.

Some problems and frustrations may travel with you as long as you have to work to eat. If you are quitting your job because of co-workers who are frustrating to work with, or hours that are too rigid, or work that is too demanding, you may find these same problems in your own business.

It is important to develop a realistic attitude toward what becoming a businessman means. It can give you more freedom, more money, and more status. It can also mean more work, more tension, more frustration, and more risks.


## DESPERATION

Necessity may be the mother of invention, but desperation is rarely the father of sound business decisions. If you turn to self-employment because you are out of work and cannot find a job, you are extremely vulnerable. You cannot help but believe things will get better, as they ultimately will, but may often overlook that things can get worse before they get better.

When Ira was laid off at the auto plant due to the recession, he looked at vending machines. "Only $13,000 and you'll never have to worry about a job again." said the vending machine salesman. "You buy the machines, place them around town, and watch the money pour in as ten cent candy is sold for twenty-five cents."

This sounds like an easy business. Vending machines can be lucrative. Several people have made a lot of money from vending machines. But, and it's a big "but," you have to have control of good locations to make money. There is a lot of competition for these good locations and usually they are gone before a newcomer hears about them. On the positive side, this is a growing business and as traffic patterns are always changing,

there is always room for one more businessperson to become successful.

This necessity of finding something can be a strong motivator and can
be used to help overcome obstacles that would stop a less committed
person.

Everyone who met Jim Mull came away convinced that they had just
met the least competent and most likely to fail man who existed. When
he came into my office to inquire if there was any legal way to prevent
the school board from firing him for incompetence, I was stunned by the
wrongness of everything he did.

Jim had been teaching for years, yet was considered to be a terrible
teacher. He never would have been hired except for a personal favor
owed to his wife by the superintendant. On several occasions Jim had
been asked to resign but he always refused. His wife had left him saying,
"It's nothing personal, but I've just gotten sick of you. You're a jerk, a
creep." Jim's wife wanted nothing from the marriage, but Jim made such
a fool of himself, alternately begging her not to leave and then following
her, lurking outside her home. She finally lost her patience, and with it
any feeling of guilt she had and left. She took everything Jim owned.
After the divorce was final Jim still made a fool of himself. At least once
he broke into her home to "borrow" some items. The police were called
and Jim confessed to breaking and entering.

It was the breaking and entering that cost Jim his job. The school
board had given up attempting to prove incompetence to a civil service
board, but they had no difficulty proving Jim had committed a crime.

After he was fired, Jim came to see me about buying a business. The
problem was he had no skill, no references, no friends, no family, no
contacts, and on top of it he made a bad first impression.

Jim ended up selling real estate. He wasn't very good, but there was a
boom in real estate and a third-rate sales company hired him because he
was available.

Jim did reasonably well. He lost a lot of sales, but he was so desperate
to succeed at something, he worked harder than anyone else at the company. Jim didn't learn very quickly, but over a period of several years he
learned enough to start buying some of the buildings that his company
listed. Because of inflation Jim eventually accumulated enough equity in
his real estate to devote full time to his investments. Jim had never been
successful in anything before, but desperation made him successful in
the end.

Desperation can provide strong motivation and enable a person to
make the most of opportunities, but it cannot create skill or opportunities.
If you are in desperate straits, exploit this strong motivation, but be sure
not to confuse desire with reality.

## INDECISION

Hundreds of people have approached me to discuss their plans for going into business. Most of them are plagued by indecision. Despite my strong encouragement and that of their friends and relatives, and despite their statements such as, "I know I should do it," "I'm not getting any younger," "I'll regret not making the move later if I don't do it now," and "I've been talking about this for years and it looks like now is better than most times," they have difficulty making the decision. Although each person's circumstances and desires are different, most aspiring entrepreneurs have difficulty overcoming one of the following barriers—the "premature burnout," the "free-lunch syndrome," and disguised fear.

The premature burnout comes from overplanning. Because the element of risk inherent in business is foreign to many wage earners, they plan and replan and plan again in a futile effort to remove all risk. Since the element of risk cannot be removed from business, the planning never ends. Will your customers like the wooden chairs you manufacture? Would they like them better if you changed the design? Would they buy more if your sign were bigger? Instead of a bigger sign should you spend the money on advertising? Or maybe tables would be a better product than chairs? Or maybe you should be buying an auto body shop instead? The questions and problems can be endless. It is possible to become fatigued and discouraged from the seemingly endless questions with no "right" answers.

No one wants to fail. It is important to evaluate all of the potential problems and prepare for them. But, if you are too cautious, dwell incessantly on what could go wrong, or keep searching for the "sure thing," you will never become a businessperson.

Ronald Roadblock has spent six years trying to develop the ultimate toy. He spends virtually every evening and most weekends in his garage planning amd making models. He is an incessant talker about how he is going to quit his job at the garage and start a toy company. His models look like good toys and the neighborhood children thoroughly enjoy them.

What started as an exciting topic of conversation for Roadblock's friends and family has grown dull—after six years it is hard to take Roadblock seriously. What Roadblock has really done is take all of the energy that should have been directed toward starting his business and expended it in overplanning. He has premature burnout.

Another common problem arises from the belief that it is possible to get something for nothing—the "free-lunch syndrome." All of us have heard thousands of times that there is no such such thing as a free lunch, but sometimes we forget. Fortunately, Freddy remembered this.

When Freddy Fastrack first discussed leaving the bank with his wife, she said, "Gee, Freddy, you've got a very good job at the bank. What happens if you start the business and fail? Will you be able to get another job paying the same salary?"

Since Freddy was familiar with the free-lunch syndrome, his response was, "Abigail, nobody receives free lunches in this life. The bank is paying me what I'm worth. If I wasn't worth every penny, they would either fire me or force me to quit. If I'm worth what they're paying me today, doesn't it stand to reason that I'll be worth at least as much tomorrow? If my business fails, I'll go back to work for a salary, and I should be able to earn about what I earn now."

There are other barriers that prevent would-be entrepreneurs from taking the first big step. Some seem gripped by chronic indecision, unable to ever make a commitment. Notwithstanding numerous declarations that they want to become businesspeople, they seem gripped by some fear that they are unable to articulate or cope with which prevents them from taking any action. If they could identify the fear they could deal with it intelligently, but something keeps it disguised just beyond the horizons of their awareness.

Gary Gumba has been a friend of mine for years. Gumba is a successful stock broker for one of the larger brokerage houses. He has watched hundreds of people quit their jobs and start their own businesses. Gumba has talked to many of these entrepreneurs about the possibility of selling stock in their business to the investing public, and when the market is up, many of them do. Gumba has witnessed the birth of many millionaires.

Gumba is making as much money as he needs to live comfortably, but is intrigued by the possibility of starting a business and excited about how much money could be made by selling stock in this business to his customers. For years he has been saying that when the "right" opportunity comes along he is going to take the step. Gumba calls me every few weeks to solicit my opinion on his latest venture. The first time he called—I remember it well because I thought it was a fantastic opportunity—a mutual friend was trying to give him a large restaurant at a busy intersection. Our mutual friend, Larry Lump, owned a shopping center. In Lump's center was a restaurant that was operated rather carelessly by an alcoholic who had a personality problem. Lump evicted the owner from the space for nonpayment of rent, and after the dust settled, Lump was left with some restaurant fixtures, inventory, a sign, and a reputation for good food but erratic hours and mediocre service. Lump called Gumba and said, "I'm a landlord. I learned a long time ago that I am not a merchant. I don't want to be a merchant. I have been getting $2.50 a foot per year for this space. If you will take over this restaurant and operate it,

I'll give you the first two months rent free. The previous owner left so I don't think you will have to purchase anything except some fresh food and some silverware. If it doesn't work out, you can just walk out—you won't owe me a cent."

Gumba debated this opportunity for weeks finally declining. The restaurant subsequently became very successful.

This was followed by the carpet distribution business that wasn't "enough of a sure thing," the lumber yard that was "a little too far away from my house," the small bank that "came at a bad time, it would have strapped me a little too much financially," and the cosmetics company that was "too cyclical."

Gumba is now 48-years old and making over $60,000 a year in his present job. He still talks about starting his own business, but I think he is too settled and comfortable to make any move. Ten years ago he would have been dynamite. Maybe if he had made the move ten years ago he wouldn't be drinking so much today and he might have the same wife.

There are many reasons why people like Gumba talk a good battle but never make the move. Part of it is excessive caution. Gumba never accepted the fact that to make the move he had to take the risk. He was convinced that around the corner was a "sure thing." I also think Gumba was a little greedy. On those days when he seemed prepared to take a risk, he seemed to be looking for too much reward; he was willing to take a risk only if he stood a good chance of making a lot of money with little effort.

It's a hard path to walk. You must be cautious enough so you don't attempt the impossible and reasonable enough so you don't expect the moon. Constantly in touch with reality, you must nevertheless be excited about the possibilities and optimistic about the future.

## THERE ARE FINANCIAL RISKS

What happens if you take the risk and fail? After all, half or more of all new business ventures do fail. If your business is one that fails, you could lose your investment, be personally responsible for the business debts, find yourself embroiled in litigation for years after the failure, and have government investigators pounding on your door for explanations or to impose penalties after the failure.

If a business fails, the owner may lose more than what he invested in the business. Payment for the equipment and supplies that were ordered for the business may be a personal obligation which you have to satisfy or be sued.

When you quit your job at the post office to start a business on Uncle

Fred's farm, the plan may be to clear the North 40 and sell the timber to builders for shakes and siding. This business requires no capital so you feel there is little to lose, other than your time. But we live in a credit-based society and sales people are highly skilled at presenting the risks of credit purchases in such a manner that they seem nonexistent.

When you start clearing the North 40, you may begin to wish you owned some commercial grade cutting equipment instead of equipment built to be used in a home hobby shop. When the lumber mill equipment salesman walks through the apple orchard and across the pasture to discuss his merchandise with you, he might be arriving just in time to make a sale.

"You know," he might say, "the equipment I'm taking out of the paper mill would cost over $80,000 new. It's in excellent condition. If I would rent a truck and take it to the equipment auction in Beaver County next month, I could sell it for $20,000 or more. The problem is, the mill wants their new equipment installed right away and I don't have any place to store their old equipment. My company gave the mill $15,000 credit for trading in the old equipment—that's its wholesale value. I'll let you have it for just what we paid. Since this is below its retail value, there is no way you can lose. If you will just sign here, I'll have it delivered tomorrow and your first payment isn't due. . . . "

You may have made a good buy and be on your way toward becoming a big time lumber man. But if you decide to go back to your old job, you may have trouble selling the equipment. Meanwhile, the payments for the equipment continue.

Business failure may also mean things that were promised will never be done, resulting in lawsuits against you for failure to perform your obligations. It is not necessary that you have a written contract to have this kind of legal problem.

When Uncle Fred heard you were going to clear his North 40 he was glad to let you do it at no cost because he wanted the land cleared. Once the land is cleared it can be used for pasture and Uncle Fred can rent it to a neighboring farmer. As soon as you started work clearing the land, Uncle Fred signed a lease with his neighbor agreeing that the neighbor could use the North 40 for pasture the next year. Now you want to get out of the business and less than one-half of the North 40 has been cleared. Uncle Fred's contract requires that the entire North 40 be cleared. If the neighbor who signed the contract with Uncle Fred insists on his legal rights, you may have a legal obligation to Fred and to the neighbor to pay the cost of finishing the clearance of the North 40.

As you attempt to extract yourself from a failed business, you may find that some disputes which would have been mere nuisances if the business had succeeded are substantial burdens when piled upon your other losses. When you didn't deliver those shakes ordered from your ill-fated timber venture by Roscoe the builder, the reason may have been because Roscoe didn't pay you for the first two shipments he received (perhaps precipitating the failure of your business). After you close your business, you may be surprised to hear that some of Roscoe's creditors are claiming that the only reason Roscoe had to file bankruptcy was because your shakes were not delivered on time (or were defective or were the wrong type of wood, etc.). You know their position is absurd, and you assume that they know their position is very weak. But both of you know that it's frequently cheaper for you to pay off than to get embroiled in years of litigation.

There are other types of problems to consider. The laws of liability are such that there may be duties and obligations imposed on you that are surprising and burdensome. Remember when Clarence Gork, Uncle Fred's next-door neighbor, talked you into selling him some of your shakes at half price? You knew you were going out of business and decided to take whatever you could get. What you didn't realize is that Gork isn't the most intelligent man in Beaver County and he used the wooden shakes (intended for roofs) for flooring his patio. Three years after Gork bought the shakes, they had become so rotten from resting against the ground that Gork's Aunt Gretta, while walking on the patio with 3-inch high heels, punctured one of the shakes, fell, and broke her ankle. Her lawyer sues Gork and he sues you. As your lawyer explains to you, the issues are: were the shakes defective, and were you negligent in not explaining to Gork that wooden shakes will rot if placed on the ground. If the answer to either questions is yes, you may owe a lot of money.

There are also various tax and governmental regulations to contend with. These laws have become so complicated that even the best intentioned are often in violation of the governmental dictates. In one test almost 40 percent of the advice given by an Internal Revenue information office was incorrect. Months after you have forgotten about your ill-fated venture, you may find federal and state inspectors beating on your door. They may have heard that you hired three college kids for two afternoons to help you move some trees. Even though you paid the kids out of your pocket and the amount of money involved was less than $200, you have committed various illegal acts. You did not withhold for state income tax purposes. You did not withhold for federal income tax purposes. You did not pay the employees' or the employer's portion of the appropriate unemployment insurance taxes (although your lawyer tells you there may be an exemption) and you did not buy any workmen's compensation insurance. You could count your blessings that the state and federal minimum wage people did not ask for an accounting and that no OSHA inspector has shown up.

When counting the various ways you can suffer loss by being involved with a failing business, don't forget to account for any loss of income that you would be otherwise earning. If you're earning $1000 a month in your present job, and if you earn nothing from your business venture, you must add $1000 a month to the tally of losses.

This is a pretty dismal list of what can go wrong. The fact is that few businesses have this many problems and there are ways to reduce the financial risk so that the impact of the problems described is minimal. Nevertheless, there will always be some risk.

Financial problems can be solved with money. The solutions to personal problems that develop when you become a businessperson, however, may not be so easy to find.

## PERSONAL RISKS, TOO

Changing from a wage earner to a businessperson will disrupt many aspects of your personal life. You will find your social activities disrupted, there will not be enough time for family and friends, preoccupation with business will further damage your relationships with others, and your health may suffer.

At the present time you have some established patterns to your life. You see your wife (or husband or roommate) for breakfast. You finish work between 4:00 and 5:00 P.M. most nights so you have supper at home every night, except for those nights when you have PTA or the bowling league or the VFW meetings. You usher at the local church and have gotten into the habit of working in the yard every Saturday morning where you enjoy exchanging pleasantries with the neighbors. When you go into business for yourself, this will change.

When you buy that hardware store, there will be daily crises. Some days you will work until midnight to prepare for the next day's sales. When the cashier is sick the same day your star salesman has taken the day off to rest up from a heavy drinking weekend, you will come home so tired from doing three people's jobs you will have no interest in dining with your family or hearing how their day was. When you do take your oldest daughter out for a Sunday afternoon private lunch your mind seems to wander, partly because of fatigue and partly because of your accountant's notice that you have underestimated your tax obligations by $7000.

"Nonsense," you might say. "My next door neighbor, Clyde Firk, has owned a motel for years, and he takes every weekend off, has more time to go to lodge meetings than I do, and appears to be a perfect father."

There is no disputing that the life of a person who owns a business is often more flexible and rewarding than that of a wage earner, but don't assume too much from how you view others.

"Sure," Claudia Firk might tell you if asked, "it seems like the ideal life now, but keep in mind I'm Clyde's second wife. He owned that motel for 12 years before he moved in next door to you. During those 12 years both Clyde and his first wife worked 7 days a week, 14 hours a day, changing beds, vacuuming, renting motel units, cooking in the coffee shop, and generally doing everything that had to be done. He's now receiving the benefits of those early years, but the price was very high. Clyde and I have talked about the price he paid and he's not sure he would do it again."

For most of us, owning your own business means long hours and the sacrifice of many vacations, weekends, holidays, and other special occasions to business. This can place quite a strain on your family. Those who don't own a successful business cannot comprehend why you devote so much time to yours. Only if you understand your own motives will you be able to stand a chance of coping successfully with these stresses. If your daughter accuses you of not loving her because you work every weekend, telling her, "I work hard so I can provide you with the things I never had," doesn't cut the mustard.

The father who understands his own motives will have a happier home life when he tells his daughter, "When I worked as assistant manager at the Holiday Inn I had regular hours and a steady paycheck, but I just wasn't happy. I liked my boss but I did not enjoy having to report to him what I was doing every minute of every day. I also had my own ideas about how the hotel could be improved. After years of being frustrated and coming home and telling your mother that I didn't like my job and I did not look forward to going to work, we decided that matters were not going to improve by themselves. That's when we cashed in the life insurance policies, sold our house, and put everything we had into the motel. We know it has been rough on you and I would have preferred to wait a few years before making the step, but if I had waited, I am afraid I wouldn't have had the energy to do it. Just like you're planning on working hard for four years in college to put you on the right track, we are planning on working very hard for a few years to get on a path that is right for me. I'm not doing it for the money or to impress anyone. I'm doing it because it's the only way I can enjoy getting up each morning."

These types of personal problems sound simple and to a rested mind they are not difficult to solve. But the tension that comes from risking everything you own on the success of your business, coupled with the excitement and challenge of running your own business, often create a preoccupation with your business worries that fills each day.

Preoccupation with your business may make it difficult to enjoy non-business endeavors and can magnify and distort personal problems. For example, you and your spouse may now enjoy a regular bridge night with your next door neighbors. When you are preoccupied with the effects of a strike and don't think to call until 7:00 to cancel the 7:00 game, a certain amount of tension on the home front is created. If you are perceptive and attentive to the effects of your business on your family and others, this tension might disappear. If you are too preoccupied with your own problems, your comments to your wife might sound like, "Listen, dear, don't bother me with things like that; I've got more important things on my mind." Such blindness to the problems of others may light the fuse leading to the destruction of marriages, friendships, or other relationships—a heavier price than most are willing to pay.

Don't forget what having your own business can do to your health. If you sleep less, your body is less able to cope with infections and diseases. If you are living with constant tension, your stomach always in knots, then you may find yourself suffering from tension headaches, developing an ulcer, and, according to some physicians, creating the climate for a heart attack. Doctors Friedman and Rosenman wrote an excellent book called *Type A Behavior and Your Heart.* Unfortunately, the person they profiled is also a likely candidate to start his own business and be successful at it.

The book describes the heart attack candidate as the compulsive over-achiever, one who is constantly setting his own deadlines ahead of what circumstances might require. The person who is subject to this constant pressure to achieve within rigid time frames should be compared to the less likely candidate for premature death who tends to judge his performance against more realistic goals.

Another disturbing finding set forth in the book is the authors' opinion that while the compulsive overachiever may be very successful in his early years, when volume of work is important, this type of personality often develops decision-making habits that result in failures in later life. The person who is always trying to do more than he can comfortably finish often develops decision-making shortcuts, categorizing problems as they are presented and then reacting with stereotyped responses. This use of stereotyped responses to similar problems is an aid if the goal is to make a lot of decisions, but the habit is hard to break if the goal changes to one of making a smaller number of decisions with a higher accuracy rate. The manager for a car dealership may make hundreds of decisions a day and is considered successful if he makes the "right" or "best" decision 70 percent of the time. The owner of the dealership needs a higher accuracy rate when deciding whether to expand, how to respond to union demands, and how to deal with a cash shortage.

An insidious health problem of hard working businesspeople is self-abuse; overwork tends to lead to overindulgence. Too little time for regular meals leads to periodic overeating; too much tension leads to too much alcohol; too little sleep leads to too much coffee. Only in mathematics do two negatives make a positive; in the real world two negatives increase the likelihood of physical a well as business failure. Remember that old merchant's proverb, "Death is nature's way of telling you to slow down."

Awareness of the possible personal problems can help you plan how to avoid them. Be prepared to severely limit your nonwork activities. Enlist the support of your family by explaining to them that you will be busy and preoccupied, but that it won't last forever. Make a conscious effort to leave your work problems at work so you can give your full attention to your friends and family when you are with them. Don't insist that the business come first for them just because it comes first for you.

## LARGE REWARDS

### Taking Charge of Your Life

The decision to go into business is a decision to take charge of your life—to assume more responsibility for what happens to you. You will lose all of your excuses ("I was passed over for a promotion because the boss wanted to promote her nephew"), but you will gain the opportunity to receive all the credit for and the benefits of your labor.

Be positive. Assume that things do go well for you. Thousands of wage earners become successful businesspeople every year.

Carl Camp has taken charge of his life and wouldn't trade places with anybody. Carl has owned a camera store down the street from the fire station for seven years now. He's able to decide what hours he works and what his job is while working. He can't retire, but Carl has never pretended to be wealthy—he claims only to be an independent businessman. He decided long ago that what he really wanted to do was show people cameras and persuade them to buy high-quality camera equipment. Everything else in the store is done by people Carl employs—he does very little ordering, advertising, bookkeeping, cleaning, and so on. Once in a while an employee leaves and Carl must change his routine, but most of the time Carl can devote his full attention to doing what he likes best. He has also been able to reduce his schedule to a 35-hour work week by hiring a second salesman on a part-time basis.

As Carl says, "I have to enjoy what I'm doing. If I don't, who can I blame? The decision of how hard to work and what to do while working is entirely my own."

Last year Carl's wife fell in love with a particular type of carpet. She told Carl that she wanted that carpet more than anything else. She realized $32 a yard was expensive, but told Carl if she could carpet the bedrooms, living room, dining room, and amusement room, she would wake up happy every day for the next five years. Carl thought that sounded like a good idea, but the price tag of $7300 was more than he could afford. Fortunately, Carl owned his own business. Carl hired his wife as a cashier when an employee unexpectedly left town, and he worked a double shift for a few months, saving the cost of putting on extra help for the Christmas season. Carl was able to increase his income in a manner that very few wage earners have available to them.

Having control over how much money you earn as a businessperson is one big advantage over being a wage earner. An equally large advantage is the freedom to "change jobs." When you were hired to sell furniture, you were hired because the boss was short one furniture salesman. If after one month you decide that you would prefer to buy furniture, work in the office, or be the decorator who designs the new displays, your boss may not cooperate—he only needs a furniture salesman, plus he knows you can sell furniture; he doesn't know if you are competent to do anything else. Your boss, however, can change his duties any time he wants. In fact, your boss may well have started selling furniture himself, and has decided he'd rather spend his time writing advertising copy, approving advertising campaigns, and overseeing the constant reshuffling of displays in the store. Why not? It's his store.

### Building Something of Value

The only thing an employee receives from the business is a salary and a few fringe benefits. The owner of the business usually makes more money, benefits as the value of the business increases from satisfied customers and inflation, and has a choice of hours and duties.

Sally is a waitress in a little town in Montana. She is paid $4 an hour, can have meals at no expense and divides all tips equally with kitchen help. She is supposed to be done with work at 6:00 but last night a big party stayed until 8:30 and she worked overtime. She wasn't very happy about working the extra time. Although Sally earned $13, she missed a party that she was looking forward to. Big Freeda, the owner of the restaurant, also stayed until 8:30 to accommodate the large party. Unlike Sally, Freeda was overjoyed. This was the first time the Ladies' Auxiliary to the Dragon Men's Honor Assembly had come to her café for their monthly meeting. Because things went well, they will probably come back every month, and in addition, now that they know her café, some of them will become regulars for lunch. Freeda saw the extra 2½ hours as a small price to pay for the possibility of increasing her annual volume by several thousand dollars a year.

Freeda bought the café because she was tired of working for a salary—she wanted to receive the full benefit of her labors. She doesn't regret missing dinner or a party because it is by her choice and for her benefit. After several years Freeda will have several thousand dollars in the bank, a restaurant that is fully paid for, a permanent job, and a source of income from a job she can't be fired from. While Freeda is accumulating money and building her business, Sally is working almost as hard but accumulating only bunions.

Look realistically at your future. Where are you now? How does this future compare with what you expect out of life? The chances are you will not achieve what you want without taking some risks. You may never be rich or famous or improve your lot in life if you buy a business, but, on the other hand, you might. What are your alternatives? Are you in a position to go back to school and become a physician or engineer? Do you have the good judgment and skill to become a commodities trader and pyramid your fortune by taking risks with borrowed money? Can you fulfill your destiny by working harder at your present job? For most, becoming a businessperson is the best and most available alternative.

## YOU CAN DO IT

Remember what every coach tells his team before the big game. To win you have to want to win and be willing to make the effort required to accomplish it. Anybody can be a loser; no effort at all is required. As Henry Ford said, "If you don't think you can do something, you can't."

Business is as competitive as a sporting contest, and if you want to be successful, you're going to have to work at it. Not being fired from a job doesn't take very much effort. More effort is required to get steady raises and promotions. Still more effort is required if you work for yourself. If you are a self-starter and can push yourself, your chances of success are greatly enhanced.

Beginning businesspeople are often tempted to quit. Although budding entrepreneurs rarely believe it, the most difficult task they may face each day is getting out of bed and showing up for another day of big problems and little rewards. Yesterday you had no business, today your only salesman quit and your bank refused to extend your loan, and tomorrow you'll have to spend all day interviewing new salesmen even though you have the flu. While you're doing this, Fred, who took your old job at the bottle factory, got a big promotion, and is vacationing in Greece. It will be tempting to say, "Who needs this," and apply for your old job.

It takes a strong commitment, a lot of drive, and no small measure of self-confidence to successfully make the transition from wage earner to capitalist, but if you earnestly want to make the necessary emotional and physical investment, you can do it. There is no substitute for positive thinking. Dozens of books have been written hammering home the simple formula, if you want to do something and you honestly believe you can do it, you will be successful.

# 2

# PLANNING THE MOVE

## BUYING PREFERRED TO STARTING

Do you want to start your own business, building something out of nothing, or does it make better sense to start with what someone else has begun? In almost all cases it is better to buy an existing business than to start from scratch, because the risks are less and the investment is smaller.

### Customers

If you don't have customers, success is impossible. There's a new shopping center in the town where I live. It's a large shopping center and in order to promote the grand opening, several famous television performers were brought to town. There were commercials on all the TV stations, billboard advertising, and extensive radio advertising for months before the official opening. Six months after they opened, they were still only two-thirds full—they had planned for 97 retail stores in the complex and they had rented space to only 62. There wasn't any need for a shopping center of that size in that part of town. No amount of advertising could create a need where none existed.

How do you know if someone wants what you have to sell? Assuming there are customers, how do you find them? When you find them, how do you talk them into trying you? Once they have tried you, how do you make them want to come back?

How will your interior decorating studio attract new customers? Some say that the only proven way is by doing good work and earning a good reputation in the community. But how do you get noticed in the first place? Maybe it would help to mail out brochures to potential customers.

What kind of brochures? What do you say? Who will help you write the promotion? How much should you spend? What would happen if you advertised on the radio or in the newspapers?

Buying an established business gives you a track record and something to build on. The odds are the former owners have tried various things to increase their customer base and you can benefit from their experience. At a minimum you have their customers to build on. You might be the best interior designer in the country, but if nobody knows about you, and if you can't get that start, all of that talent you have won't do anybody any good. It takes an extraordinary amount of energy, talent, and money to produce a quality product and at the same time plan a sales effort when you are starting with nothing—it's not impossible, just difficult.

### A Working Model

Buying an established business provides an educational opportunity—you have a working model of one way the business can be carried on. If you are buying a laundry, you'll be aware of how the facilities are operated, how the shirts are ironed, how orders are taken, how deliveries are made, what record keeping is necessary, how customers are treated, and so on. The value of this working model will vary with each person. You may already know many of these matters, and those that you don't know could perhaps be learned by watching how others run their businesses or by taking a temporary job in a similar business. Still, owning a business and being responsible for all of the aspects of its operation is different from being an employee or an observer, and for most a level of comfort is provided by starting with a functioning business that can be operated in a proven and tested way.

### Space and Location

Deciding how many square feet will be necessary to operate your business and where the best location is can be difficult and errors can be costly. If you decide to start a vacuum cleaner manufacturing company, do you need 500 square feet or 5000 square feet? Are there advantages to being near a busy intersection or will the business function just as well in the low rent part of town? Does your space have to be air-conditioned because the hot summer days might damage the inventory in storage or can you use unfinished warehouse space that's not only hot but dusty? How much parking space is necessary? How far from your customers can you be located? When you buy an operating facility you may not agree with all of the decisions that the previous owner has made, but with something specific to react to you will have a basis for deciding what changes in location and layout would be desirable.

## Employees

Finding the right employees and learning what to expect of them can be a time-consuming process. If you were to quit your job, sell your house, cash in your life insurance policy, and start a company that manufactures tents, how many employees would you need? Do you find these employees by advertising, do you hire an employment agency, or do you rely on word of mouth? How many tents can one machine operator make in a day? Is it possible to find someone who can both sell the tents and purchase the materials out of which tents are made, or do you need a different person for each job? Do you have both a bookkeeper and a secretary or can one person do both jobs? How many employees can a supervisor be reasonably responsible for? How much will you pay your employees? Do you have to buy their insurance? What vacations should they receive? Can you use part-time workers or do you need full-time employees? What will your policy be on overtime?

When you purchase the Greentree Tent Company, the former owners have already made these decisions. There is an operating history that tells you what you can expect from each employee. Their methods may not be the best and their supervision may be lax, but because the company has been in business for many years, you know that those mistakes which could ruin a company have been avoided or minimized.

## Who to Trust

Of necessity, the operation of a business requires that many people be trusted. A newcomer, with no operating history to use as a guide, is very vulnerable to exploitation. When Roxy Jumpfast went into the tent-making business, things moved quickly. She was an experienced seamstress and had been working with canvas and nylon for years. She had hardly opened her door when the business started to pour in. From one advertisement she had such a backlog of orders that she hired three extra employees to help her catch up. Six months later she was out of business. What happened?

According to the census takers, Roxy went out of business because of insufficient capital—she was showing a profit, but because she lacked the cash necessary to finance her expansion, her creditors forced her out of business. Those who were in the business before Roxy (and who are still in it) know better. They know she failed because she didn't understand the industry and because she did business with the wrong people.

Roxy didn't know at the time she chose to enter the recreational tent industry that the failure rate of retailers was higher than usual. She extended liberal credit to every failing sporting goods store and tent distributor in the country. Of course her business was booming. She was the only one in the country extending credit to anyone who asked, and the word spread like wildfire that Roxy would accept credit risks others had turned down. She didn't know these were credit risks. She had been told that everyone in the industry buys on credit, but she hadn't been told who the exceptions were. Did they repay her trust by promptly paying the invoices she sent? Of course not. How could they? These stores were in trouble—the employees had to be paid and more inventory had to be purchased from other suppliers if the stores were going to keep their doors open. After meeting payroll and paying the COD bills from other suppliers, there was little or nothing left with which to pay Roxy. When Roxy finally realized her mistake, she was unable to weed out her problem accounts quickly enough—she heard "the check was mailed two days ago and you should have it by now, but I need those tents today" and "don't worry, it was all a mistake—redeposit the check and it'll clear" a dozen times a day, right up to the day the sheriff padlocked her door.

Roxy might have been able to survive all of the bad accounts receivable if she had been able to keep the better stores as customers, but she had bad luck in that department, too. She was sold a supply of thread that weakened when it came in contact with water, a serious matter for thread used to hold a tent together. She bought thread from a persuasive salesman who explained that he could offer a special price on this thread because it was government surplus. After being manufactured for the U.S. government, the needs of the Army changed and it was never used. She lacked the experience and skill to inspect this thread and verify the salesman's explanation for why the price was so reasonable. If she had, she would have found the thread had been rejected as defective and the company that employed the salesman was notorious as the black sheep of the industry. If Roxy had purchased an existing company, she might have made some of the same mistakes, but the odds are she wouldn't have made them all. There would have been established credit procedures, a history of which customers to watch closely, and established working relationships with suppliers. In the usual purchase situation, the seller would have been able to answer questions, and would have been around the first few weeks to give advice and help her get off on the right foot.

## Details

Sally Slipso's plan to open a pet shop is fantastic, but she had a few problems getting it off the ground. She found the space immediately. She has a super name for her business. She knows how to care for all kinds of pets, knows the benefits and drawbacks of each breed, and can answer any customer's questions. She has a degree in veterinary medicine and plenty of money. If anyone should be able to start a pet store, it would be Sally. Sally did start a pet store and it was quite successful, but she says if she were to do it again, she would buy an existing business.

"You wouldn't believe the thousands of details," reports Sally. "I didn't know where to buy the animals, cages, pet food, grooming supplies, or any of the other items that I needed. When I found them, I didn't know what a fair price was or how to compare quality. I know why the customer needed each item, but I didn't know how much to charge. I also was unsure as to how much I should buy of any one item."

## PREPARING FOR PROBLEMS

When you purchase an existing business, you sometimes get more than you bargained for. You may find pleasant surprises such as inventory that wasn't listed on the balance sheet, spare parts you never expected to find, or machinery that you assumed was useless is easily repaired. But you may also find some surprises that are less pleasant. We may smile when Fred "Eager" Beaver almost goes to jail because he didn't know that in his state a specific statute requires that a licensed pharmacist must work in the prescription department of his recently purchased drugstore whenever the store is open. The problem is just as serious when the proud new owner of a vending machine route discovers how often vending machines break down, or when the parking lot entrepreneur learns the hard way how tempting all that cash is to his employees.

It is a reasonable assumption that you will face some unexpected problems in your new business. Anticipation of these problems may reduce them from catastrophes to inconveniences.

### New Skills

The idea of learning new skills can be exciting. If there are too many new skills to learn, however, the risk of failure is increased. The skills required of a businessperson are often more than anticipated.

Karl, the cook, tried to do too much when he went into the catering business. He worked for years as an assembler in a computer manufacturing plant, but Karl's real pleasure in life was gourmet cooking. His specialty was German food and he could make German pastries which everyone raved about. The secret was in the ingredients and in the hand mixing—no economizing or shortcuts for Karl.

When Karl was laid off due to a temporary cutback in production he decided to open a catering business.

"What's there to know?" replied Karl when friends asked him if he knew what he was doing. "I can cook the best German food in the state. If I sell the food for more than it costs me, how can I go wrong?"

Needless to say, things did go wrong. Never having worked for a caterer or in a restaurant, Karl had no idea of the importance of measuring how long it takes to prepare food and setting prices accordingly. He also didn't know how expensive commercial grade cookware and dishes were. The fact that paying customers didn't always pay and often complained loudly for no apparent reason was quite a surprise to Karl, not to mention employee theft, the need for good records, buying from reliable suppliers, relying on incomplete customer instructions, and so on. There was much Karl didn't know.

In fact, Karl never did learn very much about business in general or catering. He was out of business in a few weeks. He naively believed that because his food was so good he only had to make himself available and he would have more work than he could handle. He opened his business in the early summer—after the graduations and June weddings were already booked but before the novelty of outdoor barbecues had worn off. He spent almost his entire working capital, $3000, on a beautiful brochure that recited prices at least twice his nearest competitor. There was little money left with which to distribute the brochure, so Karl handed it out to his friends, none of whom could afford his prices.

What Karl did wrong could have been avoided. He could be a successful caterer today if he had only taken a few months to learn something about the catering business, not the food part necessarily but the "business" part. If he could have taken a job for a few months with a caterer or in a related business, like a restaurant, he would have greatly improved his chances of success.

### Better Mousetrap

If you invent a better mousetrap the world will beat a path to your door. True or false? True, but only if the mousetrap is priced competitively, promoted aggressively, works reliably, and if adequate funding and skilled management are available. Of course, the inventor has to worry about newer inventions making his obsolete and about a public who may feel that there is no need to buy a new mousetrap until (or if) their old one wears out.

Many inventors feel that once they have completed their invention they are done and all they have to do is sit back and wait for the money to pour in. Not true. Almost everybody has ideas that if properly developed could be the cornerstone of a new and successful business. The idea is important, but other parts of the business are equally important.

The two most common weaknesses inventors have are in the areas of finance and sales. They tend to focus on quality, unit cost, production procedures and details. The typical inventor/businessperson focuses on the product from the point of view of the user and thinks through how the product can be produced to make the customer the happiest, to the exclusion of raising the money to build the production facility, financing the production and sales, and without a lot of attention as to how the customer will be persuaded to try the product in the first place.

"I have developed a wind-driven electrical generator," said Betty to me last year, "that solves the two biggest problems that have stymied windmill development for years. I have solved the problem of low wind speed and vibration. The electric company has solved the third major problem—the storage of electrical energy. I am in the process of getting at least six patents. If I could raise $50,000 to build a prototype, I'd be on my way."

Betty was an electrical engineer with many years of engineering experience and I was sure if she said she had a good product, she did.

"I've solved the wind speed problem," continued Betty, "by augmenting the velocity through the use of a vertical surface. We have known for years that when the wind hits a building it increases in velocity as it moves up the building. By placing my windmill on top of a building instead of on a separate platform I can take advantage of this increased velocity. This means the wind speed can really be quite low and the windmill will generate a substantial amount of electricity."

"I've solved the vibration problem by securing the windmill at 20 contact points instead of the usual four or six. The storage problem for surplus electricity is solved by the electric company buying the surplus and using it for other customers."

Betty was very excited about her invention. She had made dozens of changes in standard windmill technology and they all combined to make a very efficient wind-powered electrical generator.

Betty still hasn't built a working prototype. Her difficulty is that she values her invention too highly and other skills and contributions too lightly.

The $50,000 Betty needed for a prototype would have paid for the materials, but it would not have paid for labor, space in which to build it, transportation, storage, and all the other costs of production. Nor did she have any margin for mistakes, increases in costs, or changes. A more accurate figure would have been $100,000 for one prototype.

When the prototype was built, and assuming it worked, Betty wanted to build a manufacturing plant. She assumed that prospective customers would come to see the prototype and it would sell itself. She also assumed that financing would be no problem once she had a working model because the bank would see what a safe loan it would be.

All of the investors Betty talked to wanted too much. They felt at least $250,000 would be needed to start the venture and that if she had a marketable product millions would be required. Typically, they told her that if she wanted their money she would have to give up much of the control and 60% or more of any profit. Several people told her that the amount of money required was so large that she would have to be prepared to sell out to a larger company at the first opportunity.

Betty didn't want that. She wanted to control her invention. She felt she had done the hardest part and she wanted a majority of the profits. She didn't want to sell out her interest at any time.

As I said good-bye to Betty, I wished her luck.

There are undoubtedly inventions which are so unique and so obviously needed that they sell themselves and make the inventor rich and famous in the process. I don't know of any though. Usually, an inventor who has an idea can capitalize on this idea only by giving up control and much of the profit to those who bring equally valuable skills and the necessary capital.

### Sellers Don't Volunteer Bad News

When buying a business, start by looking at things from the seller's point of view. He has owned the apartment building he is offering to sell for so long that he no longer even sees the chipped paint or peeling wallpaper. He is proud of his building—how he has kept the good tenants while getting rid of the bad ones, the new drapes, the recently resurfaced parking lot. He did the landscaping himself, buying trees and shrubs on sale and renting a truck to haul in good black dirt. He remembers the year the back steps settled, and if you look carefully you can see the line where he propped them up and patched the cracks.

This is a typical seller—a nice guy who has his share of good points. Still, the seller isn't going to tell you everything he can about the apartment building. If you ask "Does the roof leak?", he'll tell you that it does when the wind blows the rain down from the west, but if you don't ask, he won't volunteer the information.

"Yes, sir, Mr. Jones, you'll just love this building. Of course, the laundry equipment doesn't work half the time, the neighborhood is getting tougher, and the new fire codes that become effective next July will cost you a fortune because you will have to remove the incinerator, replace the fire doors, and put in smoke detectors."

How realistic is it to expect the seller to talk like this? We live in a legal and moral environment where the buyer is expected to take the initiative and the unwary or gullible are protected only from fraud or gross misrepresentations. A seller can't lie to you about the holes in the roof or hide the damage, but he can keep silent.

## Misleading Information

The courts have drawn a fine line between misrepresenting something (which is prohibited) and keeping silent (which is usually acceptable). In practice, you should assume that the seller will tell you only the good things about his business. You will have to discover any problems by yourself.

In no area is accuracy and completeness more important to you than the financial records of the business. This is also an issue that presents the greatest temptation to the seller to provide misleading information.

What Blacky Bigtoe did when he sold his saloon is typical of what many sellers are tempted to do. His building was so old and decrepit that the cost of keeping it in good enough condition so that his business wouldn't be closed by the health department, fire department, or building safety department was eating up all of the profit. He knew no one would want a business that was showing no profit, so he advertised that the saloon earned $250,000 per year gross income and liquor cost $75,000, labor (other than owner) cost $67,000, heat and electricity cost $13,000, licenses cost $3000, and rental equipment was $42,000. Prospective buyers were told that additional expenses would depend on how they ran the business. David Hummer, who eventually bought the business, had computed an additional $23,000 in costs (insurance, telephone, breakage, etc.), but he was shocked to find that repairs the first year were $26,000 alone (new roof, basement stairs, furnace, plumbing, etc.). When David consulted an attorney, he was told that he probably had no legal claim against Bigtoe because Bigtoe had not lied to David; he had clearly said that the list furnished was accurate for the items listed, but that "buyer will have to determine what additional expenses might be incurred from an inspection of the premises and his own experience."

Some sellers, leery about the consequences of giving a partial financial statement but still wanting to mislead the buyer, are declining to give any financial records and are instead delivering "projected" financial figures showing what income and expenses the seller thinks are possible for the next year. When these figures are delivered to a prospective buyer, there is sometimes a written note on the bottom stating that because the figures are predictions as to the future, the seller cannot make any guarantee that they are accurate, nor can the accountant who prepared them or the broker who delivered them. Doesn't this make you a little suspicious? It should.

The seller should be willing to show you what the actual income and the actual expenses were for the past few years (I like to see three complete years). Studying these figures carefully can tell you a lot about the problems of the business. For example, the furniture store that is projected to make $50,000 this year may have made $50,000 last year, but lost money the previous two years, indicating a cyclic pattern to the furniture business that could wipe you out if you weren't prepared for it. Or, the furniture store may have made $100,000 last year and twice that the year before, indicating that the business is deteriorating rapidly and unless something changes, you will be losing money next year.

When you study these financial statements you will need to use a lot of common sense. What were the major income items and are they likely to continue? If government purchasing, the weather or the interest rate changes, does anything happen to the gross income of the business?

While the operating history is important, sometimes it is unavailable or unusable, and in those cases you have to make up your own mind as to what the facts are. Common excuses are: "I don't keep any records so the income tax people have nothing to nail me with," "I'm selling because when my wife died, I realized there was no way for me to untangle this mess without her," and "Listen, Mac, if you want my garbage route you know the price—I'm not messing around with a lot of contracts and paper."

## Study the Numbers

Almost all big businesses and some small businesses have their financial records audited by an outside accounting firm, and if you are looking at such a business, you can normally rely on the financial records being as represented. An audit means that the accounting firm has made an inspection of the business and the financial records. This inspection will include such things as verifying that the inventory count is right and writing to accounts receivable to verify that they do in fact owe money to the business. The first page of an audited financial report will be the signed written opinion of the auditors as to the accuracy of the records. An accounting firm that signs its name to an audit report is guaranteeing that everything in the report is accurate, that nothing of material significance was left out of the report, and that the report was prepared in a manner that fairly describes the business. To reduce the legal limits of these guarantees, auditors will include in their written reports a description of what should not be relied on, called "qualifications." For example, there may be inspection of the inventory only at the end of the year, in which case the auditors would qualify their opinion by saying that since there was no verification of beginning inventory, statements as to how much inventory was used during the year should not be relied on. Potential misunderstandings are guarded against by footnoting any troublesome items and explaining the surrounding circumstances therein. Many are the battles that have been waged between auditor and businessperson over whether a particular cautionary comment needed to be included in the financial reports, or if it did, whether it belonged in the auditor's opinion as a qualification (which is usually read quite carefully) or in the footnotes (which are sometimes not read).

When the accuracy of financial records is an issue and there isn't an audit to rely on, most buyers will accept a copy of the seller's federal income tax return as verification. It is assumed that the natural desire of the seller to keep his income taxes low means that all income has been stated at the most conservative figure and all expenses have been stated at the highest possible figure. I've accepted this as verification many times, but there is an element of risk.

Problems can arise when the federal income tax return is relied on, as happened recently in the sale of a chain of pizza parlors. The buyer reviewed the operation carefully and was convinced that this pizza chain was well run and profitable—this was a business that was doing very well. The seller was deeply insulted that the buyer wanted to see the business's federal income tax returns and grudgingly gave the buyer a copy of the previous year's tax return, certified by the federal government as being as filed. The seller steadfastly refused to furnish copies of any earlier years, saying, "I'll give you this tax return because I ordered a copy for the bank, but I'll be damned if I'll write the government for a copy of any earlier returns. You tell that buyer if he doesn't trust me he doesn't have to buy my business."

The income tax return verified the books and the sale took place for a very substantial price. Despite the buyer's best efforts, he couldn't make the business profitable. The buyer's sales were only 5% less than the previous year, but expenses were 12% more. The business finally failed—another victim of spiraling costs. A few weeks after the business failed, the seller's accountant was surprised to find the seller in his office asking the accountant to prepare an amendment to the previous year's tax return. It seems the seller became confused in delivering data to the accountant and had given some erroneous information. He had neglected to include some expenses and some sales had been counted twice. The seller wanted a tax refund.

### Don't Rely on Legal Rights

Experienced businesspeople know that nothing is more important than the integrity of the businesspeople involved. If this integrity is lacking, the most thorough investigation, the best lawyers, and the most careful analysis of financial records are not sufficient to protect you. As the farmer said, "If you sleep with pigs, you will get dirty."

If you are given inaccurate information by a seller, you may have some remedies in the courtroom. There are laws designed to provide protection, but the wrongdoer has your money and can keep it until you can prove he did something wrong, perhaps a lengthy and expensive procedure. The general legal rule is that if the seller does something to mislead or trick you, he is guilty of fraud, and if the broker assists the seller, the broker is also guilty of fraud. Sometimes there will be criminal penalties ("criminal fraud"), but the more common remedies are the right to get your money back (called "recession" by the courts) or the right to receive a payment for the difference between what the business is really worth as it was sold to you and what it would be worth if the promises made to you were kept (called "loss of bargain" by the courts). The precise remedies available vary from state to state. The trouble with legal remedies is that they take years to pursue, and, in the meantime, the seller keeps the money you may need to buy groceries.

If there ever is a lawsuit, a carefully written purchase agreement can be helpful. In most situations there will be some promises made by the seller which are important to the buyer but which will be difficult to prove without a written agreement. A buyer can more easily show a court where he was misled if all important claims are written in or attached to the purchase agreement, for example, attaching a copy of the financial records being relied on to the purchase agreement and reciting in the purchase agreement that the seller represents that the attached records are complete and accurate.

Many times I have heard the comment, "The seller may not have the best reputation in the world, but I'm not going to marry him—I'm just going to buy his business. I know what I'm getting into."

I remember the carpet business that Leroy Lulu purchased. Leroy had been in the carpet business for 20 years, first as a retail salesman and later as a store manager. When Harold's Hall of Carpet came up for sale, Leroy jumped at the opportunity. He spent one whole evening negotiating terms with Harold at the Bowling Alley.

Then, because Leroy knew that Harold had a bad reputation, Leroy went to a lawyer to make sure everything was legal and in writing. This was not a wise decision. No amount of "lawyering" can protect you from crooks. Your only protection is to not do business with them. When Leroy's lawyer told him this, Leroy changed lawyers. Leroy found a lawyer who promised Leroy a "safe" contract and said if Harold didn't live up to it, he'd "throw the book at him."

The negotiations went on for days as Leroy inspected the business. Leroy had a lengthy contract where all of Harold's promises were reduced to writing.

When Leroy sold his house and paid cash for the business, he had done everything he and his lawyer could think of to protect against any of Harold's sharp practices.

It turned out that Harold hadn't been completely truthful with Leroy. Some of the suppliers hadn't been paid, even though Harold said they had been. They threatened to sue if Leroy didn't pay them. "Go see Harold," said Leroy, "he promised me that all of the bills were paid and if any turned up that he missed, he'd pay them."

Harold didn't return the telephone calls from the creditors and they returned to Leroy demanding payment. Leroy's attorney explained to Leroy that if the creditors had valid debts, they had a claim against the assets of the business, and if Leroy didn't pay them, the creditors might end up taking his business away from him.

While Leroy was trying to make up his mind what to do, irate customers started returning carpet, demanding full refunds. It seemed that Harold had been able to inflate sales the previous year by offering a 12-month full refund if the purchaser was dissatisfied for any reason. Since the carpet Harold sold was all of the lowest quality (though advertised as top-of-the-line "overruns" and "remnants"), a high percentage of last year's customers were dissatisfied.

"Let's get that dirty thief," Leroy screamed at his lawyer. "I want my money back."

"Your contract does protect you. Harold promised in the contract that all suppliers were paid in full. The contract we wrote to protect you also said," continued Leroy's attorney, pleased that he had anticipated these kinds of problems in the contract, "that Harold had no outstanding contractual obligations, and since the 12-month guarantee to customers was an 'outstanding contractual obligation,' then . . ."

"I don't care how it's done," interrupted Leroy, relieved he had the foresight to hire a good attorney and put everything in writing, "just get my money back."

"O.K., Leroy, I'll get right on it. Where is Harold?"

"I don't know. He left town."

"Well, you know I'm just licensed to practice law in this state," answered the attorney, "but when you find him, call me and I'll hire a lawyer licensed to practice in whatever state he's in. We'll get him. If you find him for us, and if Harold still has your money, we'll get it back."

"What do I do now?"

"I don't know."

Months later Leroy found Harold. Harold was back in town, selling carpet again.

It only took two days and cost $300 for Leroy's new attorney to prepare the papers to start a lawsuit against Harold. It took three months and cost another $200 for Leroy's papers to be "served" on Harold, since Harold was good at recognizing and avoiding process servers.

Shortly after Harold was served, Leroy was hit with a counterclaim alleging he had promised to pay Harold $1000 a month as a consulting fee, and no payments had been made. Harold certainly believed that the best defense was a strong offense.

"This is absurd," Leroy told his new attorney. "We did talk once about what he would work for if I needed help, and he said he'd need at least $1000 a month, but I never promised anything and I never wanted his help. It was just casual conversation. It wasn't in the written contract. How can he make this claim?"

"We like to have things in writing because then there is no dispute as to what was said. But, oral promises are legally binding, and if he can persuade a jury that you made the promise, he can enforce it. The written contract said no oral agreements would be enforceable, but there are various arguments that can be advanced to defeat this clause, such as fraud in the execution, mutual agreement to . . ."

"But I have a written contract," screamed Leroy. "I have it so there will not be any confusion as to what was agreed to. What good is a contract if he can just make things up?"

Leroy had a good question, one that is difficult to answer. It took three years for Leroy's case to get to court, and by then Leroy had several new questions.

The trial was quite a surprise for Leroy, almost as big a surprise as when he found out what his legal bill was for suing Harold.

"The carpet suppliers who weren't paid?" said Harold, under oath. "They were paid. They sent some carpeting that wasn't any good and I returned it. I didn't owe them anything. Leroy was just a pushover. They put one over on him."

"The customers who returned their carpet?" continued Harold, very much at ease in the courtroom and looking every inch like the upright citizen. "I never told any customers they could have their money back if they didn't like the carpet. I said if they weren't happy I would replace the carpet. This was a promotional gimmick. I could give the carpet away and make money on the installation charges and from selling the pad. Leroy never understood the business. That's why he went broke."

"The written contract?" continued Harold on the witness stand. "I never understood it. Leroy said it was just something he needed to have signed for the bank. It was prepared by his lawyer, but since it wasn't important, I didn't even read it. I know my word is good and I thought his was, too."

The trial went on for days. Finally, after several thousand dollars in legal bills, many days missed from work, and an ulcer, it was over. Leroy did a fine job on the witness stand, and thanks to the thorough job his first attorney did in writing the contract and the devastating effect of his second attorney's cross-examination of Harold about previous business transactions, Leroy was confident he would win.

The day following the end of the trial Leroy was waiting nervously as the jury returned to the courtroom and the foreman read from a sheet of paper, "We find for plaintiff Leroy Lulu and award him damages in the amount of $80,000 plus costs."

The judge confirmed the judgment, thanked the jury, and left. The bailiff escorted the jury out. Harold's attorney (Harold didn't bother to come to any of the trial, except on the days he was on the witness stand) congratulated Leroy's attorney and the two of them planned a golf game for the next week. Finally it was just Leroy and his attorney left in the empty courtroom.

"This is great," says Leroy. "You really did a fine job. When do I get my money?"

"I don't know," says the attorney. "All that happened was that the court agreed with you that Harold owes you some money. The court did not, and under our system of justice cannot, order Harold to pay you. You'll have to find out where Harold keeps his money, and then we can get a court order authorizing the Sheriff to go seize it for you."

"Well, then," responded Leroy, still flushed with the thrill of victory, "let's go get my money. Where do we start?"

"I don't know," answered Leroy's attorney. "I don't handle that type of legal work. No one in our firm does. You should be able to hire a good collection firm, there's lots of them around. They'll work for a percentage of what they collect. Usual fees range from 20 to 50 percent of whatever they recover, plus costs. Costs rarely exceed a few hundred dollars."

"You mean," asked Leroy, stifling the urge to scream, "that after spending almost $100,000 for a business that was worth nothing, $1200 for a lawyer to write a contract to keep me out of trouble, and an additional $7000 to get a judgment, I have to give another lawyer a third of whatever I get back?"

"Well, maybe you won't be able to hire anyone to work for a third," answered Leroy's attorney, anxious to finish with Leroy so he could go home. "They may insist on 50 percent because this looks like a difficult one to collect. They don't like to waste their time on deadbeats, so if they have too much trouble with Harold, they might refuse to continue and give the problem back to you."

After a lengthy pause, Leroy said, "When I won in court the judge said I was to get '$80,000 plus costs.' Doesn't this mean that Harold pays the cost of collection? Don't I get to recover from Harold my legal fees for the trial plus whatever I had to pay to the collection attorney?"

"Judges always give the winning party costs. They almost never give attorneys' fees. Costs mean the court costs and a few other specified costs. At the most, costs will be $200 in this matter."

"You mean," asked Leroy, "that Harold doesn't have to pay me for the expense he has cost me?"

"That's right," said Leroy's attorney. "You have to pay that yourself."

Leroy's new attorney, number three, explained things to him in terms that left no room for a misunderstanding. "If Harold doesn't have any cash or real estate in this state, your chances of ever seeing a penny are near zero. From what I've learned about Harold he is too experienced to leave anything around where you can find it. You can put him under oath and ask him about his assets, but do you really think he will tell you the truth? I won't take your case, not even if you let me keep every nickel—it's a waste of time to chase this guy; he has nothing, and if he ever did have something, he would stash it somewhere and you'd never even know about it. You know, you can't sleep with pigs without getting dirty. Next time stick with people who have a good reputation; someone who has more to lose than can be gained by lying."

# 3

# THE SEARCH

You've been thinking about taking the big step for months. You've talked to your spouse, your brothers and sisters, your parents, your friends, your neighborhood grocer, and the filling station attendant. Your mind is finally made up—you know you are going to quit your job and become a businessperson. You've spent hundreds of hours in the decision-making process. You have an idea as to what the risks are and you are willing to pay the price. You are geared up emotionally, filled with adrenalin, and you're ready to move. What's next?

## WHICH BUSINESS?

Select a business in which you have had enough experience to know the requirements for success. Too many businesspeople turn their backs on what they can do well and attempt activities for which they are ill prepared, often with disastrous consequences. The wage earner sets out to change what he doesn't like about his life. In the excitement that comes with the realization that change is possible, one may decide to change everything. This may be the right decision for some, but for many it is a decision that causes more problems than it solves. It is difficult enough to become a businessperson if you have no experience as an entrepreneur, and it is twice as difficult if you have no experience in the business you are attempting to enter.

A restaurant manager who came to see me recently comes to mind. Nathaniel Notime wanted to strike out on his own. He had tremendous energy and enthusiasm. He also had some money in the bank which he was anxious to invest. Nathaniel's first plan was to buy a real estate sales company. He had one in mind and was ready to sign a purchase agreement. Only after it was pointed out to him that he knew nothing about real estate and had very little sales experience of any kind did he realize that he had assumed little effort would be required to run the business—a malady known as "green grassism." "I thought," said Nathaniel, "that owning the company meant that I could hire a couple of salespeople and receive a check everytime they sold a house." After Nathaniel learned more about the business, he was persuaded to abandon this and search for something else.

It took Nathanial eight months and countless hours looking at dozens of businesses to accept that he should stay in a food-related business. It took him that long to realize he really enjoyed the restaurant business; it was being a wage earner he hated. Eventually Nathaniel found a grocery store, which he has since built into a small chain.

The Green Grasssism that Nathaniel suffered from is quite common. He knew all of the problems of the restaurant business—the hours, low profit, fickle customers, turnover of employees—but when examining other businesses in which he had no actual experience, he saw only opportunities. Part of the reason for this distorted vision was due to brokers and sellers, the primary source of information about alternative businesses, emphasizing only the opportunities. It took a long time for him to understand that each business has its drawbacks and risks as well as its own rewards.

Green Grassism is a chronic disease and when it is coupled with the desire to "change everything" the victim is likely to make some bad business decisions as goal setting becomes distorted, rendering opaque the real motivation behind the commitment to become self-employed. Sam Bucks was a successful and highly skilled debt collector working for a large collection agency. He spent years learning the skills of his trade—how money should be handled, the fundamental rules to follow when extending credit, how to read financial statements, methods to use when collecting from deadbeats, and how to plan and follow a budget. When he decided to take the big step, it seemed logical for him to use these skills, and his friends anticipated that he would be looking for a business like a small loan company or a small bank, or perhaps he would start his own collection agency. Instead he brought a distribution company that acted as a manufacturer's representative in the wholesaling of zippers. Sam might be successful in zippers, but the odds are that he would be more successful in a field he knew better.

All of us have unique experiences, skills, and interests, and they should be used. The telephone repairman, with a high school degree and not very much money, who quits his job to open a store selling telephone

equipment is more likely to be successful than the better financed automotive engineer, with numerous degrees and published papers, who re-
signs from General Motors to open a clothing store.

After you have determined what your strengths are, focus on which
segment of American business will best utilize them. A good starting
place is the telephone book—page through the Yellow Pages. Examine
the alternatives. Make a written list of what businesses may be suitable
for you and write out the pros and cons of each business.

When you have compiled a list of alternatives, examine each one and
see what you can extrapolate—isolate what appeals to you about each
choice and see what general guidelines you can establish. For example,
Priscilla Pips spent two days driving around the city looking at business
signs, display windows, and billboards, finding one business that appealed to her, a florist shop. Starting with this interest in a florist shop,
Priscilla analyzed why a florist shop appealed to her and what her personal strengths were. She felt that because she had been raised on a
farm, she knew all about plants, and as an avid gardener her whole life
she had a great deal of experience. Priscilla also knew that she enjoyed
being around plants, especially flowers, and got a great deal of satisfaction out of working with them. Beginning with this type of analysis, it was
easy to extrapolate and expand Priscilla's horizons. Her expanded list
included: (1) a service that cares for plants in office buildings and shopping centers—keeping them healthy and attractive; (2) operating a nursery to raise flowers for sale to florists—to be resold to the public at retail;
(3) organizing classes to teach frustrated gardeners how to avoid the most
common mistakes and how to get the most out of their garden; (4) raising
flowers for the seeds and selling the seeds to seed distribution companies; (5) starting an intensive care nursery where sick plants could be
brought for special treatment.

The possibilities for each of us are endless. The problem is not deciding what is possible; it is, instead, deciding which of many alternatives
will be the most feasible and rewarding. Once the general category is
selected, it is time to find a business to buy—and then the legwork
begins.


## ON THE STREETS

Today's the big day. The choices have been narrowed down and now
you're going to start looking at businesses to buy. All service businesses
have been ruled out because you prefer not to work with the general

public day in and day out. For the same reason you have also ruled out all retail businesses—no gas station, laundry, restaurant, motel, or drugstore for you.

Selecting an industry was difficult. You almot decided on the construction business, largely because of the three summers you helped Uncle Fred build barns, but after much soul searching, you decided that you wanted to work indoors and you did not want a seasonal business. The inspiration came one day as you were reviewing the list of alternatives previously rejected. You want a small manufacturing company that sells its product to dealers and preferably one that manufactures a product that uses electrical motors. This way you can take advantage of your military service training. You paged through the Sears catalog looking at products that use electrical motors and decided that you would like to manufacture electric drills, vacuum cleaners, automotive starters, air compressors, or some similar product.

The best place to start your search for a business to buy is the newspaper. Almost every paper has a section devoted to businesses for sale. Read each ad carefully, even the ones that are advertising businesses you have no interest in. Are there a lot of businesses for sale? This may mean that there are more sellers than buyers, causing the sellers to become anxious. Do sellers usually offer to finance the sale, or do most of them ask for cash? Among those who offer to finance, how much cash do they want and what's the interest on the balance? Which brokers seem to be the most active? Which brokers write ads that look reasonable and responsible and which brokers make improbable claims and imply unrealistic rewards? A lot can be learned from the classified ads, but at a minimum you should get a feel for local conditions and some leads.

Answer every advertisement that has any possibility of being of interest to you. "I don't know," Fussy Freddy might answer, "the company isn't what I'm looking for because it says 'distribution' of vacuum cleaners and I want a company that manufactures vacuum cleaners."

Nonsense. Call the listing agent. Go out and look at the business. Learn everything about this business that you can. Until you've looked at several businesses in the general area of your interest, you should not assume that you know the precise parameters of your interest. You'll be surprised at how much you learn from these forays.

Visits with business people who have knowledge of the business you want to enter will give you an awareness of industry trends. The vacuum cleaner sales company seller you meet may tell you that they have dropped one line and replaced it with another because the new line has a larger motor and consumers today are insisting on larger, more powerful vacuum cleaners. This may be a useful insight when you have an opportunity to buy a vacuum cleaner assembly plant, where sales have been down "because of the holidays" and the big inventory of low-horse-power vacuum cleaner motors is considered an asset because "when sales of small vacuum cleaners really take off next month, you won't have to wait for small vacuum cleaner motors like all the other compa-nies."

A great deal of data is necessary to become a businessperson, and if you are willing to make an aggressive effort to collect this data, spending time conversing with businesspeople will not be wasted. You may find out where parts are purchased, which suppliers are to be avoided, who the customers are, how much competing units sell for, and so on. Use the opportunity to ask a lot of questions. Good decisions require hard data, and a lot of it. Fill your head and your note pad with as much accurate, detailed data as you can—if you ask how powerful a motor is and are told "about a tenth of a horsepower," ask if he can check the exact rating.

Be prepared to invest some time in answering ads. Many brokers have so many activities and competing demands on their time that they attempt to discourage "window shoppers." These brokers may insist on verbal assurance that you have the money needed to buy or they may otherwise try to "qualify" you by testing your level of interest—"I can't give you any information over the phone, but if you'll meet me at my office at 6:30 A.M. tomorrow, I'll show you the plant." If you come upon one of these brokers, don't get angry and hang up. Don't sulk. Once you're "qualified" the broker will be a lot more accommodating. If you find you are unable to cope with a broker who behaved this way, you should reconsider whether you have the constitution to be a businessper-son—we can choose our friends, but in business you will oftentimes have to deal with distasteful people or situations.

Don't start your search by being apologetic, explaining how little mon-ey you have, or otherwise running yourself down. You are a prospective customer for both the broker and the seller of the business and you should be treated with respect and courtesy unless you persuade them that you should be treated otherwise.

By answering advertisements you will be educating yourself as to how the type of business you are interested in functions, which businesses are for sale, how to inspect a business, how to work with brokers and how to read between the lines when reading advertisements or hearing a busi-ness described.

Incidentally, we all know it pays to advertise, but we don't always take advantage of this knowledge. If you are in the market to buy, let the world know it. Tell your friends. Think about putting a "business wanted" advertisement in the newspaper.

Most businesses are sold with the assistance of a broker. A broker is part dream machine, part salesman, part lawyer, and part accountant. A successful relationship with him requires some awareness on your part as to how the various parts interrelate.

## THE BROKER

Most buyers end up purchasing their businesses with the assistance of a person who makes a living by putting buyers and sellers together—a broker. The qualifications and reliability of a broker vary from state to state. In some places anyone can sell businesses with little or no regulation, whereas in other areas the broker is required to pass a test, post a bond, and gain experience by working for a broker before he can engage in the sale of business. In addition to knowing the qualifications of a broker, it is important to understand that in most cases he doesn't get paid unless you buy and he does not consider it part of his job to see that you buy a business that is good for you.

Let's work through what might happen with a broker in a typical sale. After weeks of answering every advertisement that is in any manner related to what you're interested in, and after looking at so many businesses and talking to so many owners and brokers that they all blur together in your memory (fortunately you made copious notes on each investigation), you decide to make an offer to purchase the Hump Manufacturing Company, which produces Hump Vacuum Cleaners. This isn't a big business—it's run out of a double garage and has one employee. They sell only 35 vacuum cleaners a week, but you are convinced you can triple the volume of sales by improving the quality of the product and the operation generally. There is a great deal of room for improvement. The motor they use is too expensive and doesn't do the job, the bags they use often leak (permitting dirt to escape), and their distribution program is in shambles. The reputation of Hump Vacuums is not good. Several store owners you met by answering advertisements said there were problems getting delivery of the vacuums to sell when they handled Hump Vacuums, causing them to discontinue the line. You've heard that Charlie Hump is a nice guy, but he can't run the business and he never should have left his job as a tennis pro.

Hump is asking $61,000 for the business. This is a fair price and you're willing to pay it, but you wonder if you can buy the business for less. Your wife suggests that maybe you should discuss this with the broker and the broker should help you make up your mind.

"After all," your wife tells you, "that's how the broker earns his commission. If you don't ask for his advice and then follow it, you're paying his commission without his earning it." Is she right? Probably not.

In business each person is expected to look after his own interests. Consider how the broker fits into a typical sale transaction. Brokers are normally hired by the seller. The sellers pay the broker only if there is a sale. The fee to the broker is usually a percentage of the sale price. This means that everything you tell the broker could be disclosed to the seller if that will help sell the business, because that is who the broker works for and is paid by.

If you tell the broker you are willing to go to $61,000 but at the present time you are going to offer $50,000 to see what response is forthcoming from the seller, will the broker tell the seller? Ask him. Can you trust his answer? Maybe. No broker I know would lie if asked a direct question, but you aren't dealing with people I know and it may be difficult for you to know who to confide in. A good rule is if you have any doubts about sharing information, don't. Talking too much to the broker could reveal to the seller the price you are willing to pay, and cost you several thousand dollars.

Brokers may not have natural loyalty to the buyer, but they are very interested in having you make an offer that will be accepted. This can be used to your advantage. Regardless of who pays the broker's paycheck, he doesn't receive any payment unless he puts a sale together. It doesn't matter whether your offer to purchase is for more or less than the seller's initial asking price, just as long as it is high enough so that the seller will accept it. When he was hired by the seller, he was told to go out and find someone who would make an offer to purchase the seller's business for a price so high that the seller would accept it. He didn't promise to get the seller the highest or the best price, only an acceptable one.

Treat your broker as the "deal maker" that he wants to be and use him as a source of information to find out what the minimum acceptable offer might be. For example, instead of revealing all your plans and hopes and testing his loyalty by letting him know exactly where you stand, you might do some "fishing," throwing out alternatives to see what he bites on. You might say, "I have some interest in this business, but $61,000 is just too high. I'd be interested in a lower price. I'd also like the seller to give me some terms. I'm thinking about offering $50,000, ¼ down, and the balance over the next 25 months at 8 percent interest. I also want the seller to train me and to agree to work for at least three months after I buy the business." Even though you're asking for more than you expect to receive and are suggesting a price lower than you are willing to pay, the broker's response might surprise you.

The broker might respond, "$50,000 is a little low certainly, but I wouldn't be embarrased to present it. It might be accepted. His wife is sick and he's selling the business to move to Arizona, so I don't think he is going to want to stay around for three months to work, but I'm sure he'll stay long enough to train you and answer any questions that come up. I don't know what kind of terms he will accept. He's told me repeatedly he wants cash, but he might be willing to accept some financing. Let's put together an offer and if it's fair, I'll do my best to persuade him to accept it."

Given these new facts you might say, "$50,000 seems like a fair price to me. If he'll stay around for 30 days to help me get established and give me some good payment terms, we may have a deal."

At this exchange the broker might say, "I'll tell Hump that while you're firm on your price, you wanted him to stay for three months to help you get established, but I talked you down to one month. I just don't know what to say about the terms. Why don't we offer ½ down and the balance over 12 months?"

From this exchange you've learned quite a bit. You know that Hump is under pressure to sell because of his wife's illness. Reading between the lines you can assume that the realtor believes Hump will accept your price but is concerned about how fast he'll be paid. The question now becomes, does Hump need the cash or is he just uncertain about your ability to make the payments? If he is uncertain about your ability to make the payments is it because he doesn't know you very well or is it because he knows something about the business that you don't? Is he fearful that once you have an opportunity to operate the business you will not be willing (or able) to pay the rest of the purchase price?

If you come across a broker that you enjoy working with, ask him to help you. His experience can be very useful and if you keep his loyalties clear in your mind, you should not be disappointed with the assistance he gives you.

You're anxious to make your move. The broker wants you to sign an offer. The seller has another buyer waiting. Speed is as dangerous in business as it is on the highway.


## FRANCHISES

For many business people, buying a franchise has proved to be a good investment. Fast food, automobile mufflers, hotels, movie theaters, real estate sales—the list of businesses that have been "franchised" seems endless. Several franchises, such as McDonald's, have proved to be extremely lucrative. Others have proved to be of limited value.

If there is one general rule to follow when studying a franchise opportunity, it is: be careful. There appears to be almost as many franchise opportunities offered for the sole purpose of making money for the owner as there are franchise opportunities that make economic sense.

Franchises are advertised for sale in almost every publication that advertises businesses for sale. There will be no difficulty in finding a franchise to buy. The big problem will be in deciding what a specific franchise is worth.

There are 400,000 franchise businesses in the United States, making this one of the most common methods of going into business.

The apparent advantages of having a franchise are substantial. The product is better known than it could otherwise be. The seller has tested the product and knows how to best deliver it to the customer to maximize profits. Often the investment made by the purchaser of the franchise is matched by the seller as property and equipment, and sometimes inventory is leased or otherwise furnished to the purchaser under favorable terms.

The real estate sales franchises that came to town recently are a good example of a franchised system that worked.

"We paid the company $5000 when they gave us the franchise and we will give them one percent of all sales thereafter," said Michael F., realtor. "For the payment of the franchise fee we get to use the name 'American Sales' and to use forms in making sales and to use a special sign. We also received a copy of their policy manual that describes in detail how a real estate sales office should be operated. They have provided us with training materials that help us train our sales people and periodically furnish us with specialized training kits such as how to dress to be most effective."

Michael F. was very pleased. He went from a three salesperson office with no particular identity and very little class to a slick professional sales organization with contacts throughout the United States. He could specifically identify sales opportunities that would have been lost if it were not for his new image and contacts. He also felt that his sales people were better trained. His monthly profit increased dramatically as a result of his affiliation.

Not all franchise purchasers are so fortunate. There have been so many abuses that many states and the federal government have passed or are considering passing laws to regulate franchises.

Franchise abuse comes in many forms, but most commonly it comes in the form of misrepresentation at the time the franchise is purchased. The second leading form of abuse is unreasonable demands made by the seller after the franchise has been purchased.

Misrepresentation at the time a franchise is sold should be easy to detect if the purchaser takes the time to verify the seller's claims. What is being sold and how much would it cost to duplicate what is being sold elsewhere? I recently saw a franchise for sale that promised the purchaser a rewarding and lucrative career as the owner of a franchised employment agency. Upon close examination, it appeared that all the purchaser would receive is a packet of forms, most of which appeared to be copied out of standard form books which are available at any public law library. The name that was being purchased was not known and there was no customer loyalty from established accounts.

Contrast the employment agency franchise opportunity, which in this case can be considered overpriced, with the magic of purchasing the opportunity to use a well-known name like Pepsi-Cola, McDonald's, or Cadillac.

How a franchise purchaser will be treated after purchasing the franchise can best be determined by talking to existing franchise holders. This is something that should be done in any event. Anticipating this request, the seller may advise you that you are the first in your region and that is why you are receiving such a "bargain." If you are the first franchise ever sold, you have good reason to be very suspicious and should look closely at what exactly is being furnished to you. If you are not the first franchise being sold, it is possible to get on an airplane and visit one of the other existing franchise holders. It may seem like a waste to spend several hundred dollars on such a trip when you are absolutely convinced you are making the right decision, but considering the experiences of many others it would be foolhardy not to make the trip.

In the final analysis the only way to know if you are making a wise decision in purchasing a franchise is to talk to other people who have purchased such a franchise. If you allow the sellers to be your only source of information, you are taking unnecessary risks.


## TAKE YOUR TIME

The successful businessperson moves decisively but not always quickly. When you find that the business you want is on the market today, the odds are it will be on the market tomorrow. There probably isn't a salesperson alive who hasn't told his customers, "I just showed this to a fellow yesterday who seemed very interested and he told me he is going to be sending an offer today or tomorrow. If his offer comes in ahead of you, it might be accepted and this great opportunity might be gone tomorrow."

I'm not saying this is never true, but if you believe this line, then I have some swampland in South Florida that's just right for you.

Making the decision about whether to purchase a specific business requires the collection and analysis of a great deal of information. Brokers and sellers realize this and should be understanding when it takes a few days for a buyer to decide how to proceed.

If after the first razzle-dazzle urging to move quickly, you find the pressure to move quickly is increasing, you should move even more slowly. Why is Hump telling you that if you buy his business today he'll throw in his delivery truck and $3000 worth of inventory? Is it because the building inspection department has condemned the double garage his factory is in? Is it because he likes you? Is it because the Federal Trade Commission has moved to ban the sale of his product because it is unsafe? Is he nervous that you might change your mind if you don't act now? Does he know something that you don't?

# 4

# THE BUY

You search and you search and then one day, all of a sudden, you find just the business for you—a jewelry store that has been in the same location for 30 years. The decorating is beautiful, the inventory stunning, and the list of satisfied customers impressive. You and your partner, Breathless Bertha, have been looking at businesses for months and you are both convinced that if you don't buy this store, you will never find another one you like as much. The only problem is the price—the seller is asking $200,000 and no matter who you ask, the maximum value of the store, you are told, is $160,000. What do you do? The answer depends on why you are going into business. If your primary motive for the decision is a need to own something "nice" or a desire to have a work environment that makes you feel good, then recognize your motives for what they are and be prepared to pay the price for "feeling good," the same as others pay for a new car they don't need because it makes them "feel good."

"Abigail," Breathless might suggest to you, "it's such an attractive store and you and I would meet such interesting people in the jewelry business. Our friends and family would be so proud of us. If we don't come close to the asking price, it will be sold to someone else. I think we should offer $185,000."

Breathless might be right. There's more to life than money. But, if you believe that business decisions should be economic decisions, you'll want to buy this store only if the price is reasonable, a price at or below what you consider the value of the business to be. This is going to require some negotiation.

## IF YOU DON'T ASK, YOU DON'T GET

The first rule of negotiation is that you must be prepared for the seller to walk away from you and do business with someone else. If you're going to play the game, you must be prepared to lose. If you aren't willing to take this risk, don't expect too much from your efforts to negotiate a lower price or better terms.

A seller may talk a good fight as to what he will or will not accept for his business, but the truth is neither he nor the buyer knows for sure what will be accepted until an offer is submitted and the seller is in the position of accepting or rejecting what might be his only [or best] offer.

While Breathless may be deciding whether to offer $185,000 for the jewelry store, I might offer $100,000. I might be accused of trying to steal the business or even worse, but my offer might be accepted or I might get a counteroffer that is lower than the $185,000 offer Breathless is considering. I'll never know what the seller's rock bottom price is unless I've made an offer that he rejects. Even then I might be unwilling to increase my offer, preferring to wait and resubmit substantially the same offer if the business doesn't sell for several weeks and the seller starts to worry. Using this approach I once bought an apartment building for less than my original offer—after nine months with no other offers the seller became anxious, and once I became aware of this I lowered my first offer.

Unless you are under some tremendous time pressure to become a businessperson, I suggest that you be prepared to make several offers on several businesses. A prospective buyer who has only one business on his mind has a tendency to signal the seller that he is anxious. A buyer who is simultaneously considering several alternatives will project a lack of concern, causing the seller to think twice before rejecting any offer.

You can ask for anything when you are negotiating for the purchase of a business. You are limited only by your own creativity and chutzpah. I remember a manufacturing company that had been operated at a loss for several years. The owner of the company was a large corporation that each year was obligated to advance thousands of dollars to cover the previous year's losses. The company did several million dollars a year in sales and at one time had been quite profitable. It wasn't clear why it was now losing money, nor could three presidents in the past three years find a solution. Finally, the board of directors of the parent corporation decided they could no longer cover the losses and offered the company for sale. Their price was $1,000,000 cash, which represented their estimate of the replacement value of the machinery, plant, and inventory. After the business had been on the market for several months, Sidney Sharpeye started investigating it. He learned that over a dozen potential buyers had looked at the company, its operating history, assets, and books, but none had made an offer—they just wouldn't gamble $1,000,000. Sidney guessed that the money-losing company was costing its owners over $250,000 a year and assumed they were becoming increasingly anxious to sell.

Sidney had some ideas about how to make the company profitable, but there was no way to test his ideas without buying the business. Sidney wasn't prepared to gamble $1,000,000 to find out if his ideas were workable.

Although Sidney did not have $1,000,000, or even $100,000, he made an offer, one that was eventually accepted. Sidney reasoned that the company was costing its owners so much money that if they did not sell it soon, they would have no choice but to let it slip into bankruptcy. The owners would probably receive very little for their stock if that were to happen because at the bankruptcy sale the assets would go for less than their fair value. Reasoning that the sellers must have made the decision to let the subsidiary slip into bankruptcy if a buyer couldn't be found, Sidney presented an offer as an alternative to bankruptcy. He would buy the business with no cash down and the promise that if he could make it into a profitable business, the seller would receive the first $1,000,000 of profit. If Sidney could not turn the business around, all he would have lost was his time and energy. The sellers could then let the business slip into bankruptcy and they would have lost very little. If he was successful in turning the business around, he would pay the sellers $1,000,000 over a period of years, but since this money would come from the profits, he would be buying the business with its own money. It's too early to tell if Sidney will be successful.

So you ask too much? What's the harm? Is the seller going to get mad at you and never talk to you again? Nonsense. He wants to sell his business and if you're willing to pay his price, he'll sell it to you regardless of past sins. Sure someone else might buy the business while you're attempting to get the best possible deal, but that's the risk you take. On the other hand, the seller will never give you a lower price or better terms than you ask for.

## BARGAINS

The first profit you earn as a businessperson may be when you purchase your business. If you are able to purchase for less than the "real" value of the business, a price less than you could sell the business for, then you have made a profit. A dollar earned in this manner is no different from a dollar earned by operating the business. True, you can't spend this profit unless you sell the business, but you also don't pay income tax on it. It is not uncommon for a businessperson to make a profit that he can't spend. Profits will often be tied up in inventory, machinery, receivable financing, or otherwise.

If you go bargain hunting, your biggest bargaining tool will be patience. The seller will normally not jump at a rock bottom offer; he certainly won't if it appears you want to buy his business badly and are in a rush to do so. You have to wait the seller out. What does the seller do who really wants to sell; who is suddenly taken ill, divorced, beset by personal financial problems, or decides to retire? He wants to sell his business, and if it's not sold quickly, he starts to get nervous.

The seller may start out with an overly optimistic idea of what he can sell his business for, but after several weeks reality usually sets in. Many times the seller becomes as pessimistic as he was previously optimistic. He begins to imagine he will never sell the business; he sees quite clearly, perhaps for the first time, all of the negative aspects of his business— the paint peeling off the building and the sign; the absence of anything unique in his operation; growing competition; the long hours. This is when you can buy for a good price.

To buy at the right price requires a lot of work to uncover all the relevant facts, patience to wait for the right time, and determination to risk having all of your effort go for nought as the seller deliberates your offer.

A good example was the exhaust fan manufacturing company which was recently for sale in our area. I don't know how different the buyer's reactions would have been if any of these facts had been changed, but I do know he took the time to verify each of the facts and out of them constructed a strategy which was ultimately successful. Any buyer would be well advised to know as much or more before making an offer.

The Tough Job Tool Company was a small family business founded 40 years ago as a machine shop specializing in machine tooling. Their business required precision engineering and machining parts and tools that required cutting and grinding to tolerances within one thousandth of a centimeter. Their customers were manufacturing companies who were more interested in quality than price. Several years ago Tough Job had an unexpected slump—business fell off by 30 percent. During the slump one of the Tough Job vice presidents had the idea of starting an exhaust fan manufacturing company. There was plenty of room in the corner of the partly idle machine shop. There was a great deal of optimism in the beginning—valuable employees would not have to be laid off, idle space would be used, a new customer for machine tooling would be created, and the growing environmental and OSHA (a federal agency enforcing job safety rules) pressure on employers would guarantee plenty of sales as businesses rushed to purchase high-quality exhaust fans to keep the air in assembly areas fresh. As is often the case, there were some unexpected problems. Things may have been different if Tough Job had decided to duplicate what other manufacturers were doing, but their precision tooling background and lack of manufacturing experience committed them to developing a higher quality fan than presently available, one that occupied less space, moved more air per minute, used less electricity, and was quieter.

Development costs were very high but because their accounting system was not set up to keep track of the many expenses incurred while developing the fan they never knew for sure what all the costs were. They did learn it wasn't cheap; tens of thousands of dollars were spent as first one model, then another, was produced by hand, tested, and then rejected.

In time the slump ended and all of Tough Job's employees were needed for its primary business. By then Tough Job had spent so much time and money on research and development they felt they had to continue in the exhaust fan business if they expected to recover any of their investment. This was not an easy decision. They were accused by their banker of throwing good money after bad, and the two brothers who owned the company frequently argued about the decision. They put in money to increase the inventory, hired more employees, and set up a separate company in an old warehouse to produce the fans.

Ten years later the Tough Job Fan Company was producing and selling about $400,000 worth of fans annually. This wasn't big by manufacturing company standards, but it was enough to establish that the fans worked and could be sold.

As the brothers came nearer to retirement age, they wanted to slow down. They knew they lacked the marketing skills and drive to make the fan company into a substantial business. They considered hiring a top manager to run the company for them, but they were unwilling to make the kind of financial commitments such a person would demand. If they took any substantial financial risks by putting additional working capital into the fan company, their retirement plans could be destroyed.

After Emil, the older of the two brothers, had a mild heart attack and on doctor's orders cut back to working only two days a week, the brothers decided to sell the fan company.

When they reviewed the operating records of the fan company, they were shocked to find out that not once in its 10-year history had it shown a profit. Their projections showed that if they could increase sales from $400,000 to $500,000 a year they might make a $20,000 profit—assuming no cost increases or production problems. Their operating history showed they couldn't increase sales by that amount.

Emil and Sven, his younger brother, spent several weeks debating if they should raise prices. They knew if they could raise prices, the company might be profitable. They also knew that if they lost some sales because of a price increase, the operating loss might be increased. They finally decided not to raise prices because they didn't want to risk losing any customers. They would sell the business as it was and let the new, younger, and more energetic owner decide what to do.

Sven and Emil didn't know how to go about selling their business so they went to a broker. The first thing the broker asked of them was to explain exactly what it was they had for sale. They had a few thousand dollars worth of inventory, a few completed fans, and assembly equipment that could be replaced for about $25,000. The fabrication of the parts was done in their machine shop and the necessary machines were not proposed to be sold because the volume of production did not make it necessary to own this equipment. The purchaser could contract with their machine shop or any other machine shop in town to produce the parts for a reasonable price. They did have drawings of a product that worked, but despite the thousands of dollars spent on these plans, they weren't worth very much because the fan they described wasn't that much better than the competition's. They had some satisfied customers, but this was of limited value because the fans lasted so long that there was little repeat business.

On the other hand, there were more than just assets; there were some liabilities that the buyer would have to assume. Emil and Sven were willing to pay all the bills that could be identified when the business was sold, but the warranty given on every fan sold (five years for parts, one year for labor) was a problem. No one knew how many fans were still under warranty or how to compute the cost of meeting these warranty obligations in the future.

After much discussion, it was decided that the business would be advertised for sale with no price. Prospective buyers would be told to "make an offer." Emil told the broker that he hoped for a price of at least $200,000 for the business. A listing agreement was signed, where Emil and Sven agreed to accept an offer of $200,000 and pay the broker a commission of 8 percent on the sale of the business.

My good friend, Herman Cantaloupe, saw the advertisement, looked at the business, and decided it was just what he wanted. When he met with the broker, the broker confided to Cantaloupe that the sellers were hoping to receive an offer in the $300,000 range because that's what they estimated was spent in developing the product and getting established.

"Anyone starting up in this business today," continued the broker, "would easily spend $400,000. This business would be a steal at that price. Emil and Sven are too old and tired to go out and hustle. A young man like you could double or triple sales. And their prices are just too low. These guys just haven't kept up. Why, you could increase prices by 20 percent and make yourself an additional $80,000 a year. Yes sir, a business like this doesn't come along every day. I bet it'll be sold by the end of the week. My phone has been ringing off the hook ever since that ad appeared."

"I'll tell you what," said the broker, lowering his voice and moving closer. "You offer $250,000. If you do it today, it'll be the first offer in. These guys don't know what they've got. I bet they'll take it."

Cantaloupe eventually bought the business. His first offer was $50,000 cash. It was rejected and Emil was so insulted that he refused to make a counteroffer or even meet with Cantaloupe. Six months later Cantaloupe checked back, saw that the business was still on the market, and offered $60,000. By this time, Emil and Sven were becoming discouraged. They had shown the business numerous times and each inspection tour was becoming more of an effort. All of the employees knew the business was for sale and morale was slipping. The brothers made a counteroffer for $70,000, which Cantaloupe accepted.

Today you couldn't buy Cantaloupe's exhaust fan business for $1,000,000. Five years of hard work have increased sales 1000 percent. It was a great buy—a bargain.

Was Cantaloupe being too greedy when he made the initial $50,000 offer? Was he foolish to take a chance on losing a business he really wanted by refusing to pay a fair price? If the business is worth over $1,000,000 today, wasn't it really worth several hundred thousand dollars then?

"Baloney," says Cantaloupe. "For me to make a success of that business, I could not afford to give everything I owned to the seller. I needed to keep some money so I could support my family during those first few months when there was no income. No business is a bargain if you can't keep the doors open because you are out of money. The only reason it took me so long to buy the business was that so many prospective purchasers got excited about the possibility of buying a '$400,000 business' for $250,000 that the seller was encouraged to keep the price up. Fortunately for me, all the others got cold feet when it came time to sign the offer for $250,000. I was the only one who didn't pay any attention to what I was told and because of that I made the only two offers. I had no guarantees that I could do a better job than Emil and Sven. I could have lost money the same as they did. I gambled and it paid off."

Bargains do exist, but they are not easily discovered. More often than not you have to see some potential in the business that makes it worth more than the asking price or some weakness in the seller that will cause him to sell the business for an attractive price.

## THE SELLER'S PERSPECTIVE

You will greatly increase the likelihood of success if you develop the skill of seeing things the way others do. A lot of time and misdirected planning will be saved if you can determine what the seller wants to accomplish by selling his business and prepare your offer accordingly.

Several months ago, I had the good fortune of dining with the founder of the Hyatt Hotel chain, senior member of one of the wealthiest families in America, and a 1921 graduate of the Harvard Law School. Then in his eighties, he had definite ideas on what had made him successful and he was willing to share some of them with me.

"Most people think," he said, "that when you're beginning negotiations, you should decide what you want. That's wrong. You should begin with what the other person wants and what he must have to do the deal. If he wants too much, if he wants more than you can give him, then you should pass on the deal because it just won't work. You must look at the deal from his point of view before you can make up your mind what to ask for."

This is the best advice I can think of for beginning negotiations. The biggest single failing I see in negotiations is one side declaring its position or extending an offer without taking into account what the other side needs before it will make the deal. Often I see parties who are inches apart acting as if they were miles apart because neither is looking at those few issues that are of utmost importance to the other side.

When you and Breathless sit down to write out your offer for the purchase of the jewelry store, you should start with what Jethro Jeweler wants. He has an asking price of $200,000, but that is just the beginning of the important information you need. From talking to Randy Realtor, competitors, customers, and others you have determined that Jethro Jeweler: (1) feels he should have cash for his jewelry store because he is moving to Arizona and is concerned that if the new owner owes him some of the purchase price, Jethro might have to fly back and forth to collect it; (2) intends to pay $110,000 worth of business installment loans out of the proceeds of the sale, $85,000 of which has gone to buy jewelry bought for resale but not yet sold, and the balance of which was for store fixtures; (3) has sold his house and the new owner wants to move in the end of next month.

From these facts you can conclude what Jethro Jeweler will need to sell his business. Jethro has asked for a cash sale so he doesn't have to worry about being paid, not because he needs $200,000 in cash. If you can show him that you are a person of good reputation and if you pledge some security (perhaps the business you are buying; perhaps your house), Jethro may be willing to accept part cash and the balance over time. The $110,000 installment loans that Jethro wants to pay don't have to be paid when he sells the business; if Jethro were keeping the business, he would pay them over time. Again, Jethro just wants to make sure that there will be no future problems. If you agree to pay the loans for Jethro and can persuade him that you will do what you promise, you automatically reduce your cash requirements by that amount. You know that since Jethro wants to leave the state, and since he has sold his house and will have no place to live in a few weeks, he should be receptive to any reasonable offer that meets his requirements of a fair price, assurance of no future problems, and an early closing. In determining a fair price, you know that since the first $110,000 of the purchase price will be used to pay the installment loan, it would be unreasonable to offer less than $110,000. How much more than this you offer depends on your valuation of the business.

## VALUATION

The value of a business is not something that can be ascertained with mathematical precision. Value is always a matter of opinion, and as such professional appraisers talk about "estimating" value rather than "determining" value. There are several valuation techniques that can be used to arrive at an estimate of value.

### Don't Start with the Seller's Value

When you hear the asking price for a business, don't assume that it reflects the correct value of the business. The seller may know less about selling a business than you know about buying one, and his price may have been picked out of the air with no basis whatsoever. You answer an advertisement for a restaurant that grosses $300,000 a year and nets the owner $20,000 a year before taxes. The seller is asking $200,000 cash for the restaurant. Upon investigation you find that the seller does not own the building, some of his equipment is leased, and there is nothing unique about his restaurant that could not be duplicated. A fair price?

When you ask the restaurant owner how he came up with his asking price, he may tell you, "I figured that anyone would be happy with a 10 percent return on their money. I make $20,000 a year. Whoever buys from me will do as well as I've done. I've slowed down as I've gotten older and I haven't done as good a job running the restaurant as I might have. So the new owner will probably make more than I do. If the buyer is going to receive a 10 percent return, $20,000 per year is a 10 percent return on a $200,000 purchase price."

Does this method of arriving at a purchase price sound reasonable? The seller works 60 hours a week to earn $20,000 a year. The reason he's selling the restaurant is that he can no longer face the hard work and long hours. If you were to work the same hours as the seller, took no vacations, and if you could do as well as the seller, your income would be $6.42 per hour. If you are presently making $4 an hour, that might appeal to you. Even if you're making more, this analysis might sound attractive because you may believe that you can, in fact, increase the business. But wait! There is more.

If you paid $200,000 cash for the restaurant, you must include in your calculations what the use of the money is worth. Money has a value just like everything else. In today's investment market, you could easily earn 8 percent on your $200,000 by making investments where the risk is virtually nonexistent—investments that are certainly safer than putting your money into a restaurant where one case of hepatitis or food poisoning could chase all the customers away and wipe you out. Certificates of deposit at many savings and loans associations pay over 8 percent, corporate bonds for the largest corporations in the United States are paying over 8 percent. Some corporations are presently paying dividends of over 8 percent and their operating history indicates that this dividend is likely to be increased. If we assume that the $200,000 could earn at least 8 percent in an investment where no effort is required, then we could value the $200,000 at $16,000 per year and subtract that amount from the restaurant income to determine what you would be earning from your labors. When we subtract $16,000 from the $20,000 restaurant income, we see that the income that you will earn from your 60-hour work week will be $4000. This translates to $1.28 per hour. No wonder the restaurant is for sale—who would want to work for that kind of money?

The present owner is trapped. It is a fact of life for many small businesses that there is not enough income from which to pay someone to take the owner's place (if such a person could be found) and still have some profit left for the owner. Whenever the owner is away from the business, profitability seems to drop dramatically. He can't get out of the restaurant business unless he can persuade someone else to take his place in the trap. Whoever buys will similarly be trapped, destined to remain a restauranteur until someone agrees to take his place.

"But," you might say, "the seller is an old man and he's tired. I could certainly do a better job than he did. I have a better personality, I'm a better cook, and I can see at least a dozen ways that this business can be improved. So doesn't that mean that this might be a very good investment after all?"

That's true. If you thoroughly understand the food business and you're confident that you will not make any mistakes in your efforts to improve the business, this may be, in fact, a tremendous opportunity. However, it may also be that the seller has valued his business too highly.

But as is always the case with business decisions, there may be another way to look at it. Terms of payment are as important as the asking price. As a cash purchase the restaurant appears to be overpriced. If, however, the seller was willing to extend extremely generous payment terms, the price might be reasonable. An example of "extremely generous" terms would be: nothing down, no interest, $500 per month until the purchase price is paid. That calculation would give you a net of $14,000 per year ($20,000 less $6000 payments), which would leave you $4.49 per hour for your labor. This is not a high hourly wage, but it's a start and if, in fact, you feel you may increase the business volume, it may be quite a bargain. It may be that you are really making $6000 a year more because making the payments is similar to putting money in the bank, providing you can sell the business someday for at least what you paid for it. Be careful in these calculations, though, because they can be tricky. For example, if you have $20,000 profit, you have to pay taxes on this entire amount, even though you pay part of it to the seller and don't have the cash in your hand to use for payment of the taxes. On the other hand, you may be able to depreciate some of the business property, even though you haven't paid for it yet, and receive some tax benefits.

Regardless of the technique used, it is necessary to have a good understanding of each item that makes up the business being valued. The best starting place for this understanding is the financial records of the business, which can be compared to a physician beginning a physical examination with a blood sample.

## The Balance Sheet

You have found a business you want to purchase. It is a small assembly facility that produces awnings for single family homes. You have walked around the plant and have found it to be well stocked, organized, and clean. You've met the two employees and you like them; you would enjoy working with them. The seller, Sidney Slipp, has told you that he has been selling $200,000 in awnings a year, but he feels with a little effort you could double these sales.

Sidney is an insurance salesman who has been running the awning business in his spare time. He confides to you that he has really only made a few thousand dollars a year from the business, he really doesn't know how much, and that if he had it to do over again, he would have devoted more attention to this business. He had more time a few years ago, but now his insurance business is taking so much of his time that he's had to let the awning business run itself. Sidney says that everybody in the awning industry values their business at twice annual gross sales ($400,000), but because he is anxious to get the business problems off his mind, and he'd like to take a vacation, he will sell this business to you for 1½ times gross, or $300,000. You're also told that since Sidney doesn't need the cash, he'll let you have it for a small down payment, with liberal terms on the balance.

This might be it—a real opportunity. The only question is, how much is the business worth? To determine the fair value of the business the first thing to do is to ask Sidney for copies of the business's financial records. Although Sidney may have boxes of invoices, receipts, check stubs, and other types of written records, the two that should be studied first are the balance sheet and the profit and loss statement. See Sidney's balance sheet on page 56.

This balance sheet is like a photograph of Sidney's business; it is a portrayal of the financial condition of the business as of the last day of the fiscal year. Properly read it can tell a great deal about the business.

Sidney's balance sheet is not like the balance sheets found in text-books or similar to the ones the big corporations send to their share-holders. Sidney's provides less detail, does not have footnotes explaining which items merit special mention, and there is no comparison showing the changes in each item from year to year. For comparison purposes the summary financial information sent to all shareholders by a company listed on the New York Stock Exchange is in the Appendix, beginning on page 144. Cynicism is healthy in business, but don't conclude that Sidney is hiding something if his financial records do not compare favor-ably with others you have seen. In larger companies financial reports are relied on by stockholders to know what kind of job management is doing and are used by management to demonstrate to their lenders that the loan is secure. In smaller companies the need is less because the stock-holders and management are the same people and lenders are able to see

## SIDNEY SLIPP'S AWNING BUSINESS
## BALANCE SHEET
## AS OF JUNE 30

**Assets**

| | | |
|---|---:|---:|
| Cash on hand and in bank | | $ 6,447.82 |
| Accounts receivable | $21,563.46 | |
| Allowance for bad debts | (3,787.98) | 17,775.48 |
| Inventory | | 50,812.90 |
| Total current assets | | 75,036.20 |
| Furniture and fixtures | 520.16 | |
| Accumulated depreciation | (216.14) | 304.02 |
| Cars and trucks | 2,600.00 | |
| Accumulated depreciation | 1,560.00) | 1,040.00 |
| Machinery and equipment | 5,459.78 | |
| Accumulated depreciation | (2,289.94) | 3,169.84 |
| Copyright—No Compete Agreement | 77,000.00 | |
| Accumulated amortization | (23,204.02) | 53,795.98 |
| Total fixed assets | | 58,309.84 |
| Prepaid expenses | | |
| Interest | 1,621.02 | |
| Advertising | 3,799.43 | 5,420.45 |
| Total assets | | $138,766.49 |

**Liabilities**

| | |
|---|---:|
| Accounts payable—Trade | 7,693.65 |
| Accounts payable—ABC Specialties | 27,078.74 |
| Notes payable—Bank | 25,020.00 |
| Commissions payable | 939.84 |
| Accrued taxes | 832.21 |
| Total liabilities | $61,564.44 |

**Stockholders' Equity**

| | |
|---|---:|
| Common stock. | 95,000.00 |
| Retained earnings—prior years | (10,591.39) |
| Current net income (loss) | (7,206.56) |
| Total stockholders' equity | 77,202.05 |
| TOTAL liabilities and stock holders' equity | $138,766.49 |

for themselves how the company is doing. In this context management has prepared only those financial reports that are useful to the day to day management decisions. Generally accepted accounting procedures require that each asset be assigned a value equal to the lower of what that asset cost or what it could be sold for. If an asset has appreciated in value and can be sold for more than Sidney paid for it, the value of the asset should not be increased on the books; the cost of the item is the highest value that should be assigned to it. If this accounting procedure is followed, then Sidney should be able to sell his assets for at least the book value, and maybe for more.

Examining each entry of the asset column reveals that two items make up 75 percent of the asset value, Inventory at $50,812.90 and "Copyright—No Compete Agreement" at $53,795.98 ($77,000.00 less $23,204.02 amortization). These items should be studied first.

Is the inventory really worth $50,812.90? The first task is to determine exactly what constitutes the inventory. The inventory should be seen, counted, and inspected to determine if it is in usable condition and not obsolete. If possible, the cost should be verified by inspecting the invoices. It may not be reasonable to count every item in inventory or check every invoice, but it should be possible to pull out random samples and use these to test the accuracy of the seller's figures. When the existence and cost of the inventory has been established, be creative in anticipating what might cause the inventory to be worth less than cost. Was it purchased from someone who has no other connection to the seller, or could this have been a friendly sale at an inflated price? Is the amount of inventory such that it will be used up in a few weeks, or is there so much that it will last months, long enough for it to become obsolete or otherwise less valuable? Visualize how the inventory will be used and see if any problems are likely. I once inspected a plant that had over $100,000 invested in inventory, all of it new and none of it obsolete, which was worth only a fraction of the purchase price. In that case the inventory consisted of tiny control panel doors for an electronic device. The problem was that the company that manufactured these doors had a firm policy that it wouldn't sell any control panels without doors attached. No one knew how this company had obtained just the doors, but their only use was to repair doors that broke off the panels, and this was a 50-year supply.

The $53,795.98 valuation assigned to the "Copyright—No Compete Agreement" is for an intangible asset, something that has no physical properties and which cannot be readily converted into cash (like accounts receivable) or used to reduce expenses (like prepaid expenses). Sidney says that this entry describes some advertising slogans, trade names, and the obligation on the part of the person who owned these slogans and names not to compete with Sidney. What's this worth? It is common when using conservative valuation techniques to say that the intangible assets have no value under a theory that it is impossible to verify any market value for them. This is open to dispute in some cases. Slogans can have substantial value ("Things go better with Coke") as can product names ("Rolls Royce"). On the other hand, how valuable is the slogan "Sidney's awnings keep the sun out"?

The balance sheet entry labeled "Accounts receivable" describes the amount of money Sidney's customers owed him on June 30. The total of these unpaid bills (receivables) has been reduced by $3787.98, the amount Sidney estimates his customers will never pay ("Allowance for bad debts"). The value of the accounts receivable can be verified by inspecting the individual receivables, checking that the total of all the individual receivables is the same as what is shown on the books, and if there is any doubt as to the authenticity of the records, contacting a sampling of the customers to verify the amount they owe.

The "Allowance for bad debts" entry can be as important as the "Accounts receivable" entry. It is a prediction of how many receivables will not be paid. What has happened in the past is the best indication of what will happen in the future, but there is no way to be certain when predicting the future. Maybe everybody will pay; maybe nobody will pay. There are some generally accepted methods for determining which accounts receivable are questionable. If a calculation using this method gives an amount of questionable accounts receivable that is significantly higher than the amount assigned in the "Allowance for bad debts," then the seller should be asked to defend the calculations he used, preferably by showing that in the past a significant amount of the questionable accounts receivable were paid. It is generally accepted that all past due accounts receivable are of questionable value and if a customer has several accounts, the fact that one is past due means all of the accounts receivable from the customer are questionable, even the ones that are not past due. A receivable is usually considered past due if it has been on the books for 90 days, although in some types of businesses it is more reasonable to say an account is past due if it is on the books for 60 or 30 days.

The rest of the asset portion of the balance sheet can be passed over rather quickly. "Cash" can be verified by bank records. The total value assigned to "Furniture and fixtures," "Cars and trucks," and "Machinery and equipment" is quite low, and it should not be difficult to determine if, in fact, these assets have a value equal to or greater than the amount shown on the books. Incidentally, "Depreciation" on the balance sheet is supposed to reflect how much the asset decreases in value each year, but the effects of inflation and the wear and tear caused by the kind of use and care received by the asset often render the "Depreciation" figure useless for any purpose other than computing income for income tax purposes. "Prepaid expenses" are items that were paid as of June 30— interest that is due in July but prepaid in June is an example of a "Prepaid expense" asset of the company.

The itemization of "Assets" on the balance sheet may not include several tools, furniture, machinery, and other items of value that can be found scattered throughout the plant. This may be because each item was fully depreciated for book purposes and no longer has a "book" value, even though it is still of use to the company, such as the 10-year-old drill press that was only supposed to last five years. There are other reasons assets may not show up on the company's books. Although some of the purchased items should be carried as assets until fully depreciated, the company may have treated such purchases as expenses of the company which means they were not put on the book as assets. The company's motive to treat an asset purchase as an expense might be partly to reduce the bookkeeping expense and partly to reduce income taxes. When Sidney purchased an $80 wrench last week, conservative accounting and a literal reading of the federal income tax laws required him to "capitalize" this wrench, carrying it on his books as an $80 asset and depreciating it over its useful life. If the wrench is expected to last eight years, the books would reflect that $10 of the $80 purchase price would be depreciated each year. Depreciation is how the purchase price of any asset is expensed over the life of the asset. When Sidney purchases an asset that must be depreciated on his books, he does not have a deductible business expense—for tax and accounting purposes his only business expense is the annual $10 depreciation.

"That's silly," Sidney might say. "It'll cost me more than $10 a year just to keep track of the depreciation on each tool. I buy these tools all the time and they're always getting lost. There is no way I can keep track of things the way the accountants tell me I should. I'm going to treat all tools the same way I treat salaries—as an expense—and I'm not going to bother with depreciation. This means that my income (and my tax) will be reduced by $80 for each $80 tool I buy, and not the $10 depreciation the accountants tell me to take."

Accounting is as much an art form as an exact science, so there is no "right" answer to what asset adjustments are to be made. The best thing a buyer can have is some methods to use in making these adjustments.

When all adjustments are made to the asset portion of the balance sheet, with consideration given to whatever off-balance-sheet assets there might be, the liabilities portion of the balance sheet should be examined.

On Sidney's balance sheet, the biggest liabilities are accounts payable, one $7,693.65 and another $27,078.74 for a total of $34,772.39. Who is this money owed to? What is it for? When is it due? Is any of it past due?

"These accounts payable are all to suppliers who supply inventory, office supplies, and advertising services. I believe that the cheapest form of financing," says Sidney, "that any business can have is its suppliers. The bank charges interest—the suppliers don't. Every single supplier is 60 or more days past due. I don't pay until they call at least three times."

This declaration by Sidney could mean a lot of things. What Sidney is saying is true in many instances, and numerous corporate controllers view it as their duty to stretch the payment of bills out to the last possible day. But nonpayment of suppliers could also mean that Sidney is in serious financial trouble and is staving off bankruptcy by paying only the most persistent creditors. A detailed inspection will have to be conducted to determine the real facts. Special attention should be given to the payable to ABC Specialties, over two-thirds of all accounts payable. Since many suppliers give a discount if prompt payment is received, a review of the payables might show that there is a substantial cost resulting from these late payments, more than the cost would be if the money were borrowed from a bank. The payables should also be inspected to see if any of them are charging interest on amounts owing, which more suppliers are doing to encourage prompt payment. Current activities with suppliers should be checked to see if the suppliers have, in self-defense, placed Sidney on a "cash-with-order" status. If Sidney must pay cash for future supplies, the business may be headed for a serious cash shortage, as Sidney's customers continue to expect credit from Sidney while Sidney needs cash to produce the goods being sold. It may also be that some suppliers, perhaps a critical one, have refused to do any more business with Sidney because of his bad payment history or are willing to do business on a cash-with-order basis only if all prior indebtedness is paid. They may feel that if they couldn't trust Sidney to pay promptly yesterday that they are unwilling to trust Sidney to be more reliable in the future.

The entry called "Notes payable—bank" represents a $25,020 obligation. It is important to find out when these notes are due, the interest charged, and what the borrowed money was used for.

"Don't worry about that. We have a fine relationship with our bank," says Sidney. "We had a $22,000 loan to finance some of our receivables. It took us longer than we thought it would to solve our problems and we had some trouble making the payments to the bank. After we missed a few payments, we had a meeting with the bankers and they suggested that we borrow the money to pay the interest. So I signed a second note for the past due interest, which was $3020. But the bank doesn't care; they're in business to loan money. They love us."

Many questions are raised by Sidney's comments. The bank loan was for more than the accounts receivable are now. This means that either the bank loan was not for accounts receivable or accounts receivable have been reduced substantially, because banks who finance receivables will loan only a percentage of the receivables, and never more than the face amount of the receivables. Also, banks are very insistent about a borrower living up to the terms of the loan. Banks almost never agree to an abatement of interest payments, except where the borrower is in serious financial trouble, and even then, many times banks prefer taking their chances in bankruptcy court to modifying the original loan agreement. A banker who agrees to the loan agreement changes outlined by Sidney could have problems with the bank examiner who certifies that loans made by the bank were in accordance with generally accepted banking practices. It is likely that Sidney is in very serious financial trouble and that the bank is insisting that Sidney come up with a plan to pay them or they'll take legal action.

Although the entry labeled "Commissions payable" is only $939.84, it raises the question of whether commission employees are being timely paid the commissions they have earned. If Sidney is unable to pay his creditors, perhaps he is unable to pay his salespeople. How long will Sidney's sales force continue to work for him?

The entry labeled "Accrued taxes" may be relatively unimportant—it is only $832.21—but caution indicates that this item should be checked. What are these taxes for? Are they for federal income taxes, state sales taxes, social security taxes, personal property taxes, state income taxes, use taxes, real property taxes, or some other type of tax? When are they due? What happens if they aren't paid when due? The government has strong laws to collect its taxes, and if not timely paid, it is possible that all of the company's assets could be seized and sold to satisfy the tax bill. For some taxes Sidney has a personal obligation that takes precedence over most other creditors and which cannot be discharged by filing bankruptcy. These are the taxes that Sidney will be very concerned about paying.

Moving down the list of liabilities, something seems to be missing. When Sidney was showing the production facilities he said, "We make the finest awnings in the country and this quality enables us to offer our customers a 100 percent guarantee for one year. Only about 3 percent of our customers use this, but it sure helps sales." This guarantee may help sales, but it is a cost to be incurred in future years. An estimate should be made of the cost of satisfying these guarantees, and this amount should be shown on the balance sheet as a liability labeled "Reserve for returns" or "Guarantee reserve." Whatever the amount, this is a liability, the same as an account payable.

That portion of the balance sheet labeled "Stockholders Equity" states the net worth or book value of the corporation. This will always be a dollar amount equal to the difference between the assets and the liabilities. It can be a negative number if liabilities exceed assets. The first entry, "Common stock," is what Sidney (or whoever Sidney bought his stock from) paid to the company for the common stock. The size of the business is such that it is doubtful that the $95,000 listed was paid in cash. It is possible that something other than cash was delivered to the corporation for the stock; it is not necessary to pay cash for stock. For example, Sidney may have used the $77,000 "Copyright—No Compete Agreement" plus other assets of questionable value and assigned a $95,000 value for capitalization purposes. The assets portion of the balance sheet describes what is being purchased and the liabilities portion describes what obligations must be paid. So, in theory, the stockholders' equity portion is of little importance. Still, it is an insight into the historical operation of the company and should not be passed over.

The entry labeled "Retained earnings—prior years" shows that the cumulative loss for prior years was only $10,591.39. This is confusing. We have earlier decided that the business is in serious trouble. How can a business capitalized with $95,000 be in serious financial trouble with such a small loss? The answer is in the documents from which the balance sheet was prepared. This will require studying Sidney's records carefully to find out exactly what is happening.

The last item on the balance sheet is "Current net income (loss)." This shows that last year Sidney lost $7206.56. The detail as to how Sidney lost that amount can be found in the profit and loss statement, a record of income and expenses for the year.

### The Profit and Loss Statement

If the balance sheet is a photograph, showing things as they were on a certain day, a profit and loss statement is a moving picture, showing what happened during the year. This is the profit and loss statement given by Sidney:

## SIDNEY SLIPP'S AWNING BUSINESS
### Profit and Loss Statement
### For Fiscal Year Ending June 30

|  | From 7-1 to 6-30 | % To Sales | Month of June | % To Sales |
|---|---|---|---|---|
| Sales | $191,936.59 |  | $19,457.65 |  |
| Cost of goods sold | 94,672.08 | 49% | 9,364.61 | 48% |
| Gross profit | 97,264.51 | 51% | 10,093.04 | 52% |
| **Warehouse Expenses** |  |  |  |  |
| Supervision | 6,360.00 |  | 140.00 |  |
| Labor | 10,466.68 |  | 1,501.45 |  |
| Payroll taxes | 1,183.91 |  | 117.01 |  |
| Telephone and telegraph | 352.12 |  | 29.48 |  |
| Depreciation and amortization | 6,460.96 |  | 539.42 |  |
| Truck expense | 523.82 |  | 57.64 |  |
| Fuel | 875.26 |  | 5.87 |  |
| Insurance | 1,833.36 |  | 133.53 |  |
| Paint supplies | 940.15 |  | 52.50 |  |
| Shop supplies | 1,529.80 |  | 265.11 |  |
| Power and light | 628.35 |  | 37.06 |  |
| Rental | 7,200.00 |  | 600.00 |  |
| Experimental | 605.00 |  | -0- |  |
| Total warehouse expense | 38,959.41 | 20% | 3,479.07 | 18% |
| **Selling Expenses** |  |  |  |  |
| Advertising | 1,830.55 |  | 239.66 |  |
| Commissions | 12,914.92 |  | 939.84 |  |
| Trade discounts | 33,032.43 |  | 4,029.22 |  |
| Total selling expenses | 47,778.01 | 25% | 5,208.72 | 27% |
| **Administration Expenses** |  |  |  |  |
| Payroll taxes | 745.55 |  | 61.66 |  |
| Insurance | 668.62 |  | 55.70 |  |
| Postage and office supplies | 465.69 |  | 93.05 |  |
| Executive salaries | 11,400.00 |  | 900.00 |  |
| Bad debts | 962.00 |  | 97.29 |  |
| Miscellaneous expenses | 137.46 |  | 6.02 |  |
| Total administration expenses | 14,379.32 | 7% | 1,213.72 | 6% |
| Other income | 149.46 |  | -0- |  |
| Other expenses— interest | 3,503.79 |  | 267.10 |  |
| Net income or (loss) | ($7,206.56) | 4% | ($75.57) | .3% |

The profit and loss statement requires the same type of item-by-item analysis as was necessary when examining the balance sheet.

First, we notice that sales were less than $192,000, not the $200,000 Sidney represented. This will help determine how reliable Sidney's statements are in areas that cannot be checked.

Sales of $192,000 last year would mean more to us if we could find out how much sales were in previous years—is the business on the way up, flat, or on the way down? The month of June, the last month of the fiscal year, accounted for almost $20,000 in sales. If the rate of June sales were continued for an entire year, sales would be $240,000. Is June normally an above average month? Did something abnormal happen in June—some extraordinary clearance sale—that isn't likely to be repeated? Are sales steadily increasing? Maybe each month was better than the previous month.

The purpose of a profit and loss statement is to describe all income and then show what items should be subtracted from the income, the difference being profit or loss. The term "profit" is synonymous with the terms "net income" and "earnings." Items of expense deducted from income can be grouped in a variety of ways, but Sidney has elected to subtract the cost of raw materials first, the "Cost of goods sold." Notice that raw materials account for almost 50 percent of the sales price. As you inspected the operation, did you see any way to reduce this cost? A 10-percent reduction in raw material expenses could make this business profitable. Something happened in June to reduce the cost of raw materials from 49 to 48 percent. Is this attributable to new controls developed by Sidney or is it a normal fluctuation?

The rest of Sidney's profit and loss statement is broken into three major categories: "Warehouse," "Selling," and "Administration." "Warehouse" describes what it costs to assemble, store, and ship the awnings. Each entry should be examined minutely. Is the payroll expense reasonable for the labor performed, or will it have to go up (or down) in the near future? What insurance does Sidney carry? What is the $605 for "Experimental"? Sidney didn't do the arithmetic necessary to convert each individual item to a percentage of sales, but if you did such a calculation, some interesting questions might come to mind.

A business must be profitable to be successful, but a business does not have to be profitable to be able to generate enough cash to pay its bills. The depreciation and amortization expenses are $6460.96, but these are noncash expenses. Assuming that all receivables for goods sold are paid promptly, the $7206.56 loss may mean a negative cash flow last year of less than $1000. Of course, at some time the property being depreciated or amortized will have to be replaced and then a cash shortage might develop.

Sidney spends a lot to sell his awnings, and June was more expensive than earlier months; the entry labeled "Selling Expenses" was 27 percent of gross sales in June as opposed to 25 percent of gross sales for the year. The biggest portion of "Selling Expense" went for "Trade discounts," over $33,000. Are the discounts a result of reduced selling prices to distributors and manufacturers' representatives or are these discounts to accomplish some objective, such as cash with order?

"A small portion of these Trade Discounts," explains Sidney, "are discounts given to wholesalers, but most of the discounts are from the 7 percent discount we offer to all customers who send cash with order."

Does this mean that all of the accounts receivable on the books of the company are "doubtful?" Maybe. The only reason a purchaser wouldn't send cash with order to take advantage of the 7 percent discount may be that he didn't have the cash. This is worth pursuing.

Administrative expenses seem reasonable—7 percent of sales. When they are examined more carefully, though, it is obvious they can be reduced substantially.

"I take a salary of $11,400," explains Sidney, "but I really don't do much for it—I spend maybe five hours a week on the business and most of that time is spent trying to figure out what happened while I was gone. I took a salary the same as if I was spending all day selling or making the awnings, but since I did neither, my entire salary had to be changed to 'Administration Expenses.' I expect that whoever buys the business will spend more time on the business, and if they do, they can get by with less help."

If what Sidney says is true, there is the possibility that salaries can be reduced enough to make the business profitable.

With this type of analysis you may reasonably conclude that the business should be able to show a small profit with no increase in sales (by cutting expenses) and that profit together with depreciation expenses may result in a cash flow of several thousand dollars a year—cash that the owner can reinvest in the business, use for personal expenses, or use to pay Sidney for the business.

There are more financial records that could be studied, the most important of which would be a Source and Use Analysis (showing where funds come from and how they were expended), monthly operating statements from the end of the fiscal year to the date the business is being inspected (showing changes), and an analysis of how the previous year compares to earlier years (what patterns are evolving). Once all financial data have been reviewed, it is possible to "estimate" the value of the business. The three most common valuation techniques are: (1) book value, (2) income, and (3) market value.

## Book Value

In accounting terminology, book value is the difference between a company's assets and its liabilities, with all assets valued conservatively, at the lower of the assets' purchase prices or their fair market value, and with all liabilities accounted for. If a company keeps proper financial records, the book value of a business can be quickly computed by inspecting the balance sheet. In theory, every company should be valued at its book value or more. We've seen from Sidney Slipp's balance sheet that there is often a gap between theory and practice as assets like accounts receivable and covenants are carried on the books at questionable values and liabilities are being understated or left off the books. The problems with Sidney's balance sheet are not unique. Nevertheless, book value is a common point of beginning when estimating the value of a business. In some industries it is common to discuss sale prices as being some multiple of the book value—"The bank in Springfield is for sale and the price is only twice book value."

Investors who speak of a business value as being a multiple of book value are recognizing that in a going business the whole is more than the sum of the individual parts. There is a significant value created by the act of bringing together various items of inventory, equipment, and people and shaping these parts into a functioning unit.

Sometimes a business may be worth less than book value. Book value is generally determined from the perspective of the lesser of cost or what each item would sell for if sold to a willing buyer, presumably another going business that has use for that particular item. While this valuation may be reasonable if the business is sold as an operating equity or if an occasional item is sold, this value may be too high if the business is closed suddenly. In that situation, there may be many more items for sale than there are buyers. If there is a real possibility that the business will fail despite your best efforts, you should compute its value under those circumstances—what is the liquidation value of the business? The accounts receivable owed to Sidney may be entirely collectible if the business continues, but if Sidney has to close his door, would they be paid? Some customers would withhold payment because Sidney didn't fill their current orders. Some customers would take the position that since Sidney wasn't going to continue in business and honor the guarantee he gave, they were going to withhold payment. Others would just not pay their bills, hoping no one would notice in the confusion (and often no one does notice). The intangible assets would have no buyers and the other assets may have dramatically reduced value. All estimates of market value assume that there is a willing buyer and a willing seller, neither of whom are under any compulsion to buy or sell. Once a business has failed, all prospective buyers know that the seller is under pressure to sell the assets, giving buyers an advantage in negotiating the sales price. There is also the possibility that at the time a business fails, there may be no buyers who are interested in buying the business assets.

Because book value is only a starting point in estimating value, most buyers will make only the obvious, more significant adjustment to the balance sheet. With all of this, we can take Sidney's stated asset value of $138,776.49 and subtract from this liabilities of $61,564.44 (the bills to be paid) and intangibles of $53,795.98 (assets that most likely have no value) for a book value of $23,406.07.

"You might see only a $25,000 book value," Sidney says, exaggerating the number slightly, "but the real value of a business is how much you can make from it. You can't sell a college diploma for anything, but it is worth a great deal because it will increase your income. I'm talking about selling you a business that will increase your income and this is worth more than $25,000."

## Income Approach

Measuring how much profit can be earned from a business is a logical means of determining how much that business is worth. When a business has operated at a profit in the past, it is customary to use the amount of the previous year's profit as a starting point. If the previous year was abnormal in a manner not likely to be repeated, a better starting point would be the average profit for the two or three preceding years. When a business has been operated at a loss, as is the case with Sidney's business, it is necessary to assume a level of profit in the future, and this estimated amount is the beginning point. To the extent it is assumed that the new owner will make profits in a business where the previous owner failed to do so, there is an element of uncertainty injected into the computations. Assume that after considering all the facts the best estimate is that the adjusted pretax income of Sidney's business will be $10,000, which is a high number but one that is easy to work with. Using this assumed income from the business, it should be possible to estimate the value of the business.

"If you look at the daily stock reports in the Wall Street Journal," Sidney might say, "you'll see companies whose stock is valued by the stock

market at 30 or more times the per share earnings. This valuation means
that the investing public, including some of the most astute investors in
the world, values the company at 30 or more times earnings. You can see
it in the column labeled 'P.E. Ratio,' in the sections where the market
activity for listed stocks on the New York Stock Exchange and the American Stock Exchange is described. Look it up. If I used that formula here,
I would multiply my income by 30 and my business would be worth
$300,000 or more."

As is often the case with Sidney, he is partly right and partly wrong. It
is common to value a business as a multiple of earnings, and Sidney is
right about the P.E. Ratio reported in the Wall Street Journal. In fact, in
periods of economic optimism it is not uncommon for the stock market to
value businesses at 100, or more, times current earnings. But these high
multiples are a result of a belief that the income of the business will
increase dramatically in the near future and that a price of 30 or 100
times earnings today will be 10 or less times earnings tomorrow. Studying
the stock market will demonstrate that investors assign a lower P.E. Ratio
to most businesses and a substantially lower P.E. Ratio where there is a
possibility that earnings might decrease—troubled companies may be
valued at three times earnings or less.

There are some other problems with Sidney's comparison to an exchange-listed company. Reported P.E. Ratios apply to income after, not
before, tax. Sidney's calculations were applied to before-tax income.
Also, Sidney's comparison with exchange-listed companies is not as reasonable as it might appear because the listed companies are so much
larger and better established than Sidney's. A company on the New York
Stock Exchange must have assets of not less than 16 million dollars and a
company on the American Stock Exchange must have assets of not less
than 3 million dollars. Companies of this size can afford the best professional managers, have the resources to survive bad times, and have the
manpower to plan for the future. If the owner of Sidney's business were
sick for a month, the business could collapse.

Rather than starting with what stock market investors are doing to a
business using the income approach, start with what return an investor
would receive from a "safe" investment, adjust this rate of return up-
ward a sufficient amount to reflect the added risk Sidney's business represents, and convert this rate of return to a P.E. Ratio. If high-quality
corporate or government bonds are paying interest of 10 percent, then
you know you would have to invest $100,000 in those bonds to earn
$10,000 per year, the same as you would earn from Sidney's business.
Ignoring taxes this return calculates to a P.E. Ratio of 10 ($100,000 ÷
$10,000). But to encourage an investor to put money in Sidney's business,

it will be necessary for the investor to receive more than the 10 percent a safe investment pays. On the other hand, maybe the required return can be reduced if the investor believes that the income, and with it the value of the investment in the business, has the potential of increasing, unlike bonds, where income and redemption price are fixed. There is no easy formula to follow. No "expert" can do this for you. You have to use a great deal of judgment and guesswork in making this calculation to determine a reasonable rate of return. The only "fact" used in this calculation is what rate of return safe investments are earning. This fact changes from day to day, in recent years ranging from 6 to 18 percent.

Even though we have limited information on Sidney's business, let's make a guess at valuation. Since Sidney's business has been operating for several years, sometimes showing a profit and sometimes not, we can arbitrarily say that it is substantially riskier than a "safe" investment, and at least twice as much return is required, increasing from 10 to 20 percent. But the future looks very good. With good management, Sidney's Awning Business should be able to triple the profit next year and triple it again the next year. Even though a ninefold increase is anticipated, that is in the future and may never happen. It is arbitrary, but perhaps reasonable to divide the required rate of return by 3, meaning that the investor would be satisfied with a 6.67 percent (20 ÷ 3) return on his investment the first year. If projections are accurate, and earnings increase ninefold, the rate of return today of 6.67 percent will become 47.97 percent by the third year.

A rate of return equal to 6.67 percent of investment is the same as a 14.99 P.E. Ratio (1.0 ÷ .0667). Applying this P.E. Ratio to $10,000 of income means that the value of Sidney's business is estimated at $149,925. Reasonable? It rests on several assumptions and if any one fails, the computations are of no value.

"A company with this potential, with a P.E. Ratio of only 14.99, is a steal. Just look at the Wall Street Journal," Sidney might say. "You'll see how reasonable this is when you compare it to other P.E. Ratios."

I looked in the Wall Street Journal and didn't see very many companies with a P.E. Ratio this high. Even if there are a few, the comparison is still not a sound one for the reasons discussed before.

This price seems high, but this depends in part on the highly speculative nature of the estimated $10,000 first-year income. This is merely one approach to estimating value and should be weighed with other approaches and not slavishly followed.

Incidentally, don't overlook the importance of income taxes when determining what the "safe" rate is at the time you are buying. The safest investment is government bonds, but municipal and state bonds are exempt from federal income taxes and some states income taxes. Federal bonds are exempt from state income taxes. Since income taxes may be 50 percent and more, any comparison of interest rates to rate of return should have an appropriate adjustment.

The remaining common valuation technique is to determine the market value of the business; that is, what others would pay for it.

## Market Value

The market value of a business is defined as what a willing buyer would pay a willing seller, neither being under time pressure or other compulsion to act and both having knowledge of all relevant facts. Since in the marketplace there are usually time or other pressures on one or both parties, and since the parties often have incomplete knowledge of the relevant facts, this definition is somewhat theoretical.

"I don't care about theory," Sidney might say. "I've had one offer for $100,000 so I know my business is worth that much. An awning company across town recently sold for $200,000 and I think my business is similar so I'm asking $200,000. I'd be crazy to sell my business to you for less than somebody else is willing to pay."

An analysis of the sale price of comparable businesses is the best way to determine market value. If we can determine the sale price of other awning businesses that are substantially similar to Sidney's, we will have a good indicator of value. The problem is finding a substantially similar business. Usually other businesses have more sales, fewer assets, a different product line, or are otherwise sufficiently different so the sale price cannot be used to value Sidney's business. To make different businesses similar enough to be compared, appraisers use conversion standards. These conversion standards cannot be looked up in a book. They have to be created at the time using the available facts.

Someone who is buying a business can determine his own rough conversion standards. First isolate those elements of the business that are most important in determining value, for example, income, book value, gross sales, and so on. Then compute a conversion formula based on the relationship of each element to its counterpart in the other business. For example, Sandy's Shade Factory had projected pretax income of $15,000 next year, adjusted book value of $84,000, gross sales of $300,000, and sold for $275,000. Compare this to Sidney Slipp's Awning Business which has projected pretax income of $10,000 next year, adjusted book value at $23,000, and gross sales of $192,000. The conversion factor based on income is .67 ($10,000 ÷ $15,000), based on book value it is .27 ($23,000 ÷ $84,000), and based on gross sales it is .64 ($192,000 ÷ $300,000). This approach enables us to apply actual sale prices (the best available information as to value) to a business that has not been sold and causes us to conclude that Sidney's business has a market value between $74,250 (.27 × $275,000) and $184,250 (.67 × $300,000). To be more specific requires determining which factors are to be weighed most heavily. Obviously there may be other factors involved and some factors may defy conversion.

Purchasing a business for an amount equal to or less than the estimated market value provides some protection—the business can be resold for a minimal loss. There is another theory that you are protected even if you pay more than the market value. The "greater fool theory" is based on the assumption that if I, as a reasonable astute businessman, am willing to pay a specified price, then I, as a desperate, anxious seller, should be able to find another businessman who is willing to pay a comparable price—"I am not so great a fool that there are none who are greater."

These three methods—book value, income approach, and market value—should provide a range of values. If the three approaches are used by a professional, they will reinforce each other and usually will point to a very narrow range of values. Used by a nonprofessional, there may be wide ranges in the estimated values, but it should be a reasonable assumption that if you purchase Sidney's business for less than the lowest figure, you have negotiated an attractive purchase price, and if you pay more than the highest value, you have paid too much.

## Trust Your Calculations

Sidney is an enthusiastic salesman and after spending hours with him and hearing all about the things that could be done to improve the business, it is easy to become enthusiastic and excited.

"You know, I've been wanting to go back to hiring door-to-door salespeople," Sidney tells you. "Let me show you how well I did when I had one. When he quit I never could find time to hire a replacement, let alone additional salespeople. And plastic, did I show you how I intended to cut material cost by 30 percent but never found time. . . ."

Sidney may be asking a higher price than any of your calculations can justify, and you may just "know" it's a good buy at his price. After all, you may think Hank Hognose bought a similar business and after 15 years of hard work he had made so much money that he was able to retire to the French Riviera. You "know" that if you draw all your money out of the bank, sell your house, cash in your life insurance, and turn all this over to Sidney you can retire in 15 years, too. Maybe you can, but don't become so enthusiastic you forget that your best protection against a mistake is to make your decision only after dispassionate analysis of the facts and the numbers. Go back over your calculations. Find out why there is a discrepancy. Use the valuation techniques to define what it is that causes you to "know" the business is a good buy and keep working the numbers until you agree with the range of values arrived at by the appraisal techniques. If you can't make your calculations agree with the price, the price is probably too high.

## TALK IS CHEAP AND WORTH EVERY PENNY

Money does strange things to people—it makes them greedy. Just as you wouldn't tempt people's honesty by leaving cash unattended in a public place, don't leave agreements hanging, tempting the other party to change the terms.

"I've been trying to buy this stained glass company for months, and just last night, Theodore Tenuous, the owner, and I reached an agreement," I was told by Rudy Rock, aggressive businessman to be.

"I started out by offering $35,000 payable over five years," Rudy continued, "and after three hours of discussion, I agreed to pay $42,000 payable over four years. We have a deal, and we shook on it. I'm to hire a lawyer and get the terms written up, but I don't have time today because I'm meeting with the contractors about remodeling the work area. If I'm to be able to move in next month, a lot has to be done."

Two days later when Rudy took the written agreement back to Theodore to be signed, he was surprised to hear, "I'm sorry, Rudy, but I can't sign this purchase agreement. It says here that you will only pay me $42,000, and that you're going to pay this over a period of four years. I distinctly remember insisting that I be paid in cash and my memory tells me that we agreed to $47,000."

Rudy argued with Theodore for over an hour, but finally had to agree that he would pay the higher price and in cash. What Rudy should have done at this point was take out the written agreement that he had prepared and change it to reflect the new terms—drawing a line through the old price and payment schedule, and substituting "$47,000 payable in cash." Then both could have signed an agreement and the deal would have been done. Nobody ever said Rudy was a fast learner. He took the agreement back to the secretary to have it retyped before asking Theodore to sign. What happened next can be expected—Theodore was pleased at how easily he could raise the price so he decided to raise it again.

When Rudy brought the contract back the next day for signature, he was surprised to hear, "Listen, Rudy, I know we agreed to a deal, but it's not final until I sign. I've been thinking about it. I have to have $50,000 for my business. If you don't want to pay this price, I guess I'll just have to sell my business to somebody else."

Despite Rudy's protests, Theodore wouldn't budge. Rudy may have been a slow learner but he wasn't stupid. He took out his pen, wrote in the new terms, and asked Theodore to sign. An unbelievable story? It happened. Only the names have been changed to protect the foolish.

Oral offers are rarely wise. When Rudy was orally negotiating the terms for the purchase of Theodore's business, Rudy gave Theodore the chance to look into his eyes, listen to his voice, and watch his hands, all of which helped Theodore to decide how to respond to Rudy. Theodore decided that Rudy wanted Theodore's business very badly, would pay top dollar for it, backed down easily when confronted, and was very trusting. Theodore had been in business for many years and knew how to read the signs. His only regret was that he had but one business to sell Rudy. Rudy was blissfully unaware of the numerous signals he was telegraphing to Theodore's observant eyes and ears.

If Rudy would have talked less and instead submitted a written offer for a specific price, say $30,000, he could have put Theodore in a position where he would have had all the doubts that normally plague a seller when considering what will happen if an offer isn't accepted—is someone right now telling Rudy about another business he'll like better; is his wife having second thoughts about her husband quitting his secure job and taking on the risks of becoming a businessman; will Rudy change his mind? Without any way of knowing how Rudy would respond to a hard line, Theodore would have been more likely to respond favorably to Rudy's offer.

A written purchase agreement should be more than a legally binding contract that reduces misunderstandings and makes unilateral changes difficult. Properly prepared, the purchase agreement anticipates problems and forces the parties to unequivocally make commitments and decisions, for example, specifying which promises made by the seller can be relied on by the buyer and which should be discounted as mere sales "puffing." This is an important document and should not be prepared casually.

# 5

# TAXES AND PURCHASE AGREEMENTS

When you enter into an agreement to purchase a business, the written agreement should describe all of the agreements that have been made in sufficient detail so someone who wasn't there could understand what the agreement was by reading the contract with no verbal explanations. Many consider written agreements to be primarily legal documents and assume if one is written in a manner that is legally enforceable, it is well written. This is incorrect. The fact that a contract is legally enforceable isn't enough if the contract doesn't clearly say what the parties agreed to do. For this contract to be enforced the court will have to make certain assumptions about the intent of the parties when the contract was signed. These assumptions may not be accurate. The fact that we have a legally enforceable agreement for you to sell me your car for $1500 isn't enough to protect you if it is unclear and therefore arguable who has to pay the bank loan, who owns the snow tires, or who pays for the dent in the fender that wasn't there a week ago when we agreed to the price.

When preparing your purchase agreement you should think of it as a memorandum that describes what you are buying, what you are paying, what each of you promises, and what happens if something goes wrong. Consider what would be important to you if you were purchasing Verna Velveeta's Vending Company, which consists of vending machines and locations for these machines. Common sense will be a great help here. After price and terms were agreed to, for example, you might want Verna to agree in writing that (1) the financial records she showed you are accurate; (2) she owns the vending machines and there are no liens against them; (3) the vending machines are in good operating condition; (4) Verna won't go back into the vending machine business and compete with you; (5) payment to the restaurant or service station owners for permitting the vending machine on the premises is the percentage of gross receipts represented. Let's look at how other businesspeople have handled this same situation.

## THE VELVEETA PURCHASE AGREEMENT

Let's look at two different written agreements that might be used to purchase a vending machine company. Many times businesspeople are quite casual, writing very short contracts. I was once involved in the purchase of two nightclubs where the entire agreement was written on a paper napkin. This type of businessperson might write the following contract:

### Agreement

Harmon Hulk and Verna Velveeta hereby agree that Hulk purchases her vending machine company for $87,000, payable $25,000 down and the balance $1000 per month until paid in full. Interest to accrue at 8 percent. All the reports Velveeta has given Hulk are accurate.

_____

Harmon Hulk

_____

Verna Velveeta

This is a legally binding contract. Even though this agreement contains the terms most important to the parties (price and terms), it omits many items that could be problems in the future. A well-written contract is like an insurance policy—you hardly know it exists and often feel it is unnecessary when things are going well; however, it is a great comfort when matters are going poorly.

I have included a copy of the contract used to purchase Velveeta's Vending Machine Company in the Appendix on page 167. It answers many questions that might be raised.

The purchase agreement begins with four recitals that set forth the facts surrounding the purchase. These are to describe the factual context in which the agreement was entered into, making it easier for someone who wasn't there to understand what the parties wanted to accomplish, and to define some terms ("vending machines," "locations") that are used throughout the contract.

The first paragraph after the recitals describes what the purchaser is buying in detail. The vending machines are described and serial numbers are given. Spare parts, keys, and inventory are all mentioned. It is interesting and most unusual that the seller is keeping her business name even though the buyer is getting all the goodwill of the business.

The price to be paid for this business is set forth in paragraph 2. Instead of a single purchase price, each part of the business is valued separately. The purchase agreement assigns values of $40,000 for the vending machines, $4000 for the goodwill of the business, and $38,000 for the seller's agreement not to compete with the buyer. The inventory is being sold to the buyer for a price equal to the lower of cost or value, to protect the buyer against changes in the amount of or damage to the inventory before the closing.

The reason the purchase price is divided into components is the federal income tax law. Because income taxes are so high it is important for a buyer to keep in mind the differences between that portion of the purchase price that can be treated as a business expense, that portion which must be capitalized but can be depreciated or amortized, and that portion which must be capitalized but which cannot be depreciated or amortized.

Payments to the seller that can be treated as business expenses are the most attractive to the buyer because the payment can be deducted from the buyer's taxable income when it is made. An example would be payments to the seller for services rendered, such as a consulting agreement. Buyers, desirous of reducing their taxable income, will often want to allocate as much of the purchase price as possible to some such service agreement. They will sometimes ask the seller to accept an allocation of part of the purchase price to services, even though they both know the seller will not be providing any meaningful services. This is going too far. The Internal Revenue Service will generally accept the allocation of the purchase price made by the parties, but only if this allocation is reasonable. The IRS will not accept any transaction that was done for the sole purpose of minimizing taxes. If the allocation of the purchase price is rejected by the IRS, they will reallocate the purchase price and the desired tax savings may be lost.

The reason the IRS is often willing to accept purchase price allocations is that as the buyer's taxes go down, the income taxes paid by the seller increase. For the buyer to have a deductible business expense, the seller will have to receive payment for services, income that is taxed at ordinary income tax rates. If the buyer is denied business expense treatment for payments to the seller, then instead of being taxed at ordinary income rates, the seller will be taxed at capital gains rates, a significant reduction. Substantial confusion can arise as the parties negotiate allocation.

Even if the parties agree to the amount that should be allocated to a service agreement, tax complications can develop. The only way there is little likelihood of tax complications is if the seller is to be paid for only those services actually rendered during the payroll period, on a per hour or per diem basis for hours worked. Payments to the seller under these circumstances are deductible business expenses when paid, the same as payments to other employees. This is not what most purchase agreements provide. Usually the seller will be paid a predetermined amount over a period of time, regardless of the services actually provided. The seller's obligation to actually work is often very vague as the parties intend for the seller to do very little. In these cases, assuming that the IRS doesn't dispute the allocation, the IRS will require that the total amount allocated can be deducted as paid only to the extent that the payments are in the same proportion as the time elapsed; for example, if there is a five-year service agreement, but all the money is to be paid at the end of the first year, then since only 20 percent of the time for performance of the services has elapsed, only 20 percent of the payments can be deducted as business expenses, the remainder being carried as a prepaid expense with 20 percent deductible for each of the five years. The seller, however, will have taxable income when he receives the money.

In the Velveeta purchase agreement, Velveeta is to provide services, a deductible business expense, and she also agrees not to compete with the buyer, a capital asset that must be capitalized by the buyer and then amortized over the life of the agreement.

Capitalized assets do not have to be paid to be depreciated or amortized. The amount assigned for a five-year agreement not to compete can be amortized (and deducted from ordinary income) at the rate of 20 percent per year, even if there are no payments until the fifth year.

Velveeta agrees in the purchase agreement to both provide services and to not compete with the buyer, although there is no allocation between the two. There is no requirement that the parties allocate the purchase agreement into its components, and in those cases where there is no allocation, both the buyer and the seller are free to make whatever allocation they believe to be reasonable, although the IRS wants both parties to allocate in the same manner.

The IRS theory for denying an immediate income tax deduction for the purchase price of capital assets having a useful life of more than one year is that the buyer has merely exchanged one asset for another. No deduction will be permitted until the asset has been used up in some manner, and then the taxpayer is permitted an income tax deduction to the extent of his loss.

The $40,000 that Hulk is paying for the vending machines will be deductible for income tax purposes over the life of the equipment. For many items the government publishes charts that show the acceptable useful life for income tax purposes. Although there are some special tax considerations (such as the investment credit which provides a credit against income taxes for certain purchases of personal property), if the machines can be expected to be worn out or obsolete at the end of five years, then one-fifth of the purchase price ($8,000) can be deducted from taxable income as a business expense each year. This is called depreciation. If you are using up a natural resource such as gravel or coal, the process is called depletion. If an intangible asset such as a covenant not to compete is being used up, this is called amortization.

There are some capital assets that the IRS will not permit the taxpayer to depreciate, deplete, amortize, or otherwise claim are being used up. An example is goodwill. The IRS maintains that goodwill exists in almost every going business, and that goodwill is never used up. The $4000 that Hulk allocated to goodwill in the purchase agremeent with Velveeta will be carried on his books indefinitely as an asset; no portion of it will ever become deductible from Hulk's income taxes. Hulk was wise nevertheless to allocate a portion of the purchase price to goodwill. The IRS auditors have the legal power to challenge allocations that they consider unreasonable, and since they will always claim something for goodwill, the probability of a reallocation is reduced by assigning some value to goodwill. Recently some taxpayers have challenged the assertion by the IRS that goodwill always exists. In response to these challenges, the IRS's new position can be stated as follows: Every going business has some value simply because it is a going business. This value may be overshadowed by other assets and liabilities, but some portion of the purchase price must be allocated to reflect the capitalization of the costs incurred in assembling and shaping the many pieces that constitute the going business.

That portion of the purchase price that is used to purchase inventory is not deductible until the inventory has been used. When inventory is used it is called "cost of goods sold" and is deductible as a business expense. If there is any profit on the sale of the inventory, it is a capital gain item for the seller, though when the buyer resells this same inventory, any profit is taxed as ordinary income.

The seller is usually indifferent to the buyer's allocation problems because the seller has his own tax problems; he will receive ordinary income tax treatment on that portion of the purchase price allocated to the covenant not to compete and the service agreement, and capital gains treatment for the balance. The seller may become concerned about the allocation among capital assets if the seller faces some depreciation recapture from the sale of assets where he has elected accelerated depreciation on real estate or recaptured depreciation or investment credit on personal property. If these types of problems arise, the assistance of a tax advisor should be solicited before the purchase agreement is signed.

The provisions of paragraph 3 of the Velveeta purchase agreement define the restrictions on Velveeta's conduct and prohibit competition with Hulk in listed counties for 10 years. Paragraph 3 also states that if Velveeta sells any more vending equipment, she must have the purchaser of that equipment agree not to compete with Hulk. This provision may be illegal under federal antitrust and fair trade statutes which permit some agreements to not compete, but which generally make illegal many agreements to limit competition. Notwithstanding, these clauses are very common and many attorneys believe they are legal.

Paragraph 4 requires the seller to help Hulk place machines "in those locations in which Seller has placed or will place in the future any coin operated machine." It is unclear how much help is to be provided. Although the agreement appears complete, this section causes the reader to wonder how complete the agreement really is and to become a little confused about how Velveeta can agree not to compete while continuing to own coin-operated machines. It looks like the parties never thoroughly thought about the specifics of their understanding. Maybe they were in too much of a rush or maybe they told the lawyer they only needed a "fast and cheap" purchase agreement. Velveeta explains:

"Hulk is buying my food and cigarette vending business but I'm staying in pinball and electronic games. I've agreed to help Hulk wherever I have a game machine. We intended that I wouldn't have anything but a moral obligation to help Hulk, and if I introduce him and say I recommend him, I'll have done enough. The contract doesn't say this very well because we didn't explain it to the lawyer. Does it make any difference?'" It only makes a difference if Velveeta and Hulk disagree in the future as to what was promised.

The manner in which the purchase price is to be paid is described in paragraph 5. While the purchase price itself was allocated among machines, agreements to help and to not compete, and goodwill, there is no provision that defines how each monthly payment would be allocated. This means each payment would probably be divided pro rata, the same way as the purchase price. If it was the intention of the parties that the payments be allocated differently, they should have said so in the agreement.

Paragraph 5 also provides that the buyer will pay 6 percent interest on that portion of the purchase price payable over a period of time. Hulk explains:

"We really didn't want any interest to be payable and that's how we first agreed to the deal. When we met with the lawyer to write it up, he explained to us that the IRS has decided that if the payments are spread over one year or more, then some portion of what is paid to the seller must be taxed as interest income to the seller, although it is deductible as an interest expense by the buyer. I was told that the minimum interest amount that would be acceptable is 6 percent; however, if we didn't put any amount in the agreement, then the IRS would make up an amount, and they might choose an amount of interest higher than 6 percent. I don't know why the government cares; Velveeta will have more income taxable at ordinary income tax rates to the extent that there is interest, but I'll have more deductions. To get along with the government we reduced the price by an amount equal to the interest and then provided for interest."

Hulk's comments are widely believed, but slightly misleading. No interest needs to be allocated to that portion of the purchase price allocated to the agreement not to compete or to the agreement to provide services. If interest is provided for, it makes the allocation of the purchase price subject to challenge by the IRS under the theory that since the money isn't due until the service is provided or the time period for no competition has elapsed, it is appropriate that no interest be charged. When interest is, in fact, charged, as was done in Velveeta's contract, the IRS could argue that this is evidence that those payments were really for goodwill or equipment, and since the allocation of the purchase price was merely for tax purposes, it can be disregarded by the IRS for purposes of computing the federal income tax liability. There is also a question as to what rate of interest must be assigned. Your tax advisor should be consulted for the current minimum interest rate.

Paragraph 6 recites numerous representations and warranties that are made by the seller and makes clear that the buyer is relying on them. They are (1) seller owns what she is selling; (2) the bills of the business have been paid; (3) the machines are in good condition; (4) the vending machines are located where seller said they were; (5) there are no side deals with or promises to anybody; (6) all obligations of the business incurred before closing are the seller's responsibility.

In Paragraph 7 the seller agrees to help inspect the equipment, to give all keys to the buyer directly after the inspection, and to give the buyer a bill of sale wherein the seller promises good title has been delivered.

Paragraph 8 states that the buyer, Hulk, agrees that he won't compete with the seller in the game and music machine business.

Paragraph 9 provides that the closing will take place after the buyer has had an opportunity to verify some claims made by the seller.

Paragraph 10 provides that Hulk and his wife will be "jointly and severally" responsible for the payments to Velveeta. This means if a payment isn't made on time, Velveeta can sue either Hulk or his wife, removing any temptation that Hulk might otherwise have to avoid his obligations by "giving" all of his property to his wife if things were going badly.

There are many items packed into this purchase agreement, but it is intended as an example of a purchase agreement that was used, not as a model to be followed. It contains some errors, but this is true of many purchase agreements. The trick is not to make costly mistakes. The more money at stake, the more carefully written (and longer) the purchase agreement.

In this particular purchase agreement, there was no discussion of who was responsible for maintaining insurance coverage on the equipment and the inventory. The closing proceeded as scheduled and that same evening Hulk was supposed to go to Velveeta's storerooms to pick up the inventory. Velveeta said she would load the inventory on one of her trucks and leave the truck outside the warehouse, on the street, because the warehouse would be closed by the time Hulk would arrive. She gave Hulk a key to the truck since it would be locked.

As it turned out, Hulk wasn't able to pick up his inventory until after midnight. That night, about 11:00 p.m., the truck was burglarized and the inventory was stolen. Neither Velveeta nor Hulk had insurance on the inventory at the time it was stolen, as each assumed that insurance was the other's responsibility. The purchase agreement did not spell out the obligations of the parties to obtain insurance, and it was not clear if Velveeta had agreed to store the inventory for Hulk until he picked it up (making her responsible for the loss), or if Hulk had, in effect, borrowed a truck from Velveeta and stored the inventory in it (making him responsible). As their lawyers explained, there were many possible legal claims from negligence to assumption of risk. The combined legal fees for resolving this dispute were estimated to be more than the value of the inventory lost. There was a great deal of anger, but finally, after much squabbling, Hulk decided he needed Velveeta's help more han he needed the money, so he assumed responsibility for the loss.

## LONG AND SHORT PURCHASE AGREEMENTS

When preparing a purchase agreement it is important to anticipate potential problems, but at what point does protection against potential problems become so burdensome that common sense indicates it would be better to take the risk? This is a difficult decision, one that depends on the particular facts of each purchase. Most businesspeople want the purchase agreement to accurately state their agreement and to answer all questions that are likely to arise as the agreement is being performed. They are much less concerned about the purchase agreement dealing with problems that might arise, but probably won't.

At a minimum, the purchase agreement should state the price and terms of payment, identify the buyer and seller, and describe what is being sold. Expected problems and common questions should also be dealt with, for example, what bills will the seller pay before closing; or what happens to the buyer's earnest money if the buyer decides not to or is unable to complete the purchase.

There are also a host of problems that could develop, but which probably won't, for example, the buyer or seller dying before the closing, an employee strike before closing, or the business is destroyed.

Most of the frustrations that arise in the preparation of a purchase agreement come from dealing with problems that could, but which probably won't, develop. Both parties know it is impossible to deal with all the potential problems, yet when discussed in the right environment each potential problem seems important.

"Why, I remember one time," your attorney says, "when the parties had a falling out and because the purchase agreement wasn't thorough enough, thousands of dollars were needlessly spent resolving the dispute. I was the attorney for the seller. When he sold the business it was an important matter that the person he was selling to was financially reliable so he had the buyer represent that he had paid all of his bills on time for the past five years, and I put this representation in the purchase agreement. After the closing which involved payments to be made to the seller over several years, the seller found out that he had been lied to. The buyer had paid his bills on time, but only for the last 10 months. Before that the buyer didn't pay anybody on time and, in fact, had been forced to file bankruptcy about a year before.

"Anyhow," the attorney continues, "the seller didn't want to trust the buyer to make the payments with that kind of a history, so he called me up to see if he could get out of the agreement, get back the business, and give the buyer his money back. The first problem I saw was notifying the buyer that a problem existed. The courts always require notice of some kind. The purchase agreement didn't provide how notices could be given from one party to the other, and since the buyer was constantly traveling on business, we had no address to send the notice to. If the agreement had given mailing addresses for the parties and had provided that all notices could be by mail, we could have sent the notice to that address, and even if the buyer never saw it because he was traveling, it would have been legal notice."

"We also had a problem because the buyer and seller lived in separate states and the law in each state was different as to whether or not the seller could rescind the agreement under these facts. If the contract had only said which state's law applied, it would have been simpler and cheaper to solve this problem.

"There were additional problems," your attorney continues, seemingly oblivious to the fact that you are alternating between boredom and frustration, bordering on hostility, as you wonder if things had to be this complicated, "arising from an alleged verbal agreement which the buyer claimed changed the written purchase agreement. The buyer claimed that over dinner one night he and the seller agreed that where the purchase agreement said he had 'paid his bills on time for five years,' the 'five years' would be changed to 'six months.' Now if the contract had said that it could only be modified or terminated by a written agreement signed by both parites, then he would be prohibited from telling this ridiculous story in court."

Any experienced attorney can speak for hours, listing all the horrible things that could happen when a business is being purchased, but this same attorney should have in his files standard language that he recommends using to provide a reasonable level of protection. This standard language is commonly referred to as "boiler plate" and it is commonly added to all purchase agreements prepared by that attorney. Because this language is used so often by the attorney, he is very familiar with it, enabling him to add or subtract pages of boiler plate quickly and inexpensively. In the appendix on page 179 is a sample purchase agreement that was prepared for the buyer to purchase a small corporation. It contains a substantial amount of boiler plate that was included solely for the buyer's benefit. Some of the boiler plate deals with: (1) the legality of the corporate existence; (2) detailed description of taxes paid and liabilities disclosed; (3) accuracy and completeness of the corporate records; (4) legal authority to sign contract; (5) attorney's opinions; (6) notices; (7) governing law. This agreement affords a great deal more protection to the buyer than the Velveeta contract, both because of the boiler plate and because of the number of representations made by the seller. This is a sample of how more protection can be given than was given in the Velveeta contract. Your attorney has his own forms and should be able to write a contract and add just the amount of boiler plate to protect you against possible risks, without overburdening the documentation by attempting to unreasonably protect you.

Don't confuse boiler plate paragraphs with a well-written purchase agreement. Too much boiler plate can be confusing, causing the parties to overlook important matters. Your attorney won't know what the most important parts of your purchase agreement are unless you tell him, and you shouldn't be lulled into believing that he understands and has dealt with all the important issues merely because the purchase agreement has pages and pages of boiler plate. Before you begin to read his draft and become bogged down in the details of the purchase agreement, think through what is really important to you. In the purchase of this vending machine company, for example, what happens if you find that business is not what you thought it was and you don't want to make all of the payments? Do you want the right to sell the machines to somebody else before they are paid for? How about if things go very badly for you and you find yourself losing money in the vending machine business? It may be possible to negotiate language that says you have no personal liability to make the payments and that if you fail to make any of the payments, all the seller can do is take back the business, the inventory, and the machines, keeping what you have already paid.

Sometimes it is a businessperson's judgment that for one reason or another he doesn't want a lengthy purchase agreement. An agreement can be brief and still provide a great deal of protection for the buyer. An example of this is the four-page-letter purchase agreement in the Appendix beginning on page 193, which is a short purchase agreement, employment agreement, and agreement not to compete. This confirms most of the essential terms defined in the 13-page purchase agreement on page 179 in the Appendix. In the long purchase agreement the buyer did not know the seller very well and wanted a high level of protection for a transaction involving hundreds of thousands of dollars. In the short purchase agreement the parties had a history of working together, there was a high degree of trust, and less than $100,000 was at stake.

# 6

# BECOMING A DEBTOR

### PREPARE THYSELF

After weeks of soul searching and months of scanning the newspapers you have found the business for you—Mike's Maternity Shop. You have spent weeks inspecting the business and discussing the terms with Mike. You are satisfied that there will be no problems with the purchase agreement. The asking price is only $60,000 and you know it is a bargain. If you can just buy Mike's, you will have the beginning of something substantial; many more maternity shops will follow.

The only problem is money. You don't have $60,000 in cash and Mike needs cash to finance his new career as a stock car racer. No matter how many times you add up your checking account, savings account, credit union balance, and cash surrender value on your life insurance, you have only $11,000. Maybe you could take a second job driving a cab in the evening and in seven or eight years you might be able to save the $49,000 you need. The problem is that if you don't buy Mike's soon, somebody else will. What do you do?

You must start with a clear idea of your assets and liabilities. To do this you should prepare a personal balance sheet. A sample appears on p. 86.

## BALANCE SHEET

**Assets**

| | |
|---|---:|
| Cash in checking account at First National Bank | $ 700.00 |
| Cash in savings account at State Mutual | 3,000.00 |
| Credit Union savings account | 4,250.00 |
| Life insurance cash surrender value | 3,050.00 |
| House fair market value | 63,000.00 |
| 1977 car | 1,700.00 |
| Furniture and personal effects | 7,500.00 |
| Coin collection | 900.00 |
| Total assets | $84,100.00 |

**Liabilities**

| | |
|---|---:|
| Department store account balance | $ 600.00 |
| Balance owing on automobile loan | 875.00 |
| Home mortgage | 31,000.00 |
| Total liabilities | $32,475.00 |
| Net worth | $51,625.00 |

In this example you have a net worth of $51,625. If everything you own were sold and all of your bills paid, that is the amount of money that would be left for you.

After you have made up your balance sheet, stop for a few moments and see if you have missed anything. Are there any assets or liabilities that are missing from your list? Have you omitted any jewelry, silverware, common stock, stamps, valuable antiques, or pension rights? How about debts that are not listed, such as doctor bills that are being paid monthly or the bill that hasn't yet come in the mail for the new furniture. Since you'll be using this balance sheet to borrow money, it is important to be accurate and complete, disclosing all liabilities as well as all assets. Using a financial statement that is misleading to borrow money can subject you to criminal penalties. Additionally, the obligation to repay money borrowed by use of fraudulent financial statements cannot be discharged by bankruptcy.

When you are examining a business's financial records you want the records to be conservative in the values used, and it is reasonable to expect that they will be prepared in accordance with "generally accepted accounting procedures," known by the acronym GAAP. Prospective lenders do not appear to insist on GAAP from individuals, although the same lender will insist on GAAP when dealing with a business. When you prepare your personal financial statements it is acceptable to put your best foot forward by not strictly following GAAP. For example, you may have purchased your house three years ago for $43,000. It is now worth $63,000. GAAP requires that you list your house at the lower of cost or fair market value, in this case $43,000. I suggest you use the higher figure, but show clearly that this is market value, not cost.

When you inspect the financial records of a business you look at a profit and loss analysis together with the balance sheet. Similarly, whoever inspects your financial condition to determine if you are a good candidate for a personal loan will want to see a type of profit and loss analysis from you. Prepare an analysis of your income together with what it costs you to live each month. Estimate your average monthly cash requirements, including food, automobile, clothing, laundry, telephone, entertainment, medical, dental, and installment loan payments. When your cash requirements are subtracted from your income, the difference is called "cash flow." This is the amount that you can use every month to repay the loan.

You now have your personal financial preparation done—you know your assets, liabilities, monthly obligations, and cash flow. Now put yourself in the position of a prospective lender. How would you react to yourself and your proposal to borrow money?

The lender will first look at the business, the purpose of the loan. You have analyzed the business from the perspective of someone who will be on the premises every day, who will have intimate knowledge of all the business details, and who will be able to react to problems as they arise. The lender will not want to become involved in the operation of the business, but he will want to be assured that you have done your homework and that you are competent to run the business. The only way the lender can receive these assurances is to question you. Do you know how much it will cost per month for the business to stay open? How much business do you have to do every month to pay these bills? Have the previous owners done that much business in the past? How much money will be left over for you? What is the provision for contingencies? When are employees due for raises? What costs will go up next year? You must do some written projections, forecasting what you think the business's income and expenses will be month to month. The lender will cross-examine you about the reasonableness of these projections. He will be especially interested in your cash flow analysis and in how profitable your business will be.

Any lender will want you to have considered what will happen if the unexpected happens. What resources are you holding in reserve, that is, if a problem arises, will you take a part-time job, file bankruptcy, reduce personal expenses, reduce business expenses, or sell your house?

When you have completed your personal financial review, done your projections, and considered what your response will be to obvious questions, then you are prepared to begin discussions with your lender.


## THY BANKER

### Bankers Don't Like Risks

In the usual situation, banks will only loan money to those individuals who do not need it—as the bank might have said to Alice in Wonderland, "Only if you can prove to me that you don't need a loan will I know you are a good credit risk, worthy of receiving a loan. If you need a loan, don't bother to ask me because I won't give it to you."

When you approach your friendly neighborhood banker to borrow money, he will have two major concerns. The first is how you will repay the loan and the second is what the bank can do if you do not repay the loan.

When you ask your banker he will want to ascertain how realistic your income figures are. Will you be able to repay the loan as fast as you say? A bank wants its money back fast. A savings and loan association may give you 30 or more years to pay for your home, but your bank will want you to repay a personal loan to buy a business much faster, sometimes in 12 months. If Mike's Maternity Shop is to be a part-time venture for you and you will be able to keep your present job, it may be possible to obtain a loan with the understanding that you will pay the money back out of your salary. The same is true if your spouse has a job. If you need a part-time job to make ends meet while your business is getting off the ground, the lender will want some assurances that you will be able to obtain new employment. If you can't demonstrate the required income, you won't get the loan. Even if you have a good job today, if you have a history of quitting jobs or being fired, you will not get the loan unless you can somehow demonstrate that you will certainly be keeping this job.

If your primary source of income will be your business, then you must satisfy the lender that your expectations are realistic. The history of the business you are purchasing will be given great weight, but if the business is new or hasn't been profitable in the past, you must demonstrate to the lender that your experience in the business is substantial, your reputation is good, and the projections are realistic.

Once your banker is satisfied that you have the financial ability to repay the loan, his next question will be what happens if after you borrow the money you don't want to or can't repay the loan? What will happen, for example, to your desire to repay the loan if your projections are wrong and the business is a complete failure? The banker will remember the time Clyde Humpbuck borrowed $49,000 to buy a store selling records. What Clyde and the bank didn't know was that the complete stock of records was rapidly becoming obsolete as consumers were rejecting Clyde's 78 rpm records in favor of the smaller 45's and the longer playing 33 ⅓'s. After three months, Clyde closed the store and sold the inventory for $7000. At that time he had paid very little back to the bank and his attitude about working the next several years, giving most of his income to the bank, wasn't very good. "Why should I," said the note left behind, "work for nothing? I'm leaving town to start over somewhere far away." When Clyde left he took everything he owned except his house, but since he had recently gotten a second mortgage on that, his equity was only about $3000.

You have to give the banker reason to believe that even if your investment fails, you will pay the bank back, either because the bank can keep something of value until the loan is repaid or because there is something that would prevent you from fleeing, filing bankruptcy, or otherwise avoiding payment. The banker knows that the laws are written to protect you, and if he loaned money to the wrong person, one who can't or who doesn't want to repay the loan, collection can be very difficult. In most states, your home, furniture, clothing, personal items, and other property cannot be taken away from you by a creditor (with limited exceptions), and you can even file bankruptcy without losing them.

Even if you are wealthy the bank may be unwilling to make a loan if they suspect you may resist repayment. What can the bank do if you do not pay? Unless they are holding something that can be sold to pay the loan, the only remedy available is a lawsuit, which is very costly and usually takes years to resolve.

The banker will look closely at the factors, if any, that would keep you from leaving town or filing for bankruptcy. It may not be enough to be well known and respected. Filing for bankruptcy no longer carries the social stigma it once did. Each year over 214,000 individuals file for bankruptcy in the United States. The theory of bankruptcy legislation was that debtors should not carry the burdens of bad decisions their whole lives. In practice, the existence of liberal bankruptcy laws sometimes makes it difficult to borrow money. Incidentally, a promise not to file for bankruptcy is not enforceable.

Just because you are willing to pledge assets worth more than the amount of the loan as security, do not assume that you will receive a loan.

The bank may believe that you will not be able to repay the loan and that they would have to foreclose on the security to get paid. Banks do not like to foreclose and take your assets. Banks look at the security pledged for a loan more as an additional incentive for you to pay than as something to be sold by the bank if you don't pay. If you lack the ability to repay the loan, the additional incentive is meaningless. If the property that you are proposing as security for the loan will likely have to be sold to pay the bank loan, the bank would prefer that the customer sell it in the beginning and never involve the bank. The bank may offer a very short-term loan to be repaid out of the proceeds from the sale of the property if it has been sold to raise cash but payment will not take place for a few weeks. This type of loan is commonly called a "swing loan."

"How can that be?" you might scream at a banker. "I am willing to pledge my entire net worth of $51,625 for a lousy $49,000 loan. How can you possibly lose? If I keep my job, I'll be able to pay off the loan. If the business does well, I'll be able to pay the loan out of the proceeds from the business, and the income from my job will be extra. If I miss a payment, you can foreclose and take all of my property. I thought you were in business to loan money. How can you ever make money if you don't loan it out?"

If the banker answered candidly, she would say, "We think you are cutting it too close on your projected living expenses. If any unexpected items, such as medical expenses, were to occur, you could not make your loan payments unless the business was very profitable. We are unwilling to base the loan on your business being a smashing success. In addition to the fact that we make loans primarily on the borrower's ability to repay the loan, a requirement that you fail to meet. The security you mentioned is not enough. Valuation is a matter of judgment and there is always a possibility of a substantial error in the values assigned. Also, if we have to foreclose, the sale proceeds must be reduced by the costs of the foreclosure and the costs of the sale, a substantial sum. Most important, "fair market value," the basis of your financial statement valuations, assumes a willing buyer, who is under no compulsion to buy, and a willing seller, who is under no pressure to sell. In the foreclosure context, the bank would be under great pressure to sell (what would we do with your home or your automobile except sell them?), and based on our experience, we would sell your property for only a small fraction of what it might really be worth. We also have a great deal of concern because you are asking us to put more cash into the business ($49,000) than you are putting into the business ($11,000). Taking all of these things into account, we prefer to loan our money to someone else."

"OK," the customer might respond. "Since you won't do business with me any other way, I'll have my brother pledge the $100,000 worth of negotiable bonds he owns as additional security. He doesn't want to sell them unless he has to because he would have some taxable gain on the sale, but he has said he will pledge them as security if necessary. He has a good income and has also said that he will be a cosigner with me if necessary. Can we do business then?"

'A "yes" may not be automatic even with promises of additional security. Suspicions of dishonesty often plague bankers. You may know that you are of the highest integrity, but how is your banker to know it? Whenever a stranger comes into a bank the banker will consider the possibility that the loan is being sought with no intention of repaying it. Each banker will look at those signs which he believes demonstrate you are trustworthy. Have you ever borrowed money from a bank before? Is your checkbook ever overdrawn? How often do you move? How easily can your assets be converted to cash or packed in the station wagon and driven out of state? How quickly can the business you are buying be liquidated? How does the bank know you really own the house you live in?

Around my office, we're still talking about the time that Freddy and Teddy, two gentlemen from Chicago, came to town with no business connections and left a few weeks later with several hundred thousand dollars given to them by a local bank. Their scheme started in another city where they pretended to be the naive progeny of two wealthy British families, recently arrived from London. Presenting themselves to the largest bank in that city, they asked that the bank handle the "details" of keeping track of their income from family investments. Dropping the names of the wealthy and the famous, they turned over to the curious banker several official-looking bonds, and other official-looking documents, all of which indicated that large sums of money would be paid at regular intervals and that these payments were guaranteed by substantial British companies.

"We certainly don't need any money from you," said Freddy to the banker, "but we would like you to collect the money as it comes in, transfer it to our checking account, and give us periodic reports of where we are financially. We'd like it handled by your trust department and we expect to pay the usual trust fees."

As the banker could see no risk, he accepted the charge. Freddy periodically sent money to the bank, disguising the source and thereby causing the bank to believe this represented payment on bonds. The bank sent all the money it received, less the trust department fee, to Freddy together with a handsome report from the trust department which showed the phony bond as "assets on deposit with the trust department, secured bonds having a face amount of $2,475,200."

Freddy and Teddy then came to my town and within a week they had signed an agreement to purchase a large building and had engaged a prominent architect to do tens of thousands of dollars worth of plans showing how the building was to be remodeled. The next week they moved into a $350,000 house, leased a limousine, and appeared at a local bank.

"We're new in town," they said, still posing as the sophisticated and fast-moving businessmen progeny of wealthy British families. "We are impressed with your city and your people and want to move our center of business here. As you can see from this bank trust department report, we have several million dollars in trust. As you can see from our architectural plans, we've already invested a lot in this building that we're going to remodel. Will you loan us $250,000 for the next few weeks so that we can go ahead with our project? We'll pledge our trust assets."

The bank looked at their house, their car, the $2.4 million in trust, the extensive plans, and loaned them $250,000.

A few weeks later Freddy and Teddy were arrested for fraud—they apparently had three or more similar schemes going at the same time and someone caught on. Bail was fixed at $100,000 each and the next day they were released. A week later they were gone, bail forfeited to the court. None of the bank's $250,000 was found.

When the dust settled we discovered they had gotten a bail bondsman to post bail for them without either of them putting up a cent; they pledged their $350,000 house. But they didn't own the house. The documents of title they had given the bail bondsman were phony. He was out $200,000. The owner of the house they were renting had been persuaded by them to accept possession of a small box of diamonds as security for rent payments. "You hold these diamonds," Teddy had said, "until our next trust check comes. Here's an appraisal showing that they're worth $75,000, several times our rent." The diamonds were phony. Needless to say, the architect was never paid and the check written on a London bank as earnest money for the purchase of the building was returned with "account closed" stamped on it. It was a clean sweep; no one was paid for anything.

Don't be offended by the distrust of your banker as he gets to know you. He's only protecting what everyone seems to want: his money. Once the preliminaries are over, your banker can be a real help to you, acting both as a lender and as a trusted financial adviser. He has seen how many successful businesspeople operate and he has also seen the kind of mistakes that often cause businesses to fail.

## Some Loan Terms

When your bank has decided that you are a worthy risk and an amount has been agreed to, several issues remain to be resolved. When will payments begin? How large will they be? If the loan is an installment loan, a fixed amount will be due every month, the interest rate will be high, and generally the entire loan will be repaid in less than four years. Installment loans are very common; an installment loan is what most people use when they buy an automobile.

Notes that are often used with established bank customers are short-term or demand notes. A short-term note may be for 30, 60, or 90 days. A demand note is one that is due whenever the bank asks for the money. There may be an informal understanding between the bank and the borrower that this demand or short-term note will remain unpaid for several years. Paying a short-term note that is due by using the proceeds from a new one is called "rolling over" the note and is not uncommon. There are advantages to the bank having a demand note or a short-term note. Even though it is intended that the note will not be repaid for a year or more, the bank can ask for a higher interest rate periodically, and if concern develops over the borrower's ability to repay the loan, the bank can demand payment before matters become worse. Frequently, demand or short-term notes are used with informal repayment schedules. The customer may agree with the banker that he will repay the entire indebtedness within four years, and every 90 days he will sit down with the banker, roll over the note, and make whatever payments he is then capable of making.

A less common small loan is called the term loan. In this case the bank agrees that you may keep the money for several years and make periodic payments to retire it. This is similar to an installment in that regular payments are made, but the term may be longer than an installment loan, payments may vary in amount, and term-loan payments may be made quarterly or semiannually, whereas installment loan payments are usually made monthly. Banks are short-term lenders and prefer loans where the money is repaid quickly. If you need a real estate loan for 30 years, your banker will probably refer you to an insurance company or other long-term lenders. But if you need the money for eight years, a bank may be able to help with a term loan.

Any of these three types of loans—installment, demand, or term—can be secured or unsecured and can bear whatever interest rate and contain whatever terms and conditions as are permitted by the banking regulations.

The bank will want every protection possible in the loan documents you sign. As a small borrower your business may  not be important enough to the bank for it to modify its procedures for giving loans. You can either take what the bank wants to give you or go elsewhere. An example of the kind of requirements that the bank will impose is the somewhat standard loan document clause which provides that notwithstanding the length of the loan term, if the bank determines that in its opinion circumstances have changed and the loan is "at risk," then the bank can declare all monies due. If the customer has any other checking or savings accounts in the bank, the money in them may be seized by the bank to pay the loan. The bank often wants this right, even if all required payments have been made on time.

Occasionally I'll see an advertisement that states if you send the advertiser a few dollars, he will explain to you how you can borrow money from the bank and have no obligation to pay it back. If you send for his advice, you will be told that since the shareholders and officers of a corporation have no obligation to pay the bills of the corporation, you can get the benefit of the loan without having to pay it back by forming a corporation to borrow the money. It is true that corporate employees and shareholders are not liable for the debts of the corporation. However, a bank won't loan money to a corporation unless it has substantial assets or unless someone of substance cosigns or guarantees the loan.

Bankers are creative. They have invented many ways for you to borrow money in a manner that reduces their risk. Let's say, for example, that Mike's Maternity Shop takes in $100,000 a month. You haven't paid much attention to this because historically Mike's Maternity Shop has paid out $98,000 every month in salaries, bills, and inventory purchases. What good is $100,000 in deposits? This may be important to your banker because it means the business may have a substantial "float" in its checking account. If you deposit money on the first and immediately write a check, that check may not be presented to the bank for payment for several days—you have to write it, mail it, the receiver has to deposit it into his bank, and his bank has to present it to your bank. The money that is in the business checking account to cover that check when presented is the float. This may mean that on an average day Mike's Maternity Shop has only a few hundred dollars in its checking account, according to the checkbook where all checks are subtracted when written, but for the bank's purposes (having seen only the deposits, not the checks that are in the mail) the account balance is $30,000. If you were to borrow $30,000 from the bank, the bank might have a totally secured loan because on an average day the bank could seize all of the money in Mike's Maternity

Shop's checking account and be paid in full. This dramatically reduces the bank's risk.

Bankers can sometimes find value in business assets where the owner finds none. Mike's Maternity Shop has inventory that costs $25,000 and receivables (money owing from customers for purchases) of $15,000. There are also unpaid bills of $40,000. Since the amount of unpaid bills equals the value of the inventory and the receivables, the owner of Mike's Maternity Shop has a zero net worth if just these items are considered. The owner is more interested in the location of the store, the list of loyal customers, the store fixtures, and the good business reputation with suppliers. The bank, however, may see $40,000 of security where the owner sees a zero net worth.

"You must remember," banker Tyrone Tillsworthy says, "that the $40,000 in bills you are talking about are all unsecured creditors. They are the rent, electricity, telephone, office supplies, advertising, and similar bills. Secured creditors have priority over unsecured creditors. If we make a loan to you and take as security, the inventory and the receivables, we can seize the inventory and sell it, and keep the money from the receivables, even if the other creditors loaned you money first and even if they receive nothing. If we add these assets to your other property, we may be able to give you a secured installment loan."

Bankers are often quick to spot techniques for increasing their income while causing as little pain as possible to the businessperson. Two widely used techniques are compensating balance requirements and use of a lock box.

The loan agreement may require the borrower to keep a certain amount of money in his checking account for the life of the loan. The money required to be kept in the account is called a compensating balance. Since the bank doesn't pay interest on money deposited into business checking accounts (although many personal checking accounts bear interest), this "free money" given to the bank effectively increases the rate of interest it earns. Since it is difficult for the businessperson to compute the value of these compensating balances, frequently he will assign no value to the requirement. This is unfortunate because compensating balance requirements will increase the interest rate by ½ percent or more, a significant amount when comparing the cost of alternative sources of money.

Other loan agreements use a so-called lock box arrangement. All the money received by the business is deposited into a special noninterest bearing account (the lock box), and when released from the lock box the money is immediately used to reduce the loan balance. When the business writes checks, the bank loans additional money to pay the checks. Elmer Tiddle has a lock box for his fishing supply business. Elmer says, "Three or four times a year we have a tremendous surge in orders and we need to borrow up to $200,000 from the bank to have enough material and workers to fill these orders. The rest of the time we don't need any money from the bank. Rather than having to negotiate a new loan every time we need money, the bank has said that we can borrow up to $200,000 anytime, but that this is expected to be paid back as the fishing supplies are sold to stores around the country. When we owe the bank money all of our cash receipts must be deposited in a lock box account, and if, for example, $90,000 comes in one week, then $90,000 will be applied to our loan balance. If we need $110,000 to pay our bills that week, we must increase our loan by that amount—we have no cash because every cent we took in went to the lock box. The only thing that bothers me is that the bank refuses to transfer the money from the lock box to reduce the loan the same day the checks come in. They wait up to four days to see if there will be any problem when the checks are presented to the payer's bank. When these checks are paid they become 'collected funds.' "

"This makes me kind of mad," continued Elmer, "because the bank doesn't insist on collected funds in other situations. I don't know what it costs me in extra interest because the bank won't accept an uncollected check, but I bet it's plenty." The cost of lock boxes depends on the length of delay in transferring funds, and this varies as banks have different policies.

Creative as your banker might be, he may be unwilling to help you, in which case there are several alternatives.

## ALTERNATIVE LENDERS

If your banker can't help you, ask him to recommend someone you should approach.

I often hear borrowers discussing the Small Business Administration, known as SBA. The SBA is a federally funded agency that is charged with helping small businesses obtain loans. Although the SBA is able to help only a small number of businesses, you may be one of those helped. Your banker should be willing to help you apply for SBA help. One requirement to apply for SBA assistance is that a bank must certify that it has turned you down for a loan. If you are accepted by SBA, they will guarantee your loan from the bank. The SBA is designed to assist all small business concerns with special attention to (1) businesses that are located in areas where there is a high percentage of unemployment, (2) businesses owned by low-income individuals, (3) businesses damaged by floods or other catastrophes, and (4) businesses displaced by federal government action. Because of these special requirements, the typical small businessperson can expect little help from the SBA. Even if you qualify for special attention, the SBA has not lived up to its potential. The paperwork, governmental restrictions, and local practices pose many obstacles.

If the SBA is not for you, take a look at those people who are in the business of loaning money. Look in the telephone book yellow pages under "Loans" or similar headings. Call and explain your needs. Visit with several lenders. If one can't help, ask who they recommend. Shop for money the same way you shop for an apartment or a new car. Talk to several people, ask questions, and ask for advice.

The way you approach your bank is a good model to follow for all lenders. The same questions will be asked by all of them, but their response to your answers may be different. Some lenders are in business to earn a higher profit than banks attempt to earn and they are willing to risk losing their money to earn these higher rewards. A bank is first concerned about protecting its money and secondly concerned with making a profit. Because of this banks will not accept some loans, regardless of the amount of potential profit; you cannot persuade your banker to extend a loan to you by increasing the amount of interest you are willing to pay. The banker's philosophy is if a loan is so risky that it has to bear a very high interest rate, the loan does not belong in a commerical bank. He has depositors' money to protect and bank regulations to comply with—not so with many small loan companies.

When dealing with professional lenders make sure you limit your dealings to companies that have good reputations and that you understand everything you sign. Check the reputation of the lending company by asking the opinion of other lenders and those who regularly borrow money. If all else fails, ask the lender who it would give as references and as satisfied customers. It takes some effort to determine reputations, but if you have once dealt with a disreputable lender, you will realize its importance.

Banks are highly regulated and the customer generally receives fair treatment. High-risk lenders are regulated very little, if at all. These lenders handle many more problem loans than banks do, and they can be tough to deal with if you don't repay your loan as agreed to.

Occasionally you will hear of a lender who is willing to take a percentage of your profit as additional interest. He explains to you that this is the "sweetner" or "kicker" that enables him to take more risk than other lenders. This is requested by multibillion dollar insurance companies as well as the small loan company. These lenders occasionally want to play an active role in the business, for example, they want to help you set credit policy, determine how much inventory to keep on hand, and decide salaries. This can be of great help to you if you and the lender have the same philosophy, but it can be a source of tremendous conflict if the two of you do not see things the same way.

Before you accept the terms demanded by Honest Harry's Loan Company consider who else may be willing to loan you money, perhaps a lender who does not loan money as a business.

### Everybody's Favorite

So Mike wants $60,000 for his Maternity Shop. The newspaper ad said, "Cash only," and the broker has told you that Mike wants to cash out. Do you believe everything you read and hear? Of course Mike wants cash—if he can get it.

The seller is often the most available, interested, knowledgeable, able, and willing lender. What does Mike want the money for? If he needs it to make the down payment for his new house, you may have difficulty persuading him to loan you money by accepting a promissory note for part of the purchase price. That is rarely the case. Almost always the seller will be able to forego a portion of the cash, and all you have to do is persuade him.

Work as hard to persuade the seller as you would have to persuade a bank. When you put your offer together, offer to give Mike a second mortgage on your house and tell him that if you miss the payment, he can take the business back and resell it. If he resells the business for more than you owe him, he has made a profit. If he resells it for less than you owe him, he can collect the difference from your house. Show him how you expect the business to succeed and where the income will come from to pay him.

Remember, the seller has a problem: he owns a business and he wants to sell it. A buyer doesn't have a problem; he has desire and some money. If a buyer is going to help a seller solve the seller's problem, it is reasonable to assume that the seller will be flexible.

Most purchasers assume that when a business is for sale the buyer must either buy the entire business or buy none of it. This is not true. Buying only a portion of the business assets can be one way of resolving a disagreement between the buyer and seller as to the value of the business, and this technique can also be used to enable a buyer to acquire a business he couldn't otherwise afford.

Accounts receivable and real estate are two business assets that the sellers commonly want to sell but often can be persuaded to keep.

"There's not a doubt in my mind," Sidney might say, "that every dollar of the $21,563.46 accounts receivable will be collected. That 'Allowance for Bad Debts' is just something the accountant made up. I don't care if every receivable is 90 days past due, awning people are good people and they pay their bills."

If you believe Sidney's accounts receivable are worth 10 cents on the dollar, arguing the point with him can degenerate into you implying that either his business judgment is bad or he's lying to you in an effort to inflate the value of the business. It would be better to tell Sidney he can keep the receivables. This would reduce the purchase price by that amount.

This technique of buying only a portion of the business can be extended to other assets of the business, for example, real estate or cash.

Sellers are often willing to keep the land and buildings used in a business, provided they receive a fair rental. When Kathy Kernal looked at the tavern on Old Smokey Road, she felt that the $70,000 asking price was a bargain, but even so it was more than she could afford. Upon investigation, she found that although the seller had not considered it before, he was willing to sell the business and lease the building on a 20-year lease when she proposed this. One incentive for the seller to do this was Kathy's agreement to pay a higher rent than the building would normally rent for. After several hours of calculations they decided if Kathy paid $30,000 cash for the business plus $1,000 per month rent, both would have what they wanted. Kathy would be paying a higher rent, but she would have the opportunity to purchase a business she couldn't otherwise afford. The seller was retiring without the security of cash in the bank, but the rent was more than he would earn on a savings account, so he felt the risk was worth it.

A variation on the technique of leasing a seller's building is to use the buyer's lease to increase the value of the property sufficiently so that the seller can obtain a portion of the purchase price by refinancing the building. The buyer's lease payments would then repay the mortgage.

"At one point in the negotiations," explains Kathy, "Waldo, the fellow I was buying from, felt he needed a minimum of $55,000 cash from me, and that almost ended our discussions. He went to the bank to see how much he could borrow on the building. They told him he could increase his mortgage by only $15,000. Stalemate! I could give him $30,000, but even with refinancing the building he was $10,000 short. Then Waldo had this great idea. We drew up a lease saying I would pay $1000 per month rent for the building and took that to the bank. The bank told Waldo that with an experienced tavern operator like myself they could feel confident that the rent would be paid. That made me feel pretty good. They also told Waldo that they could give him the additional $10,000 because my lease made the building more valuable. They said that with no one renting the building they had to estimate the sale price for loan purposes, but now that it was rented they could take the income from the building into account, and this gave it a higher value.

### The Anticipation Waltz

When you buy a business, the amount of cash you can afford to give the seller is limited by the amount of available cash that must be held back to fund unexpected events or to use as working capital. If a lender offered to loan you money for contingencies and working capital, the effect would be similar to a loan to purchase the business. For many businesses, there is such a lender.

Although it cannot be used to purchase a business, using the anticipation waltz will provide working capital, permitting a buyer to devote more of his limited resources to the purchase.

Suppliers who sell to businesses anticipate that from time to time these businesses will 'waltz' them past the due date, delaying payment until the last possible moment. Those you buy from, whether you are buying dresses, lumber, oranges, insurance, advertising or plumbing repairs, are willing to extend liberal credit, but they rarely volunteer to do so.

Too many businesspeople carry over the attitudes they developed as a consumer toward paying bills. If you are spending $10 a month at the local hardware store and your charge account isn't promptly paid, strong letters or telephone calls may ensue, causing you to pay the bill. The hardware store may be strident in their demands because there are thousands of potential customers who will spend $10 per month and your business isn't that important. You may pay promptly, even if you're short of cash, because it is easier than dealing with an aggressive businessperson.

When you buy as a businessperson the roles are reversed. The supplier wants your business more because you are buying more. It is often cheaper for him to extend liberal credit to you in anticipation of future sales than to take a chance on losing your goodwill.

For those suppliers who are so big that they don't care if you remain a customer, a willingness on your part to discuss payment calmly and with precision will do much to increase your credit line.

"You're 60 days past due," snarls the credit manager for the dress company. "If you don't pay today I'm turning this over to our law-yers."

"I'd pay you today but I don't have the cash. We've loaded the store up with inventory for the Christmas season. I won't be able to send you any money for another three weeks, but then you'll be paid in full." If that doesn't mollify the credit manager, you can get tough yourself by con-tinuing, "When I bought these dresses the salesman told me I would have a reasonable time to pay. If you don't want to honor that you'll just have to sue me. Of course, if you do I'm going to defend myself, and it could be several years before you are paid." The possibility of that threat, often unspoken, is what keeps many suppliers reasonable. Many successful (and reputable) companies have one or more people assigned to do noth-ing but talk to creditors and delay payment for as long as possible—remember that if you ever become a supplier selling to a business.

This possible source of funds can serve as a cushion, protecting you against unexpected cash shortages. You've had a bad month. The month after Christmas is always bad, but there were two snow storms that stopped everything. You know you have to make a $1000 payment to the seller of the business and the payroll has to be met. Where does the money come from? Take everyone you owe money to and put them in order of priority. Pay only the highest priority creditors. If there are a lot of different bills, businesses will often divide them into categories, for example, must be paid in full, must pay 1/2, must pay 10%, and must telephone. Another technique is to pay no one until they call twice, and then never pay them in full. This may not be the nicest way to run a business, but it is sometimes necessary. Communication is the key to keeping a creditor from suing or taking other drastic action. He knows you owe him money, but he doesn't know anything else until you tell him.

It is possible to estimate the amount in reserve from suppliers by examining past payment history. Is your average payable paid in 15 days? Assume that this can be extended to an average of 45 days. This is the same as a 30-day loan of that amount. Since new payment obligations are incurred every month, this loan remains in effect indefinitely. If the business has been paying out $25,000 every 15 days, extending the aver-age payable period to 45 days results in a permanent $50,000 loan. The cost of this loan may be high, involving lost discounts as well as service and interest charges, but that can be computed in advance. Regardless of the cost, any loan must be compared to the alternative.

# 7

# FORM—AS IMPORTANT AS SUBSTANCE

You have decided to go into business. How will you conduct your business affairs? Will you be a sole proprietorship, a corporation, or a partnership? Each has its advantages and disadvantages.

## PROPRIETORSHIPS

The proprietorship is the simplest form of business. Legally a proprietorship means that one person does business in his own right, though he may use a fictitious name. The meaning of "proprietor" is synonymous with "owner." There are no forms to complete to become a sole proprietorship. You just do it as 11 million others do.

When Sally Schwartz purchases Mike's Maternity Shop, she has no partners, is not a corporation, and all legal transactions are in the name of "Sally Schwartz doing business as Mike's Maternity Shop." She keeps all the business profits and is legally obligated to pay all the business bills.

If Sally wants someone else to own part of the business, she will have to incorporate or form a partnership. If she wants to avoid being personally responsible for the bills incurred by the business, she will have to form a corporation. If she wants to minimize her income taxes, perhaps she should incorporate. If she wants to keep her accounting and legal fees low, she should remain a sole proprietorship.

As a businesswoman she will be entitled to income tax deductions denied to her as a wage earner, for example, business entertainment. Of course, as a wage earner she wouldn't have these expenses, so it's a mixed blessing.

The consequences of a proprietorship are best understood by comparing it to corporations and partnerships.

## CORPORATIONS

A corporation is an artificial person, having an existence separate from its creators. A corporation comes into existence by governmental charter, almost always state, and is subject to the limitations imposed upon it by its charter and applicable state or federal laws. Although in most states one person can incorporate, a corporation is more often a collection of several individuals who have decided to join together to engage in business. A corporation can sign contracts, be sued, institute legal actions, file tax returns, and continue as an entity indefinitely, unaffected by the death of its owners. There are over two million corporations in the United States and several thousand new corporations are formed every year.

The owners of a corporation are its shareholders. In most states there can be any number of shareholders, ranging from one to millions. The primary duty of the shareholders is to elect a board of directors, which usually occurs annually, and to approve any changes made in the state charter (amendments to the articles of incorporation). A shareholder has no legal responsibility for the operations of the corporation and no right to the profits until a dividend has been declared by the board of directors. A shareholder has a limited right to inspect corporate records and some limited rights in the event the corporate board of directors abuses its discretion by behaving in an obviously unreasonable fashion, for example, refusing an extremely generous merger offer and then accepting one that is less favorable to the shareholders because corporate management will have more secure and higher paying jobs under the terms of the second merger offer.

The affairs of a corporation are overseen by the board of directors. Elected by the shareholders, the board of directors in smaller corporations has the primary function of electing the corporate officers, who in turn are responsible for the day-to-day management of the corporation. In larger corporations the board of directors might be quite active, meeting regularly to oversee senior management and set policy. In some states a director must be a shareholder, but in most there is no such requirement. In a typical, small, closely held corporation (a corporation where the stock is owned by a small number of people), the corporate president and a small number of additional corporate officers or members of their immediate family are the directors. In closely held corporations it is not uncommon for all of the stockholders to be directors and officers of the corporation. Bankers and other institutional lenders generally feel that the corporation is better served if there are some members of the board of directors who are not major shareholders or employees of the corporation and who are in a position to exercise independent judgment free of self-interest. These people are called "outside directors." Outside directors are present, often the majority, on the board of directors of almost all large corporations. There are some limits on the number of directors a corporation can have and this varies from state to state. Commonly corporations have from 3 to 15 directors, although some have only one director and some more than 20. Directors can be held accountable for the improper activities of the corporate officers. A recent surge of lawsuits in this area, alleging improper supervision of the corporate officers, has caused many individuals to hesitate before becoming a director. Directors' liability insurance is available to protect individual directors from lawsuits, but the premium is quite high, effectively making such insurance unavailable to directors of small corporations.

The day-to-day business of the corporation is run by its officers. The customary officers are a president, treasurer, secretary, and one or more vice-presidents. The corporation may also have assistant vice-presidents, assistant secretaries, and assistant treasurers. While the board of directors elects officers, the officers in turn hire and fire all of the other employees of the corporation.

The primary reasons people form a corporation are to obtain limited liability, reduced income taxes, ease in transferring ownership, and clear lines of management authority.

### Limited Liability

Limited liability is perhaps the biggest single reason why small businesses incorporate. If Mike's Maternity Shop is a proprietorship, the proprietor is personally responsible for all of the bills of the business. If a shipment of dresses can't be sold and consequently the business can't pay for them, the proprietor is legally responsible and will have to pay. When a corporation does business, it is the only one responsible for paying the bills—the employees, officers, directors, and shareholders have no personal liability for these bills. All the owners of the business can lose if the business is unable to pay its bills is what they have invested in the corporation. If the owner of Mike's Maternity Shop had incorporated, he could walk away from the business if there wasn't enough money to pay the bills and let the creditors fight over what's left; none of the creditors could hold him personally responsible for the bills.

Just as the owner of a corporation is protected from the claims of creditors, he is also protected from lawsuits for negligence, breach of contract, product liability, and other actions, although under some circumstances this protection is not complete. Protection from lawsuits is especially important in this day of litigation if you are in a business where insurance is not available or costs too much. Clara's Ceramic Shop might never be sued, but on the other hand, Clara might be sued by the user of a ceramic plate who claims the coloring agent in the plate poisoned his food. There might be a good case against the manufacturer of the coloring agent, but regardless of the merits of the claim against Clara, the legal costs to Clara might be so high that Clara would be well advised to walk away from her business and start over again, especially if this is a part-time basement operation involving only a few hundred dollars worth of equipment. If she's incorporated, she may have the choice of walking away; if she isn't incorporated, she has no choice.

The exception to the general rule that the owner of a corporation has no liability for the debts of the corporation is when the owner directly participates in actions that cause injury or damage to another, was negligent, committed fraud, or intentionally caused injury. If the owner is driving an automobile owned by the corporation and carelessly runs over a pedestrian, it is no defense for the owner to claim that he is not legally responsible for the accident because he was on company business.

### Taxes

Another reason for incorporating is the federal income tax laws, which offer tax incentives to corporations by imposing a lower tax rate on corporate income than on individuals. Moreover, some tax deductions permitted for corporations are denied to individuals.

A corporation pays income taxes on the income it earns according to this table prepared from the Economic Recovery Tax Act of 1981

| Taxable Income | Tax Rate | |
| --- | --- | --- |
| | 1982 | 1983 |
| -0-to $25,000 | 16% | 15% |
| $25,000 to $50,000 | 19% | 18% |
| $50,000 to $75,000 | 30% | 30% |
| $75,000 to $100,000 | 40% | 40% |
| over $100,000 | 46% | 46% |

Many times there is a tax savings by having the corporation pay these taxes, because if the income were added to the taxable income of the owner, the rate would be higher. The income taxes payable by a married couple filing a joint return according to the tax rates from the Economic Recovery Tax Act of 1981

| | Tax Rate | | |
|---|---|---|---|
| Taxable Income | 1982 | 1983 | 1984 |
| $3,400 to $5,500 | 12% | 11% | 11% |
| $5,500 to $7,600 | 14% | 13% | 12% |
| $7,600 to $11,900 | 16% | 15% | 14% |
| $11,900 to $16,000 | 19% | 17% | 16% |
| $16,000 to $20,200 | 22% | 19% | 18% |
| $20,200 to $24,600 | 25% | 23% | 22% |
| $24,600 to $29,900 | 29% | 26% | 25% |
| $29,900 to $35,200 | 33% | 30% | 28% |
| $35,200 to $45,800 | 39% | 35% | 33% |
| $45,800 to $60,000 | 44% | 40% | 38% |
| $60,000 to $85,600 | 49% | 44% | 42% |
| $85,600 to $109,400 | 50% | 48% | 45% |
| $109,400 to $162,400 | 50% | 50% | 49% |
| over $162,400 | 50% | 50% | 50% |

Beginning in 1985 personal income tax brackets will be indexed to reflect the effects of inflation. Comparing these tax tables shows how tax savings can be accomplished by shifting income from personal to corporate or by dividing taxable income between the two. If a business is conducted as a corporation, these are some potential tax problems, for example, excessive salaries, constructive dividends, unreasonable accumulations, and the personal holding company surtax.

One big incentive is deductibility of medical expenses. The employee pays no income tax on this benefit. If the employee were to pay the medical expenses personally, only a small portion would be deductible from his taxable income.

Corporate retirement plans are given more favorable tax treatment than individual, partnership, or proprietorship retirement plans and larger contributions can be deducted. An individual who does not own a business can set up an Individual Retirement Account and deposit the lesser of $2000 or an amount equal to his taxable income into the plan (although if an employer makes the contributions to a simplified employee pension the limit becomes the lesser of $7500 or 15 percent of taxable income). When the money is put into the plan it is deductible from taxable income. Interest on the money deposited into the plan is free from income tax as the interest is earned, all income tax being deferred until the plan comes to an end. The benefits of this tax deferral are substantial. If we assume you have $1000 a year to save for retirement, can earn 10-percent interest, and are in the 50-percent income tax bracket, then if you have no qualified retirement plan you have to give 50 percent to the government. You can save $500 per year (50 percent of the $1000 available) and earn 5 percent (50 percent of the 10 percent earned) on your savings after taxes. Because of income tax deferral, if you adopt a qualified retirement plan, the amount saved each year will be doubled ($1000 instead of $500) and the amount earned as interest will be increased fourfold (10 percent of 1000 instead of 5 percent of 500). This money must be deposited in a commercial bank of similar depository.

Partnerships and proprietorships can adopt Keough Plans, which have the same tax benefits as Individual Retirement Accounts except the dollar amount that can be deposited is larger, 15 percent of the salary earned up to a maximum annual deposit of $15,000. The choices of where to deposit the money are quite broad, including the stock market and real estate. It is a tax law requirement that the plan not discriminate in favor of the more highly paid employees. That must be weighed against the tax benefits, but isn't a factor if the owner is the only employee, as is often the case.

Corporations have all the benefits of partnership plans, and under the Employee Retirement Income Security Act the employee can receive as much as 15 percent of his salary as additional compensation paid into a profit-sharing plan by the employer. If the employer has both a qualified profit-sharing and pension plan, up to 25 percent of the employee's compensation can be paid into the plans. For some types of plans there is a maximum dollar amount that can be contributed annually. For other plans the only limitation is that the pension being funded can't provide for annual retirement income to the employee in excess of the lesser of the salary of the employee or a dollar amount.

A variety of business deductions seem to be easier to justify if a business is incorporated, for example, if your automobile is in the corporation's name, the IRS auditors tend to permit you to deduct it more readily than if the automobile was in your name and you claimed a deduction because it was used for business purposes. There are also some tax gimmicks that are often mentioned but which may not be proper, such as using your corporate form to give low cost loans to yourself or educational grants to children.

There are also some tax advantages to consider if the business is not successful. A stockholder cannot normally deduct corporate operating losses from the stockholder's personal income tax return. However, there are some exceptions. If a corporation elects to be taxed as a partnership (called a Subchapter S Corporation), corporate losses can be deducted by the stockholders. There are a few restrictions on which corporations can make the election; for example, a corporation cannot elect to be taxed as a partnership if it has more than 25 shareholders.

The biggest advantage of the Subchapter S election is that operating losses are deductible. In some cases there are advantages to having the stockholders report the taxable income on their personal income tax returns. This depends on the tax rates applicable to both.

There are several disadvantages to Subchapter S status. A Subchapter S corporation cannot adopt a corporate retirement plan and dividends from other corporations are taxed at a higher rate if received by Subchapter S corporations.

In addition to Subchapter S status (or as an alternative), a corporation may elect to adopt a 1244 plan. If the corporation adops a 1244 plan, stockholders who own 1244 stock are not permitted to deduct corporate operating losses (unless there has also been a Subchapter S election) but they can deduct any loss when they sell their stock. If the corporation does badly, the stock can easily be sold for $1.00. The maximum amount that can be deducted is $50,000 ($100,000 if a joint return is filed) in any one taxable year. Any corporation can adopt a 1244 plan if the price for the stock to be issued does not exceed $500,000 and if the total equity capital of the corporation does not exceed $1,000,000. If a 1244 plan is adopted, the loss is deductible from ordinary income; if a 1244 plan is not adopted, the loss is a capital loss, which is only deductible against capital gains with a portion deductible from ordinary income to a maximum of $3000 per year. There are no disadvantages to a 1244 plan, and if a corporation qualifies it should adopt one before selling stock.

## Transferability of Ownership

When you are doing business as a corporation it is a simple matter to transfer all or part of your interest in the business. By merely issing more stock or selling some of the stock already issued the transfer is accomplished. It is a very simple procedure, evidenced by the fact that millions of shares change hands daily on the stock exchanges.

It is quite a different matter to transfer an interest in a partnership. There are many questions to be answered that do not arise in the corporate form. For example, what percentage of the partnership income will the new partner receive; when will the profits be distributed; what duties will the partner have to perform; what personal liabilities is the new partner assuming; how will partnership decisions be made? In the usual corporation these questions have clear answers. The new stockholder owns a certain percentage of the corporation stock and the same percentage of the property of the corporation, whereas it is not uncommon for a partner to put in one percentage of the money, own a different percentage of the partnership assets, and receive a different percentage of the partnership profits. Corporate profits will only be distributed when declared by the board of directors, whereas in a partnership it is unclear when profits will be distributed unless there is a written partnership agreement that answers this question. No personal liabilities are assumed by stock ownership, whereas a partner immediately becomes personally liable for all of the debts of the partnership. In a corporation, policy decisions are made by the board of directors and day-to-day management decisions are made by the chief executive officer, usually the president. In a partnership each partner can make decisions independent of the other.

All of this means it can be quite confusing, time consuming, and expensive to transfer an interest in a partnership.

It is possible to structure a partnership very much like a corporation, with a managing partner, clear division of profits, and so on. To the extent that the partnership agreement anticipates and deals with all of the questions a buyer may have, it is possible to transfer partnership interests in a manner somewhat similar to transferring stock. The major difference, and a major drawback, is the fact that the partnership is a matter of contract and the buyer must study a lengthy agreement to be satisfied that all relevant issues have been dealt with.

The corporate form also provides flexibility in how you structure equity participation. The alternatives range from the use of warrants (which give the holder the right to purchase stock at a future date and which can be traded the same as stock) to nonvoting stock to instruments as complicated as "cumulative, nonparticipating, callable, convertible preferred stock." This lengthy title is a shorthand method of describing that if dividends are not paid every year, they will accumulate until they are paid, the owners of the preferred stock will not receive any extra dividend, even if corporate profits are substantial enough for the common stockholders to receive a larger dividend than the preferred stockholders, the preferred stock can be repurchased by the issuing corporation on demand, and the preferred stock can be converted into common stock on demand of the stockholder. Complex ownership arrangements can be made quite quickly and immediately understood.

Easy transferability is often a goal as a businessperson wants to permit employees, friends, or relatives to share in ownership. The corporate form provides a vehicle for this that is simpler, less expensive, and easier to understand than the partnership form.

## Lines of Authority

One of the advantages of a corporation is that it requires the creation of a clear line of authority, expediting the decision-making process and defining each person's responsibilities. For example, you and your two cousins decide to go into business. Cousin Henry is going to put in a little more money and it is expected that you will assume more responsibility for running the maternity shop. What is the procedure and who has the authority when it comes to hiring or firing people, buying inventory, or setting prices for your goods? If the three of you buy the business together (a partnership), none of these questions may be answered. Forming a corporation won't resolve all questions of authority, but with its built-in hierarchical structure, which requires the selection of a board of directors and the naming of officers, the issue is discussed and dealt with before a problem develops.

## Simple to Form

Forming a corporation is quite simple, although the assistance of an attorney is usually necessary. The corporation is in existence when the organizer obtains a charter from the Secretary of State in any state in the United States. To obtain a charter in most states a short document, called articles of incorporation or certificate of incorporation, is filed, and some filing fees are paid. A charter is automatically issued. The Appendix contains a sample certificate for a business in Delaware. This is the most popular state for forming corporations because its laws are designed to cope with modern corporate problems and because most lawyers are familiar with Delaware's corporation statutes. Although the form in the Appendix is one of many alternatives, it complies with Delaware law while revealing very little about your corporation or your business plans—only the corporation's name, address, authorized number of shares, and name of the incorporator are disclosed. In most states it is not necessary to tell the state very much about your business to obtain a corporate charter.

Before you select a name for the corporation and go to the expense of filing for a charter, you sould check with the appropriate state officials to make sure the name is available. Normally, you cannot get a charter for a name that is likely to be confused with another corporation chartered by that state.

To get a charter your corporation must have a mailing address, but this doesn't mean you have to be open for business to get a charter. In many states the address of the corporation can be your home, your lawyer's office, or the business office. It is merely an address that can be used for locating the corporation. If you want to incorporate in a state that you do not do business in, you should be aware that in some states it is necessary to appoint someone in that state as "resident agent" to accept legal notices and to be available as your agent in the state. Also, some states require that one or more directors be a resident of the state of incorporation.

Someone will have to sign the papers forming the corporation. This person is called variously the promoter, organizer, or incorporator. In some states more than one incorporator is required. The incorporator will be you, unless you do not want your name on public record associated with the corporation, in which case you can use a nominee, someone whose name is used but whose involvement ceases as soon as the papers have been filed.

The charter issued by the state will authorize the corporation to sell up to a certain number of shares of stock for a minimum price. Without this authority the corporation lacks the legal power to issue and sell stock. The amount a state charges for granting a charter usually goes up as the amount of stock the corporation wants to sell increases. For a closely held corporation the number of shares authorized is often irrelevant. For example, if I and three others are going to form a corporation and be equal shareholders, it makes no difference if we each own 10 shares or 10,000 shares, as long as we each own 25 percent of all of the stock that has been sold by the corporation. Although fractional shares are common, sometimes a high number of authorized shares of stock is requested to avoid this. For example, if daughter Debbie is going to be given 1 percent of the stock of your corporation as a gift, 1000 shares sounds better than one-tenth of a share, although both could represent the same value.

## PARTNERSHIPS

### Some Comparisons

If more than one person is going to own a business, the owners must usually choose between sharing their ownership as stockholders in a corporation or as partners. Other forms of relationships, for example, joint adventurers, cooperatives, trusts, or syndicates, are used only rarely.

On the surface a partnership is an easy relationship to understand. Partnership agreements do not have to be in writing; they can be formed with a verbal agreement made over the telephone. Two people decide to go into business together and their agreement is that all profits and all losses will be divided equally. This is enough to create a partnership, and with this comes a complex relationship that is best illustrated by examining the alternative.

The primary differences between a partnership and a corporation are: stockholders have no obligation to pay the debts of the corporation, whereas each partner has the legal obligation to pay all of the debts of the partnership; corporate profits are taxed twice, whereas partnership profits are taxed only once; corporations continue indefinitely, whereas partnerships end when the partners die; ownership of an interest in a corporation (stock) is freely transferable, whereas partnership interests are not; the management of a corporation's affairs is centralized, with the board of directors selecting a chief executive officer, whereas partnership management is divided among the partners; corporations are created by state action, whereas partnerships are created by agreement between the partners. These differences sound clear and easy to follow, but the line between a corporation and a partnership is not a clear one. Sometimes business relationships will have characteristics of both a partnership and a corporation, making it difficult to tell if a business is a partnership or a corporation.

Not only is a partner liable for all of the business debts, he is legally responsible for the conduct of all the partners while on partnership business. If Larry, Lois, and Lance are partners in a window-cleaning service, they may have agreed among themselves that each would be responsible for one-third of any loss, but if Larry, without telling his partners, signs a contract to wash windows for a price so low that the partnership will lose money, or if Lance comes to work drunk and from the tenth floor of an office building drops a pail of water on someone passing, Lois is legally responsible. She may have to pay the cost of performing the contract and compensating the injured person. Her legal liability is 100 percent, not one-third as agreed to by the partners. If they were incorporated, Lois would have no liability. Lois also could have limited her liability if she had been a "limited" partner in a limited partnership, an entity that is called a partnership but which has some similiarities to a corporation.

If a limited partnership is formed, some of the partners will have no personal liability for business indebtedness or the acts of their partners.

The partners who have this limited liability are called "limited partners." To have a limited partnership there must be at least one "general" partner who is legally responsible for all business indebtedness and the acts of all general partners. The primary drawback to using a limited partnership is the requirement that limited partners cannot play an active role in the management of the business or the partnership affairs. Limited partnerships are like corporations in several respects. There is limited liability, the partnership can continue after the death of a partner (unless there is only one general partner and he dies), limited partnership interests are often freely transferable like stock certificates, management of partnership affairs is centralized with the general partner, and limited partnerships must be in writing and filed with the state before the limited partnership becomes effective. Limited partnerships are used most often when the partners want to have the incidents of a corporation but pay income taxes as a partnership. For example, a real estate investment where the investors want to take advantage of the artificial accounting loss afforded by accelerated depreciation but do not want to become involved in the management of the real estate or have any responsibility for debts incurred by the general partner.

The single biggest reason for choosing the partnership form over the corporate form is the double income tax burden imposed on corporations. Partnerships have to file income tax returns, but the partnership itself pays no income tax. Instead, each partner pays the tax on his share. If the Larry, Lois, and Lance partnership is a smashing success and they make $300,000 one year, each of the three partners will have $100,000 of taxable income which they will add to their other income when computing the amount of tax they owe. If they were incorporated and wanted to pay this $300,000 in profit out in dividends, the corporation would first have to pay $118,250 in corporate income taxes (1982 rates). After taxes, there would be $181,750 or $60,583 per shareholder that could be paid out as dividends. This dividend income would be added to each shareholder's taxable income and taxed. The shareholder would then have almost $40,000 less income.

Many closely held corporations attempt to avoid this double tax by using all profits to pay salaries (which reduces the taxable income of the corporation) to the shareholders instead of dividends. Salaries are deductible business expenses and reduce the taxable income of the corporation; dividends are not deductible and must be paid out of after tax income. The IRS imposes several restrictions on this. If payment of salaries is found by the IRS to be a substitute for dividends, the IRS can ignore what the payments are called and tax them as dividends. This means that a salary can be paid only if services are performed for the corporation and the salary must be reasonable. While the IRS never complains that a salary is too low, it will often object that a salary is too high. If the salary is deemed to be too high by the IRS, it will impose the single tax only on the portion it considers reasonable as salary and levy the double tax on the balance. This is a very disturbing problem for many talented and highly paid businesspeople. When I suggested to Clyde Thurk that he incorporate, he had some strong objections based on this IRS policy of deciding what salaries are reasonable. He said, "I've worked for 30 years to build my business up to where it is now. I work 7 days a week, 10 hours a day. My manufacturer's representative business is profitable only if I work this hard, because my customers all want to see me, not one of my employees. I will make almost $200,000 this year, slightly more than I would make as a commission salesman working for one of my suppliers. If I worked a normal week, I'd probably only make about $100,000 a year, and if I weren't the best in the business, I'd make less than $50,000 a year, no matter how many hours I worked."

"I don't like to blow my own horn, but I think I'm worth what I earn. If I incorporated I'd probably have some IRS auditor who is a kid right out of school who has never worked more than 37-½ hours a week and who has no idea of what my business is about or what my skills are. I can just see this fellow trying to understand what a reasonable salary is. All he really knows is what his salary is. He's probably jealous of anyone who makes more. I don't need the hassle. I'd like limited liability and I'd like some of the other features of being incorporated, but I just don't want to take the risk."

These are legitimate concerns and if you are in the position of Clyde, you should review with your tax adviser how realistic these concerns are for you, what it would cost to fight the IRS, what the probable outcome would be, how much might be saved in taxes if you incorporated, and so on. It is not possible to give a general answer to these questions.

If an IRS agent does challenge a salary as being unreasonable, this can be disputed by pointing out other similar businesspeople who earn as much. You are entitled to pay yourself as much as others earn. This is helpful if you are a member of a group where statistics are published and if you fit within the statistical range, but if you aren't, you may have to bring to court businesspeople who are paid similar salaries for similar work to testify about their compensation. Even if you can find these businesspeople, often they will refuse to help because their tax advisors have told them that if they testify they will be next on the list for a visit by the IRS. Regardless of whether this fear of being on an IRS "enemy" list is valid, it is difficult to get this kind of testimony.

Sometimes corporations attempt to defer the double tax by leaving the money in the business, paying out neither salary nor dividends. This way only the corporate income tax is paid and sometimes this is less than an individual would pay. This is a good idea if the money is used for the business, but the IRS has the power to claim that this was done merely to avoid income taxes and impose a special tax on the "excess" accumulated earnings. Again, an IRS agent will inspect the operation of the business and decide how much is needed to be kept by the corporation, for example, $250,000 in accumulated profit is too much for a beauty salon but not too much for an active, medium sized, home builder.

For many small businesses the profits are such that there is no difficulty in paying out all of the profits as salary, so there is no income tax reason to prefer the partnership form of doing business, but the complexity and potential for problems created by the federal income tax law is enough to keep them away from corporations.

"I know that it can be done today," one partner in a $500,000 plus net profit business told me. "And in fact there are good tax reasons for incorporating. But they change the laws so often that what's legal today might be illegal tomorrow. I don't want to have to be constantly checking with my accountant and my attorney before making business decisions. I want to be left alone to run my business and I don't want to get tangled up in something that may be as hard to untangle as a corporation."

How you react depends on your temperment and how much is at stake. All tax planning involves an element of uncertainty, but so does all business. Generally, successful businesspeople feel that money made by saving on taxes is no different from money made by operating their business, and they spend just as much time minimizing taxes as they do maximizing operating profits.

### A Sample

When two or more people decide to become partners there are numerous points that should be agreed to. The sample partnership agreement in the appendix on page 199 can be used as a beginning when determining what the issues should be. As you can see, the list of matters dealt with in this partnership agreement is long, covering such items as how much money each partner is to put into the partnership, what happens if more money is required, how and when profits are to be distributed, whether the partners can receive salaries, what happens if a partner dies, files for bankruptcy, or withdraws, how partnership interests can be transferred, and how partnership profits are to be divided. Each of these matters could be resolved in a variety of ways.

How much money each partner is to contribute to the partnership can be a problem, but there are several related questions. Must each partner contribute cash or can he contribute work having the same value? What happens if there is a disagreement over the need for additional contributions to the partnership; is this to be resolved by unanimous agreement, majority vote, arbitration, or other methods? What happens if a partner promises to contribute more money and then can't deliver? In the sample partnership agreement it is contemplated that the contributions will be written out in advance and will be in cash ("Amount of Contribution" on Exhibit B). No additional contributions need to be made unless both partners agree (paragraph 2.02). If a partner promises to make a contribution and then fails to do so, he is forced out of the partnership at a reduced sale price (paragraph 2.02).

Are the partnership profits to be kept in the business or distributed? The partnership agreement should anticipate and deal with this question.

"We have $7000 in the bank now," Albert might say to Alfred, his partner, "and all our bills are paid. I've been repairing television sets and radios 12 hours a day for weeks. I want to go to Hawaii and relax. Let's take out $2500 each; that'll leave enough in the business for emergencies."

"Now Albert," Alfred might respond, "let's not do anything hasty. I've been thinking if we can save a little more we might be able to open a second store. I don't need a vacation now. Let's leave the money where it is for a while."

Paragraph 4.01 of the sample partnership agreement provides that no profits can be taken out of the partnership unless both parties agree.

In a partnership, the partners are not entitled to salaries unless the partnership agreement specifically so provides. If Alfred and Albert are equal partners, they divide all profits equally, even if Albert works 60 hours a week and Alfred only 20 hours a week. This type of inequity can be resolved by providing that each partner will be paid for his services to the partnership and what is left will be divided equally. Paragraph 4.04 of the sample partnership agreement provides that salaries will be paid to the partners only to the extent that the partners unanimously agree.

Death of a partner may terminate a partnership, but his estate will then own an interest in the assets of the partnership. This can pose a variety of problems as the surviving partner has to deal with someone who may know nothing about the business but who has a half interest in the machinery and other property formerly owned by the partnership. Article 8 of the sample partnership agreement deals with this issue by spelling out a detailed procedure for winding up the affairs of the partnership if a partner dies.

Problems can occur if there is a bankruptcy and the bankruptcy court distributes one partner's interest in the partnership to creditors in payment of bills. Paragraph 8.03 in the sample partnership agreement provides for the termination of the partnership if this should happen. Under the recently enacted Federal Bankruptcy Act this language may not be enforceable.

What happens if one partner quits the partnership? If Alfred and Albert can't agree, then can Albert say, "I've had it. I quit. You either buy me out or we'll sell the business"? There are many ways to deal with this issue, but in the sample partnership agreement the withdrawal of one partner terminates the partnership.

Can one partner sell his interest in the partnership?

"I need," said Albert, "some way to convert my partnership interest to cash. One way would be for me to sell my one-half interest in the store to my son. Let's agree that I can sell my one-half interest to anybody at any time."

"No way," responded Alfred. "Your son is fine, but what if you sold out to somebody I didn't trust or I couldn't work with?"

The sample partnership agreement, paragraph 7.01, gives each partner a right of first refusal if any other partner wants to sell his interest. Paragraph 7.02 provides that a buyer of a partnership interest is entitled to a proportionate share of the profits, but does not have any of the other rights that go with being a partner. Paragraph 7.03 provides that new partners are admitted to the partnership only upon the unanimous agreement of the partners.

Unless there is a specific agreement to the contrary, all of the partners in a partnership share the partnership profits and losses equally. When Bill Bump and Ned Knott formed a partnership to manufacture screens, Bill put in $20,000 and Ned put in $15,000 to buy the business. If the first year of operation shows a profit of $30,000, each account will receive $15,000. They could have decided to divide profits any way they wanted to, for example, in the same proportion as the initial contributions of money (15/20), in proportion to the services rendered to the partnership, in any arbitrary ratio, or there could be a ratio that is recomputed each year based on the capital account ratio at that time. In the sample partnership agreement a ratio is determined in Exhibit A; that ratio continues until the partners agree otherwise.

There are no limits on the number of partners that a business can have. Some accounting firms have hundreds of partners, and businesses with dozens of partners are commonplace.

# 8

# Some Advisors

## NUMBERS

The accounting system used by most wage earners for their personal finances is not suitable for business. A good accountant can be invaluable in analyzing the financial records of the business you want to buy, in preparing pro forma financial statements that estimate for the future, and in assisting you after you buy the business.

The "cash-basis" method is the most widely used accounting system and is the one we use when we balance our checkbook and pay bills. If we have paid out $400 in one month, we say our "expenses" were $400 and the $200 left is available for other items. Cash-basis accounting is typified by monitoring only cash transactions.

Cash-basis accounting is adequate for personal expenses, but even there, it is not an accurate form of accounting. When operating a business, both the increased complexity and the need for more accurate accounting records require that you periodically review your financial situation using the "accrual method" of accounting. In accrual accounting the operative event is earning the income and incurring the obligation to pay, even if no cash changes hands. When you have your automobile repaired in June, but aren't able to pay the bill until September, accrual accounting would reflect automobile expense at the time the bill was received (June), whereas cash accounting would reflect automobile expense when the bill is paid (September).

When dealing with an automobile repair, the difference between cash and accrual accounting is easy to compute, but when applied to a business, matters can become complicated very quickly.

When you are preparing pro formas for Mike's Maternity Shop, you may decide that based on prior sales you will sell $11,000 worth of clothing the first month of operation. If the total bills that you expect to pay the first month are $6000, does this mean there has been a $5000 profit? To answer this question it will be necessary to accrue all expenses and income. For example, the casualty and liability insurance annual premiums will be paid, but since only eleven-twelfths of the benefit of the insurance will be received in the next 11 months, only one-twelfth of the annual premium should be expensed in the month it is paid. The landlord has required two month's rent in advance, which means that the $1000 in rent paid shouldn't be called an expense the first month—one-half of the total payment is rent expense for the first month, and one-half is as asset of the business called "prepaid expense." The $1500 in inventory purchased the first month is not an item of "expense" and that amount is not deducted from profit. For accounting purposes it is as if you substituted dresses for cash, both being assets of the business. Only as each dress is sold will its cost be expensed as "cost of goods sold." The $350 used cash register, paid for the first month, isn't a $350 expense. The cash register will last for three years (36 months) and therefore it will be expensed at one-thirty-sixth of the purchase price each month. The $312.50 telephone bill for the first month of service hasn't come yet, but nevertheless it is an item to be charged to the first month's expenses.

Accountants can see things from the financial records of a business that are not apparent to others.

Herman, a good friend, had owned his construction company for several years before he hired an accountant. Herman told me that sales had increased tenfold in the past three years and it was time he had some professional help.

"You know," Herman had said many times before, "the best accountant in the world can't increase sales by one dollar. In this business if you have the sales, the profit will follow. I'll only hire an accountant when I'm too busy to keep the books myself."

Herman's accountant analyzed where the money came from and where it went, applying accounting procedures that were new to Herman, although as each accounting theory was explained to him, he had to admit they made sense. What the accountant found was quite a surprise to Herman.

"I'm really broke," Herman moaned, "before I hired that accountant I was rich; now I'm broke. I'll have to sell my plane and we won't be able to build that new house I've been planning. I just don't know how I could have been so wrong. He showed me how I'm losing money on one out of three construction jobs. He also showed me that the recent growth was about all we could handle, and if we didn't stop growing for a few months, there wouldn't be any cash to pay the bills."

Herman was lucky. He didn't end up in bankruptcy court, although he came close to it.

What happened to Herman happens to many businesses. They're selling something for one dollar and the material and labor used to make it costs less than one dollar. They "know" the more they sell the more profitable they'll be. This analysis is often erroneous because of cash shortages created by growth and hidden costs.

Three years ago, when Herman was billing $100,000 per year, his accounts receivable averaged $10,000. By the time Herman was billing $2,000,000 per year his accounts receivable had grown to $200,000. $200,000 in accounts receivable is similar to Herman loaning his customers $200,000. To finance this loan to customers Herman had to borrow $200,000 from the bank, at an interest rate of four points over the prime rate. The accountant pointed out that the interest Herman paid was more than the profit he earned. In addition, he was almost out of credit. The maximum the bank would loan Herman was $225,000. He was rapidly approaching a critical cash shortage.

Herman took some steps to solve his problem. Among other things, he insisted that all of his customers pay within 30 days, increased prices slightly, began to charge his customers interest on amounts they owed him, paid those suppliers who offered discounts for prompt payments, and paid other suppliers only after 60 days. He also stopped chasing business indiscriminately, declining to bid on those jobs where there was a substantial element of risk.

## Specific Accounting Services

A wide variety of services are performed by accountants, but they can be roughly divided into these four areas: write-up services, audits, income taxes, and management services.

Write-up services include keeping the day-to-day records of a business and recording each item of expense and income. Most smaller accounting firms will do write-up work, and for many it is the primary source of income. Traditionally the larger accounting firms don't do write-up work. They prefer not to, because if they do, the ethical rules accountants operate under may prevent them from doing an audit; that is, they would be auditing their own work and this could affect their independence and objectivity. In addition, their clients don't need them for write-up work in the same way a smaller business might. Their clients are large enough to employ in-house bookkeepers or accountants on a full-time basis to keep their daily financial records.

Regardless of whether done internally or by an outside accounting firm, each businessperson needs a write-up system to keep track of income and expenses. In some businesses the system consists of having the accountant visit the premises periodically and go through the check-book and sales records. From this the accountant prepares a balance sheet and a profit and loss statement. This is time consuming and expensive because of the many questions that may arise during the review, that is, a check may not have been written in the register because the businessperson was in a hurry and now he can't remember who the check was made out to, how much it was, or what it was for. There is also a problem of identifying what the cash expenditures were for.

Many small businesses are well served with a write-up system consisting of voucher checks, a chart of accounts, and access to a small inexpensive computer.

Voucher checks come in carbon packs, so as each check is written, one or more carbons are simultaneously made, and the check is large enough to have room for a careful description of why it is begin written. This gives a simultaneous and accurate record of the payee, date, amount, and reason for writing the check. One carbon is sent to the accountant, from which financial records are prepared. For this system to work, cash expenditures must be at a minimum, limited to petty cash items.

Because even the most conscientious businessperson will sometimes write descriptions on the voucher checks that are meaningful only to him, the businessperson often adds numbers to the description on the voucher check. These numbers are arbitrarily assigned to each category of expense, for example, all telephone expenses are number 5197, all advertising expenses are number 5103, and so on. The chart of account headings are the same as those used in the balance sheet and income and expense statement, so preparing these reports is simplified. A sample chart of accounts is in the appendix on page        .

The income records can be kept by depositing all receipts into the business's checking account and keeping a record of such deposits with the appropriate chart of account numbers.

A computer is not necessary to keep good financial records, but access to computers and computer programs to keep business journals and prepare financial reports has become so inexpensive that it usually costs less for a small businessperson to computerize than to hire a bookkeeper. Most accountants who do write-up work use a computer, and the cost of programming the computer and getting monthly computer reports can be as low as $75.00 per month. The computer reports will typically restate every transaction so that you'll have a journal of what happened day to day (e.g., each check written or deposit made), a balance sheet, and an income and expense statement. Because of the computer's tremendous capacity to manipulate data, the information can be presented in a variety of ways designed to assist in financial planning.

"That computer," said Waldo, new owner of a paint store, "tells me everything. Each item of expense is given in dollars as well as a percentage of gross receipts, and with the current month is a comparison of a year ago and the year to date. In my June report, for example, I see that returns of paint were $625. The computer has compared this amount to total June sales and it tells me that in June returns were 7 percent of sales. The computer also tells me that so far this year total returns of paint were $2000 and that this is 3 percent of all sales this year. More paint was returned this June than in an average month. As I examine the rest of the computer report I see that if I look only at June a year ago, returns of paint were $250, which was only 2 percent of sales. This shows me that returns of paint were higher than normal this June and that I should look into it."

Audit activities are the largest single source of fee income for most large accounting firms and for some smaller accounting firms. When an accountant audits a business he issues a written report certifying that the financial records were prepared in accordance with generally accepted accounting procedures which were consistently applied and that the financial records accurately and fairly reflect the financial condition of the business. If there are any potential errors of misleading statements, the accountant will either "qualify" his opinion or write footnotes that explain the problem in sufficient detail for the reader to be fully advised. An example of qualification might be a sentence that says, albeit more tactfully, the following: "Since we did not have an opportunity to inspect the inventory on the premises of Mike's Maternity Shop at the beginning of the year, we are obligated to rely upon the representations of the present owner, and if the present owner was erroneous and gave us the wrong beginning inventory figures, then the analysis of income and loss is erroneous and therefore we express no opinion as to the accuracy and fairness of these financial statements." This type of qualification puts anyone who uses the financial statements on notice that they should not be relied on. An example of an unqualified opinion appears in the appendix on page 166. This is the type of opinion that auditors prefer to give and businesspeople prefer to receive. It tells the world that these figures can be relied on.

Sometimes there is additional information that the auditors believe should be given to anyone who reads the financial statements, as they might draw the wrong conclusions from the financial statements if the information is omitted. This information is added as footnotes to the financial statements. There are examples of footnotes in the appendix beginning on page 150.

An audited financial report is a valuable tool for businesses to have. Because the audited report is relied on by lenders, investors, and anyone else who needs independent assurances that the reports are accurate, auditors have developed ethical standards that require them to maintain their independence from the businessperson. This independence creates an environment where many times the auditor has to refuse to do things that the businessperson who hired him wants done.

"Herman," the accountant begins, "we have a serious problem certifying your financial statements. The problem is the warranty reserve. You give a full two-year guarantee on all swimming pools you sell, and this could amount to a lot of money. There could be a bad winter or some unknown problem could appear. Since you just started giving this guarantee last year, we really don't know how much money is involved. I think we're going to have to qualify our opinion."

"You can't do that!" responds Herman. "My bank will get very nervous if they see a qualified opinion. They need numbers they can rely on. If you qualify, it could cause the bank to refuse my request for a bigger bank line, and that could be disastrous."

"Let's do this," continues Herman. "I've been in business for over 20 years. I know this guarantee will be used by less than 5 percent of my customers. It just doesn't amount to very much money. Let's put it in a footnote. I don't think my banker reads the footnotes very carefully. Even if he does, he won't be as nervous if he sees it there."

"If we know how much money is at stake," says the accountant, then we should show that much on the books as a warranty reserve. You sell about $8,000,000 a year, and if you have returns of 5 percent for two years, you have returns of $800,000 ($400,000 for each year). Maybe we could add an $800,000 liability instead of qualifying, assuming we can verify that amount as being reasonable."

"That's too much. That's more than my profit. $80,000 would be more like it. Most of the time it just costs a few hundred dollars to repair the pool. Besides it's way less than 5 percent of the pools that will ever call me," says Herman, becoming agitated. "Why don't we just leave it out of the financial statements—it's too small."

"We can't leave it out unless we know it's an immaterial amount," says the accountant. "Since you don't have any records on calls from customers with problems, we are unable to verify that the amount is immaterial."

"I don't have any records," screams Herman, "because I get so few calls. If it was important I'd have the records, but it's not important. Not very much money is involved. If you make a big deal of it in my financial report, everybody will think a lot of money is involved and I'll be hurt."

"Well," says the accountant, "the guarantee you give must be dis-closed somewhere in your financial reports."

As Herman found out, an accountant performing an audit has an obli-gation to be fair; he cannot be an advocate for the interests of the busi-nessman. In the other accounting functions the accountant can more agressively pursue the interests of the businessperson.

Accountants provide a great deal of assistance in dealing with income taxes. The tax laws applicable to a businessperson are incredibly com-plex, and without a good accountant a businessperson will pay more than necessary. Because the federal and state governments will take up to one-half and sometimes more of your profit as income taxes, you should consider the tax impact of every business decision; the government is a substantial partner in your enterprise. Do you want to acquire a delivery van for Mike's Maternity Shop? You tax advisor will help you decide if you should lease or buy a van. Do you want to expand your credit policy? Check with your tax advisor first. If you are on the accrual basis, the tax laws force you to pay the income taxes on credit sales weeks or possibly months before you are paid. This could create a serious cash shortage if credit is expanded. Do you want to buy health insurance for your em-ployees, if it is not done as part of a "qualified" group health plan, there may be adverse tax consequences. What are the rules for business enter-taining? What kind of records must be kept on the company car? What are the rules for business gifts?

Once the tax advice is received it must be followed up with proper preparation of the business income tax return. Accountants prepare mil-lions of tax returns every year. Any competent businessperson can follow the instructions for preparing an income tax return, but a good accoun-tant will more than earn his fee by applying those laws and interpreta-tions that aren't in the instructions written by the government.

Some accountants also give advice on how a business should be oper-ated. This is called management services. Management services is a new phenomenon in American accounting. For years accounting firms found themselves embroiled in management problems; their opinion was sought on various operational matters because of the broad experience they had gained from performing services for so many different busi-nesses. In response to this need many accounting firms offer business advice in such diverse areas as recruitment, use of computers, manage-ment training, and inventory control, to name a few. Because manage-ment decision-making is quite different from the traditional accounting function, many accounting firms set up separate departments to provide these management services.

"I'm going to buy the Book Worm Book Store and I've been told by a computer salesman that I can cut inventory costs by 30 percent if I buy his computer," said Barry Geres, new businessman. "So I called the accountant I'd hired to look over the financials. His office had a computer expert and in just three hours I had all the answers I needed."

## Selecting an Accountant

There are over 525,000 public accountants in the United States. When you need some professional assistance, how do you select the one that is best suited for your needs?

As you look for an accountant, ask other businesspeople who they use. Your best source of information is a satisfied customer.

The accountant you select will know more about your finances than any other person. He will help you analyze the financial records of your business before you buy it and in some cases he will prepare these records for you. He will also do your personal and business income tax returns, prepare pro forma financial statements, and assist you in providing financial statements that your lenders will rely on. You must trust his judgment and be able to communicate easily with him. As you are meeting with the accountant who was recommended to you, does he talk so he can be understood or does he hide behind labels and technical terminology? Does he listen to you when you talk? Do you respect him enough to do something you don't want to do merely because he says it has to be done?

Accountants are divided into two groups: those who are Certified Public Accounts (CPA) and those who are not certified. Less than 180,000 of the 525,000 accountants in the United States are certified. Certification is awarded by the state in which he or she wishes to practice and verifies that the recipient has completed a two-year apprenticeship under the direct supervision of a CPA and has passed a series of lengthy and difficult tests in the areas of auditing, accounting, accounting theory, and business law. By retaining a CPA, you are assured that your accountant has a high level of skill.

However, it is not necessary to retain a CPA to have a competent accountant. There are several reasons why an accountant may not be certified. In some cases a lack of formal training in one or more of the areas to be tested means that expensive educational efforts in those areas must be made in preparation for the tests. If these areas are of little interest to the accountant he may feel that certification isn't worth the effort it would take. In other cases accountants may have gone directly from school into private industry. The required apprenticeship may not have been important to them at the time they left school, and now they may feel their skills in some areas are so rusty that it would take more effort to prepare for the written exams than certification is worth.

Another method of categorizing the accounting profession is by the number of accountants in the firm. The accounting requirements of large businesses are so extensive that very large accounting firms are necessary. This has led to the creation of several national accounting firms with thousands of accountants and hundreds of offices throughout the United States and many foreign countries. The largest accounting firms, commonly referred to as "The Big Eight," are Arthur Young & Co.; Arthur Anderson & Co.; Ernst Whinney; Deloitte, Haskins, & Sells; Coopers and Lybrand; Price Waterhouse & Co.; Peat, Marwick, Mitchell & Co; and Toche, Ross & Co. While these firms often represent smaller businesses, the bulk of their professional fees are earned by serving the needs of the larger national and international businesses. The regional accounting firms are smaller in size and scope than the national firms, generally limiting their activities to one region of the United States. Local accounting firms are the smallest, generally limiting their practice to smaller accounts and their acitivites to one urban area. An accountant who practices in a smaller accounting firm may have a broad range of talents and experience due to the many hats he is required to wear, and may be sensitive to the needs of the small entrepreneur because he is part of a small business. On the other hand, the small office may be unavailable when you need help the most, and it may lack the necessary training, experience, or manpower to handle unusual or complex problems. Large businesses need huge accounting firms with offices in dozens of cities and expertise in all areas. Mike's Maternity Shop may be adequately served by one of the local accounting firms.

What an accountant will cost is of great concern. Accountants customarily charge by the hour for services rendered with hourly rates typically ranging from $20.00 for an accountant who is just out of school and not yet certified to $120.00 for a middle partner in a national accounting firm. A senior member in a large accounting firm may be more expensive than a senior member in a small accounting firm, but the larger firm is more likely to have a younger, less experienced and less expensive accountant available to assign time-consuming routine matters to, often producing a lower total accounting bill.

## PROTECTION

"Who needs insurance?" says Humble Bumble. "If this business doesn't succeed, everything I own is gone. If things don't work out, I'll have to go on welfare."

It's difficult to dispute Humble's analysis. He only had a few hundred dollars to begin with and every cent of that is tied up in the service station he is leasing. He has taken a big chance in quitting his job at the box factory and he has no intention of starting to hedge his bets now.

Few businesses start on such a slender shoestring as Humble Bumble and most realize the need for insurance protection. There are many different types of insurance. Years could be spent understanding the nuances between competing policies, but the basic coverage is relatively simple to understand. Even if you aren't able to purchase all of the insurance you would like to have, it is important to know what insurance is available.

## Worker's Compensation

An employer is legally responsible for injury to his employees on the job. The benefits to be received by the employee are determined by state law, for example if a finger is lost, the employee will receive specified benefits, such as a percentage of the employee's salary (if the loss of finger puts the employee out of work) retraining funds (if necessary for a new career), and a specified dollar amount (for the loss). To make sure that the employee is paid, employers may be required to purchase worker's compensation insurance. The premium for such insurance is usually a percentage of the total salaries paid by the employer, with the percentage increasing for the more hazardous occupations.

If an employer does not purchase worker's compensation insurance, he may be subject to civil and criminal penalties. In addition to the penalties, if it is discovered that an employer has not been purchasing worker's compensation insurance, he may be required to pay all back premiums for the period such insurance should have been in force. In some states failure to provide worker's compensation insurance may give the employee the right to sue the employer for more money than would have been permitted if the insurance had been in effect.

## Casualty

Casualty insurance provides protection against your business being damaged or destroyed. It is necessary to protect your investment, and if one of the reasons the bank loaned you money to purchase the business was a belief that the business was good security for the loan, they will insist on adequate insurance protection. You should have extended coverage protecting against fire, vandalism, water damage, wind damage, and other types of casualties.

This can be complicated insurance. For example, most policies insure against water damage only where the damage occurred suddenly, for example, a window is blown out and it rains into your store. If you are concerned about plumbing leaks or other forms of gradual water damage (which can be serious), you must purchase a rider providing such protection.

Another confusing question is how much to insure for. Most companies offer a choice between replacement cost and market value. Replacement cost is usually more than market value, so the premium for replacement cost is higher. If there is a total loss, the market value should be enough to replace the destroyed property, so there is no need for the higher premiums required of replacement cost. But there is a real problem if the property is only partially destroyed.

"My bowling alley only cost me $240,000," said Jim Julius, "and that was a fair price. But if I were to build a new one just like it the cost would be $325,000. The problem is no one would build a bowling alley just like this again because there have been so many improvements in design. So I bought insurance on the market value. The next year almost a fourth of the alley was destroyed. It cost me almost $90,000 to replace the destroyed part but the insurance company would give me only a fourth of the market value, $60,000. If I had understood this could happen, I would have paid the higher premium and obtained adequate insurance against partial damage."

There are also problems with coinsurance clauses, which require that the value for insurance purposes be realistic and keep pace with inflation. You also may want to consider a business interruption rider designed to provide some income if the business is closed down because of damage or destruction.

All in all, the services of a competent and experienced insurance agent who presents the alternatives in an understandable fashion are necessary so that you can make an intelligent choice when evaluating how much and what type of casualty insurance is right for you.

### Liability

Liability insurance protects you from claims made by people who were hurt as a result of how you run your business. If someone trips over a box your employee carelessly left in an aisle, you are protected.

Liability insurance also protects you from the burden of legal fees incurred in defending against claims. When a claim is made the insurance company will assume responsibility for the defense, hiring and paying for the necessary legal assistance. As attorneys cost $500 per day and more, this is valuable protection.

If there is no liability insurance, even litigation where you know you will win can tie all of your assets up, making the operation of your business difficult. There may be liens filed by the person suing you; it may be necessary for you to post a bond; creditors may refuse credit to you because they believe if you lose the lawsuit you will not be able to pay your bills. Because of this most lenders insist on liability insurance as a condition of loaning money. Landlords have become increasingly concerned about being sued, so today most sophisticated landlords will not rent space to a business unless it purchases liability insurance protecting both the business and the landlord from any claims.

## Theft

Theft in business is a serious problem. A robbery or burglary can cripple a business, and the need for such insurance is easily understood. Not so obvious is protection against theft by employees. Although employees steal more than shoplifters and employee honesty coverage is reasonably priced and readily available, few businesses carry it.

"It can't happen," you say. "I only have three employees and I've known them all for years. Why, just look at them. Do they look like thieves to you?"

Your employees do look like nice, honest citizens. Of course, I have never heard of a businessman who knowingly hires an embezzler. In fact, if the embezzler looked like an embezzler the employer would have watched him closer and there wouldn't have been any embezzlement.

As any insurance agent will tell you, some of the largest losses come from employee thefts. Thousands and thousands of dollars can be stolen, a few dollars at a time. As the thief falsifies documents to cover the theft, customer lists, accounting records, inventory records, credit reports, and other business records that are the data base for the conduct of the business become unreliable. Sometimes it is impossible to correct enough of the false entries to make the records usable, requiring that the businessman start over at tremendous cost.

I was involved with a theft in which three teenage girls were stealing hundreds of dollars a week. The owner had a good accounting system that called attention to the fact that gross receipts were down, but he had several employees and couldn't pinpoint who the thieves were. The loss was substantial by the time the culprits were caught. The insurance company was helpful in finding out who the culprits were and in designing controls to make such theft more difficult in the future. The help and advice from the insurance company was worth as much to the owner as the check from the insurance company reimbursing him for his loss.

## Errors

Depending on the type of business you're in, you might be sued for making a mistake. An automobile repair garage might fail to repair the brakes on an automobile properly and in such event both the owner of the garage and the mechanic who did the repair work may be legally responsible for the deaths and injuries that occur, just as a doctor who removes the wrong organ during an operation is legally responsible.

Anyone who sells judgment and competence should consider errors and omissions (malpractice) insurance. In the past such insurance protection was sought only by individuals whose sole product was competence, for example, physicians, attorneys, dentists, engineers, and architects. In recent years an attitude has evolved that if a person is hurt or suffers economic loss, someone must be at fault. The consumer expects the supplier to bear all the risks of any errors or mistakes, and the potential for claims is substantial.

Whether you are installing fire alarms or selling automobile mufflers, you should consider the risks of not being insured. If the only opportunity for making such an error after you buy Mike's Maternity Shop is to sell a maternity dress to a lady who isn't pregnant, you may not need insurance, but don't jump to any conclusions. If a maternity dress burns, injuring the owner, can you be sued for not telling a smoker the dress she is buying is flammable?

## Product Liability

Product liability insurance protects the manufacturer of a product from claims that the product is unsafe. Every item sold must be safe to use if the directions are followed.

Every day manufacturers are sued for selling unsafe products. It is no defense that the manufacturer was very careful and exercised good business judgment. If baby food is contaminated and a baby dies, the manufacturer pays. If there is a nail in the soda pop, pebbles in the popcorn, or if a defective piece of pottery splits when filled with hot soup, the manufacturer pays.

Product liability insurance tends to be expensive, so look carefully before deciding you need the protection. If the worst that can happen is a defective dress seam that splits, maybe you don't need the protection. Those who sell products produced by another may not need the protection, either because the manufacturer is willing and able to stand behind its product or because the legal liability for a product manufactured by another is limited.

## Life

When you borrow money, the lender is going to be concerned about what happens if you die before the loan is paid. Does early death mean the business will close? If it does, where will the money to pay the loan come from?

The concerns of lenders are satisifed by purchasing life insurance. When purchasing life insurance for business purposes there are several decisions to be made.

When you purchase personal life insurance, no portion of your insurance premium may be deducted from your taxable income. If you could deduct your insurance premium you would be able to buy your insurance at a lower cost because you would then be using before-tax dollars, dollars that have not been reduced by the government taking its share. If the insurance is for some business purposes, premiums can be deducted as a business expense. You can purchase, for example, up to $50,000 in life insurance and deduct the premium as a business expense without incurring any taxable income, provided you comply with government regulations as to which employees also get insurance. When you discuss this with your insurance agent you may find that it is less expensive to buy insurance for several of your employees and deduct the entire premium than to purchase insurance on just yourself.

If your business is incorporated, the laws are such that it may be cheaper for the corporation to buy life insurance, even if the premium is not a deductible business expense. If the taxes paid by your corporation are lower than the taxes paid by you personally, then each corporate dollar has had a small amount taken out and can buy more than if the corporation paid the same amount to you as salary (a corporate deductible business expense) and you then used your salary (less income taxes) to buy the insurance. The IRS requires that unless this insurance is of some benefit to the corporation the premiums will constitute taxable income to you, but in most cases it is possible to document a benefit to the corporation, for example, to fund a stock redemption plan in which the corporation buys some of the stock owned by a deceased shareholder to provide cash for payment of death taxes. Such a plan can be used even when there is only one shareholder.

There may be a tax benefit to having your corporation purchase your life insurance even when there is no business purpose and this is taxable income to you. The corporation will be able to deduct the premiums just as if it had paid you a bonus, and you will pay income taxes on the value of the insurance, as you would if the corporation paid you a bonus. The difference is that the IRS has written regulations declaring the value of the life insurance, regardless of what the premiums actually are. It is this value that is used when computing your taxable income, and since the premiums are usually more than what is on the government tables, there may be a tax saving.

The number of different types of life insurance policies has grown geometrically since the days when the only choice was whether to buy whole life or term insurance. Plan on spending some time learning about the alternatives.

## Medical

There may be significant tax advantages to purchasing medical insurance through the business rather than purchasing it personally. When medical insurance is purchased individually, one policy is written; the premiums are not deductible from your taxable income, except to the extent your medical expenses and medical insurance premiums exceed a percentage of your adjusted gross income. When a business purchases medical insurance it purchases group medical insurance, usually with a lower premium than individual medical insurance, and depending on the type of group plan, the premium may be tax deductible.

### Selecting an Agent

Because there are so many types of insurance, and because insurance is expensive, it is critical that you work with an insurance agent or agents that you trust and respect. You need someone who can quickly and clearly explain the benefits of insurance you may not have considered (umbrella coverage, disability insurance) and then follow your instructions without trying to sell you something you have decided you don't want. Don't buy insurance from someone just because he knocks on your door.

Each business's needs vary so greatly it is difficult to generalize about insurance agencies. What is right for you depends on your community, what is available to you, and how many people in the insurance field you know and trust.

If you have an insurance agent you have been working with for years, know well and trust, then you should seek his advice as to how to proceed. While he may limit his insurance activities to one or two areas, he undoubtedly has contacts and trusted friends in related areas. Working with him, you should be able to put together a competent insurance team that you can rely on. One cautionary note: while commission splitting is sometimes illegal, many agents pay "referral fees" for insurance business referred to them. If you suspect this is the case on the referral of your business, go slowly. A reference bought and paid for is not much of a reference.

An alternative to working with several different agents, each specializing in different areas, is to work with one larger agency that handles all forms of insurance. Insurance is so complicated that you will still be meeting with different specialists, but they will all have the same employer. The advantages of dealing with a larger agency are that all of your needs can be met at one place, you may be a more valued customer because you are purchasing all of your insurance from one place, and the agency has greater resources both in solving difficult insurance matters and in dealing with insurance companies. On the other hand, you may be a small customer by comparison to the other customers of the agency and you may be treated impersonally as you are transferred among the various departments.

Insurance agents will jump at the opportunity to talk to a prospective customer. You should shop around and talk to various individuals. It is difficult, expensive, and time consuming to decide which agents will serve you best, but if you are careful at this stage, meeting future insurance needs will be that much easier.

## LAW

You should have the assistance of an attorney when you purchase the business. If you will be forming a partnership or a corporation to operate the business, an attorney will be necessary—both to create the partnership or corporation and to advise you of the legal consequences. If you have tax problems, you may use an attorney instead of your accountant. Whether or not you need an attorney after that depends on the business you are in. The owner of a dress store may need advice from his accountant every week, meet with his insurance agent every few months, but not see his attorney for years. Highly regulated industries (e.g., bus companies) and businesses that use many contracts (e.g., equipment leasing companies) may need legal advice every day.

Attorneys come in all shapes and sizes, some of which would be perfect for you and some of which would create more problems than they would solve. It is a common complaint that attorneys can create problems out of thin air. They are skilled at describing all of the terrible things that might go wrong and producing complex documents to deal with each terrible possibility. Some clients, for example, banks or large corporations where millions of dollars are at stake, want their attorneys to think of and deal with every conceivable problem. These clients view the attorney's job as protecting them from all risks. Other businesspeople are willing to take some risks; they want their attorney to write the deal the way the parties discussed it, with attorney-initiated changes limited to substantial problems. These clients feel the attorney's job is to describe the problem; the businessperson's is to decide if the risk is worth taking.

Selection of an attorney is made more difficult by the absence of any easy way to recognize skill or training. In theory, all attorneys are equal. There is no system where some attorneys are certified and others aren't, as is the case with accountants. Each state licenses the attorneys who practice in that state, and to obtain this license an attorney must display a minimum level of competence. Once an attorney receives a license to practice law he is deemed competent to practice in all areas of law (except for some exceptional areas such as admiralty and patent law). After the attorney has received a license from any state, he can, upon application, automatically obtain a license to appear in federal court, to appear in tax court, to appear before various administrative agencies, and after five years, he can automatically receive a license to practice before the U.S. Supreme Court. Thus an attorney who does little more than appear in traffic court can display a wall full of licenses that could give the appearance of broad experience and competence in many areas.

While some attorneys specialize in one or more areas of law, in some places they are prohibited by the canons of ethics from advertising their specialties. When attorneys do advertise a specialty there is generally only their representation to rely on. There are no educational or on-the-job training programs leading to a specialist's designation in the legal profession, unlike the medical profession.

There is an independent source of information about attorneys that may be helpful to you. It is a seven-volume set of books titled *Martindale-Hubbell Law Directory*. Most attorneys in the United States are listed with information about their date of birth, education, who they practice law with, who their clients are, and a rating system showing how other attorneys view their level of competence and integrity. This set is available in any law library and in many law firms and banks. These books are updated and replaced every year, so the information in them should be current. In the *Martindale-Hubbell Law Directory* attorneys are given the opportunity to purchase space to describe their area of practice and to list typical clients. There are no standards of competence for listing areas of practice, and when you read a description, the only safe conclusion is that the attorney has an interest in that area. The list of representative clients published in the *Martindale-Hubbell Law Direc-*

tory may be an indicator of the firm's degree of specialization. If you find, for example, that the law firm you are considering represents several trucking companies, it is safe to conclude that they have some expertise in representing you in your purchase of a trucking company. If, on the other hand, the law firm represents only insurance companies, it is possible that they are not the best law firm for you to hire.

## Selecting an Attorney

Before you hire an attorney visit with him and ask questions about how he would represent your interests. Most attorneys will be pleased to meet with you for this purpose and any fee charged will usually be quite small.

When choosing your attorney, you should look for someone whom you trust and can work with, and whose fees you consider reasonable. Trust is believing that the attorney can do the job, that he is competent, and that he will use his competence in your best interests. This is determined by general reputation, satisfied clients' recommendations, and by your feeling that the attorney knows what he is talking about and cares about helping you.

Whether or not you can work with a particular attorney depends on the personalities involved. If the right chemistry isn't there, if you find it an effort to discuss matters with an attorney, then keep looking.

The legal fee you will be paying is also important. Attorneys are expensive and you should know what you are getting into before you hire one. At the first meeting, ask the attorney how much it will cost for him to perform the services you desire. This is important when hiring any professional, but it is especially important when hiring an attorney because fees vary so widely. Many attornys compute their fees based on how many hours a task will take. Some attorneys will work for $40 an hour, others charge $150 an hour or more. The lowest hourly rate is not always the lowest total bill so instead of asking about hourly fees, ask for an estimate of what the fee will be for the entire job. If an attorney is not familiar with the legal problems in purchasing a business he may spend a lot of time learning what to do. When he looks at the lease that Mike's Maternity Shop has signed, does he immediately recognize many of the clauses as standard in his jurisdiction and understand how they will be interpreted? Or does he have to study each line of the lease and figure out what it probably means? When you tell him there is an existing pension plan, does he know how to check to determine the extent of any liens that may be imposed against the business assets by virtue of the plan, or does he have to search through reference works to find out something about pension plan law? When you ask him to prepare a purchase agreement, does he have a checklist and opinions as to how to proceed based on years of experience, or does he have to search through his books to find a form that he hopes will work and then hammer this form into usable shape?

Just as you wouldn't go to the cheapest physician if your child were ill, don't select an attorney based solely on price. On the other hand, to continue the medical analogy, you wouldn't hire a prominent surgeon to remove a wart.

## Working with Attorneys

There is a great deal of discretion involved as an attorney does his job. In the accounting profession there is something called "generally accepted accounting procedures," and when your accountant prepares your books he has these standards to rely on. They are written down in a publication called *Financial Accounting Standards* published by the Financial Accounting Standards Board, the rule-making body of the American Institute of Certified Public Accountants. While these standards may not be strictly followed, they do provide a guide.

Legal services are the last of the "cottage industries"; each item is custom made, much the way many manufactured products used to be made in the workers' homes. Imagine how much more expensive insurance would be if each policy was custom written, with the language negotiated between the insurance company and yourself.

If you meet with your attorney to discuss the purchase of Mike's Maternity Shop and tell him that you have known Mike for years, you know he is reputable, you are very familiar with his business, you know the business is not in financial trouble, and you want a purchase agreement that provides reasonable protection at the least possible cost, he will likely prepare a brief and not too detailed purchase agreement. This purchase agreement will cover only the usual kinds of problems and it may overlook some potential problems unique to this transaction, but it will be inexpensive and probably adequate.

If, on the other hand, you appraoch your attorney saying that you know Mike as a very bad person and you know his business is in trouble, he will give you a more complex and more detailed purchase agreement. When he is suspicious, for example, he may provide that the earnest money be held in escrow, not to be delivered until the closing, or he may insist that the description of what is being purchased be more complete. I remember the purchase of a grocery store where the buyers' attorney wrote in the purchase agreement, "shelves to be filled." They did not take possession until after they had paid the entire purchase price to the seller and they were surprised to find that all of the food and other merchandise had been removed and that every shelf was filled with toilet paper. The attorney could have written "store to be fully stocked with the same merchandise in the same condition as inspected by the parties on June 30, 1979," but he had been told the sellers were honest and he was to provide the lowest priced purchase agreement. Had the buyers known that they were dealing with this kind of a seller, their attorney should have itemized the inventory listing both the quantity and quality. If the attorney wanted to be really prepared to deal with inventory shortages, the purchase agreement should have then gone on to spell out how any adjustments in inventory would be handled. The agreement might have said, "The parties shall inspect the inventory immediately prior to the closing and if the inventory shall have a wholesale value more or less than the wholesale value set forth herein, then the purchase price shall be adjusted by an equivalent amount, provided however, if there shall be a substantial change in the nature of the inventory or if the adjustment shall be more than $500, then the buyers may elect not to proceed with the purchase and the earnest money herein paid shall be returned and neither parties shall have further liability to the other."

It is easy to see what was missed after a problem develops. It is not so easy to sit in an attorney's office, decide what problems are possible, which ones should be guarded against, and then how far to go in providing protection.

# 9

# FOLLOW THROUGH

## ONE COMMON PROBLEM

A very common problem among small businesspeople is that in an effort to be successful they start too many diverse endeavors to be very good in any of them. When business is slow or when an opportunity presents itself, they plunge ahead, not considering the negative effect this may have on their existing business. Skills are lost or never fully developed, and customers chafe at the decline in service. There is a significant value to continuity, reliability, and experience in a specific area.

It takes time to develop a business. Slow periods are to be expected and endured. Not all opportunities can be seized. I remember Dennis Diddle very well because he never agreed with this.

Diddle was a real nice, hard-working, personable fellow who after years of selling insurance for one of the big agencies decided he wanted to be his own boss. Because of his vast experience in the casualty insurance field, he opened an agency that handled casualty insurance. His business was growing and many of his old customers were in the process of switching to Dennis when his next door neighbor asked if Diddle would like to help him remodel a house to sell at a substantial profit. This sounded like a good idea to Diddle. As he explained it to me, his mornings were generally free anyway, and would probably continued to be free until his business doubled. He also wanted to protect himself in case his business didn't work out—he was committed enough to quit his job, but thought that diversification was only good sense, to "insure" against failure. Diddle started spending about half of his time on house remodeling and did make a few thousand dollars this way. Because Diddle thought there was a future in real estate and because his sales ability was such that he could sell anything, he took the test for a real estate salesman's license and passed. He was an excited man when he put up a real estate agent's sign next to his insurance agency sign. From then forward whenever the insurance business was slow, he would concentrate on the real estate business (sometimes sales, sometimes remodeling) and vice versa. Diddle was active in everything. The Jaycees even gave him an award for being so active and for helping them find a hall to rent. Although Diddle had been a friend of mine for years, I never did very much business with him. I did buy some casualty insurance on a building I owned, but my experience with Diddle was such that I believed that, despite his good intentions, he was unable to provide the type of service I required. When I tried to reach him to discuss insurance it always seemed he was out, working on another "deal" of his. I also doubted that Diddle was spending enough time keeping up with changes in the insurance field. While other agents were attending educational seminars or sitting in their office reading the latest pamphlets distributed by the insurance companies, Diddle was driving around looking for houses to remodel. Diddle never did really understand how the insurance industry changed when the Tax Reform Act of 1976 was passed, and I doubt he was aware of any of the subsequent changes in the tax laws. From talking to mutual friends, I know that many of Diddle's clients were unhappy with the service he provided and many of them changed agents when their affairs became so complex that they felt Diddle was no longer competent to handle them—the dynamic growing accounts outgrew Diddle because he stopped growing and they didn't.

Diddle's remodeling business fizzled out. He did two or three houses a year for about five years. Then money got tight at the same time the cost of labor and materials went up. Eventually Diddle found it was easier to buy the houses for the "right" price and then resell them at a profit without making any significant improvements.

Diddle's real estate sales business did reasonably well, but Diddle was never successful enough to add any more salespeople and it remained basically a one-man operation. Diddle was also unable to expand beyond the lower priced single family homes—he just wasn't able to spend enough time to cultivate the skill, following, and style required to sell more expensive homes. For the same reason he was unable to expand into commercial property or apartment buildings. Diddle also had trouble attracting loyalty from his customers—he would sell someone a house and then be surprised to find a few years later that when they decided to sell they went to another realtor. When Diddle's sister and brother-in-law bought through another realtor Diddle was outraged. It didn't lessen his frustration to be told, "We're sorry, Diddle. We always thought of you as an insurance agent who remodeled and sold houses as a hobby. We never thought of you as a realtor."

When I ran into Diddle in a local saloon the other day, Diddle described his life in glowing terms. He had an option out on a house that he was going to repaint, and once it looked better he expected to make $10,000 on that one transaction alone. He got a new listing on a house last week and he was sure he would sell it next month (but there was another realtor who also had it listed and he might sell it first). The insurance business was doing fine, almost 80 percent of his customers renewed and he was submitting a proposal to a big manufacturing company next month to try to become the agent writing their health insurance. Diddle honestly believed he had maximized all of his opportunities by having his fingers in a lot of pies. Perhaps he had. But, looking at the economic side, Diddle has limited his potential. He has lost his better insurance customers while at the same time he has not expanded his remodeling skills, nor has he built a real estate sales organization or developed a real estate sales following. He started with a lot of balls in the air and he still has a lot of balls in the air. If his goal in becoming a businessman was to have a wide variety of activities and the excitement of constant change, he has been successful. If his goal was economic security from an established, growing business and job satisfaction from a professional job done well, he has been less successful.

Diddle is a nervous Nellie. If things are slow, he has to run out and do something. There are thousands of Diddles in business throughout America. Most are content with their lot. Some are wearing themselves out by the tremendous emotional and physical energy they expend trying to keep so many balls in the air. Many would be happier if they could learn to use the slow periods to regroup and prepare for the busy periods.

## INTELLIGENT HEDGING

All of us have different drives, skills, and resources. For some it is best to enter the business mainstream cautiously, hedging against business risks whenever possible.

Donald Do Right is a good example of this type of businessperson. When he first stopped by to discuss his business venture with me, he worked for the city as a fireman. It was never clear why he wanted to go into business, but his plan of action was very simple and he carefully insulated himself against the risks of failure. Donald set up a small shop in his basement where he manufactured miniature furniture for doll houses. He used only the finest materials and catered to the upper end of the market. Rather than hiring salespeople or spending his time going from store to store to solicit sales, he advertised in a few of the publications that catered to the type of buyer he was interested in and sent direct-mail solicitations to a few of the more exclusive shops. Due to low overhead, good management, and proper positioning in the marketplace, Donald's profit is 50 percent of his gross sales. He feels when his sales volume is $50,000 a year, he can comfortably quit his job, give up his pension and other fringe benefits, and devote full time to this business. His present volume of business is $20,000 a year, and although Do Right knows if he quit his job today he could probably double his volume in a few short months, he doesn't want to rush into anything and doesn't feel the need to take any unnecessary risks. Both Do Right and his family are very happy with the present arrangements, and in the final analysis Do Right may never leave is job as a fireman—knowing he has the option to leave anytime has made being a fireman so much more enjoyable that he may have lost his primary reason for wanting to leave.

Others are plungers. The only way they can make a move is to jump right in, burning all bridges behind themselves. An exaggerated example of a plunger is Harold "Hasty" Hepwirth, who once used his wife's automobile accident insurance settlement and their life savings to purchase a roller rink, sight unseen. Hasty had never been in a roller rink, did not know how to skate, and was allergic to dust. To run the roller rink he quit his tenured job as a school teacher, knowing full well that the surplus of teachers in his specialty made it a certainty that he would never be able to return to that school system. Harold plunged so deeply he had to be successful to eat, and he was—he now owns three roller rinks and is planning a fourth.

Those who hedge their bets are less likely to suffer from the painful, tension inducing "six-month syndrome." An example of the "six-month syndrome" is Fred Farkle's plan to have the issue of success or failure resolved in six months. Says Fred, "By borrowing against my insurance, using our savings, cutting expenses, and if Maggie goes back to work two days a week, we can survive for six months. If I haven't cut it by then, I'll hang it up and go back to the cookie factory folding boxes."

# ══ CONCLUSION ══

Deciding to become a businessperson is not an easy decision, and it isn't for everyone. There are significant financial and other risks involved. On the other hand, there are substantial benefits to be gained.

The real question is do you want to go into business for yourself? All it takes is planning, hard work, common sense, and determination. If 11 million Americans can go into business, so can you.

You can minimize your risks by: (1) buying wisely, (2) surrounding yourself with reliable and competent advisors, (3) having contingency plans if the unexpected happens, and (4) preparing yourself and your family for the stresses that will be created.

# ═══ APPENDIX ═══

# SAMPLE OF FINANCIAL INFORMATION

## CONSOLIDATED BALANCE SHEETS
### JULY 31, 1978 AND 1977

|  | 1978 | 1977 |
|---|---|---|
| **Assets** | | |
| Current Assets: | | |
| Cash (Note 2) | $ 8,057,117 | $ 4,310,122 |
| Receivables: | | |
| Customers | 53,770,388 | 36,177,522 |
| Current portion of notes receivable | 1,099,734 | 374,120 |
| Other | 3,926,045 | 3,034,759 |
|  | 58,796,167 | 39,586,401 |
| Less allowance for doubtful accounts | 966,504 | 925,847 |
| Inventories | 39,325,556 | 29,349,323 |
| Prepaid expenses | 1,976,719 | 913,929 |
| Total current assets | 107,189,055 | 73,233,928 |
| Property, plant and equipment (Note 3) | | |
| Land and land improvements | 975,862 | 969,574 |
| Buildings and leasehold improvements | 11,098,198 | 9,024,134 |
| Equipment, including tooling | 23,324,054 | 17,849,072 |
| Construction in progress | 574,267 | 881,362 |
|  | 35,972,381 | 28,724,142 |
| Less accumulated depreciation and amortization | 14,102,217 | 11,818,225 |
|  | 21,870,164 | 16,905,917 |
| Restricted cash (Note 3) | 344,402 | 323,625 |
| Notes receivable and other investments | 2,229,960 | 3,119,275 |
| Deferred charges and miscellaneous assets | 837,793 | 691,963 |
| Excess of cost over net assets of purchased businesses and other intangibles | 534,405 | 633,765 |
| Total assets | $133,005,779 | $94,908,473 |

|                                                    | 1978        | 1977        |
| -------------------------------------------------- | ----------- | ----------- |
| **Liabilities and Shareholders' Equity**           |             |             |
| Current liabilities:                               |             |             |
| Current portion of long-term debt                  | $     —     | $   300,000 |
| Trade accounts payable                             | 14,444,276  | 8,997,811   |
| Customer advance payments                          | 8,974,318   | 3,036,855   |
| Accrued salaries and wages                         | 2,141,094   | 1,297,864   |
| Accrued profit-sharing contributions               |             |             |
| (Note 8)                                           | 2,202,619   | 1,018,436   |
| Other payables and accrued expenses                | 11,848,497  | 7,627,429   |
| Accrued income taxes (including                    |             |             |
| deferred income taxes of $3,754,605                |             |             |
| and $2,929,375, respectively)                      | 10,410,934  | 4,361,657   |
| Total current liabilities                          | 50,021,738  | 26,640,052  |
| Long-term debt (Note 3)                            | 28,650,000  | 23,100,000  |
| Shareholders' equity (Notes 3, 5 and 6)            |             |             |
| Common stock of $1 par value per                   |             |             |
| share.                                             |             |             |
| Authorized 5,000,000 shares; issued                |             |             |
| 2,648,592 shares                                   |             |             |
| in 1978, 2,636,490 in 1977                         | 2,648,592   | 2,636,490   |
| Additional paid-in capital                         | 3,914,428   | 3,810,857   |
| Retained earnings                                  | 47,771,021  | 38,721,074  |
| Total shareholders' equity                         | 54,334,041  | 45,168,421  |
| Commitments (Notes 10 and 11)                      |             |             |
| Total liabilities and shareholders'                |             |             |
| equity                                             | $133,005,779 | $94,908,473 |

See accompanying notes to consolidated financial statements.

## SUMMARY OF CONSOLIDATED EARNINGS
### (DOLLARS IN THOUSANDS)

| | Years ended July 31, | | | | |
|---|---|---|---|---|---|
| | 1978 | 1977 | 1976 | 1975 | 1974 |
| Net sales | $227,403 | $161,043 | $137,513 | $133,734 | $114,592 |
| Cost of sales | 150,610 | 108,226 | 93,168 | 96,434 | 78,949 |
| Gross profit | 76,793 | 52,817 | 44,345 | 37,300 | 35,643 |
| Gross profit % | 33.8% | 32.8% | 32.2% | 27.9% | 31.1% |
| Selling, general, and administrative expense | 51,851 | 39,586 | 33,718 | 29,566 | 24,349 |
| Interest expense | 3,843 | 3,346 | 3,965 | 4,332 | 2,415 |
| Other expense (income) | 876 | 607 | 484 | 22 | (88) |
| Provision for income taxes | 9,138 | 3,923 | 2,580 | 1,601 | 4,395 |
| Earnings from continuing operations | 11,085 | 5,355 | 3,598 | 1,779 | 4,572 |
| Earnings from discontinued operations less income taxes of $—0—; $229; $674; $115; $790; respectively | — | 234 | 805 | 701 | 773 |
| Net earnings | $ 11,085 | $ 5,589 | $ 4,403 | $ 2,480 | $ 5,345 |
| Earnings per common share and common stock equivalent: | | | | | |
| Continuing operations | $4.12 | $2.05 | $1.41 | $ .72 | $1.84 |
| Discontinued operations | — | .09 | .31 | .28 | .31 |
| Net earnings | $4.12 | $2.14 | $1.72 | $1.00* | $2.15 |
| Earnings per common share assuming full dilution: | | | | | |
| Continuing operations | $4.05 | $2.04 | $1.41 | $ .72 | $1.83 |
| Discontinued operations | — | .09 | .31 | .28 | .31 |
| Net earnings | $4.05 | $2.13 | $1.72 | $1.00* | $2.14 |
| Dividends per share of common stock outstanding | $ .77 | $ .58 | $.515 | $ .50 | $ .44 |

*Earnings per share were lowered by $.69 in 1975 as a result of the change to the last-in, first-out (LIFO) cost method of accounting for substantially all inventories.

## SALES BY PRODUCT LINE
### (DOLLARS IN THOUSANDS)

| | Years ended July 31, | | | | |
|---|---|---|---|---|---|
| | 1978 | 1977 | 1976 | 1975 | 1974 |
| Consumer lawn equipment | $103,048 | $ 66,711 | $ 62,596 | $ 69,478 | $ 62,326 |
| Snow removal equipment | 49,325 | 30,449 | 17,633 | 13,573 | 10,355 |
| Professional turf equipment | 40,111 | 30,120 | 24,924 | 30,222 | 23,583 |
| Turf irrigation equipment | 24,182 | 17,045 | 13,873 | 10,728 | 12,472 |
| Center pivot irrigation systems | 3,550 | 7,133 | 7,535 | 2,108 | — |
| Toro-owned distributors | 19,457 | 27,331 | 26,556 | 20,721 | 19,872 |
| Intercompany sales | (12,270) | (17,746) | (15,604) | (13,096) | (14,017) |
| Total* | $227,403 | $161,043 | $137,513 | $133,734 | $114,592 |
| *Includes international sales of | $ 33,000 | $ 28,303 | $ 24,800 | $ 24,746 | $ 20,023 |

## OTHER STATISTICS
### (DOLLARS IN THOUSANDS)

| | Years ended July 31, | | | | |
|---|---|---|---|---|---|
| | 1978 | 1977 | 1976 | 1975 | 1974 |
| Gross expenditures for property, plant and equipment | $ 7,527 | $ 3,683 | $ 1,514 | $ 7,866 | $ 3,192 |
| Research and development | $ 5,831 | $ 4,424 | $ 4,006 | $ 3,698 | $ 2,784 |
| Advertising costs | $ 7,964 | $ 5,388 | $ 3,981 | $ 4,555 | $ 4,385 |
| Wages and salaries | $33,032 | $28,333 | $25,607 | $22,749 | $19,064 |
| Average number of employees | 2,620 | 1,986 | 2,246 | 1,977 | 1,820 |

## CONSOLIDATED STATEMENTS OF
## EARNINGS AND RETAINED EARNINGS
### YEARS ENDED JULY 31, 1978 AND 1977

|  | 1978 | 1977 |
|---|---|---|
| Net sales | $227,402,996 | $161,043,572 |
| Cost of sales | 150,609,830 | 108,225,963 |
| Gross profit | 76,793,166 | 52,817,609 |
| Selling, general, and administrative expense (Note 8) | 51,851,625 | 39,586,275 |
| Operating income | 24,941,541 | 13,231,334 |
| Other expense (income): |  |  |
| Interest expense (Notes 2 and 3) | 3,843,332 | 3,346,395 |
| Other expense | 2,165,507 | 1,446,535 |
| Other income | (1,289,860) | (839,924) |
| Earnings from continuing operations before income taxes | 20,222,562 | 9,278,328 |
| Provision for income taxes (Note 4) | 9,137,730 | 3,923,133 |
| Earnings from continuing operations | 11,084,832 | 5,355,195 |
| Discontinued operations (Note 12): |  |  |
| Loss from discontinued operations less income taxes of $167,630 | — | (181,599) |
| Gain on disposal of discontinued operations less income taxes of $396,569 | — | 415,332 |
|  | — | 233,733 |
| Net earnings | 11,084,832 | 5,588,928 |
| Retained earnings at beginning of year | 38,721,074 | 34,628,844 |
| Cash dividends on common stock, $.77 per share ($.58 in 1977) | (2,034,885) | (1,496,698) |
| Retained earnings at end of year | $ 47,771,021 | $ 38,721,074 |
| Earnings per common share and common stock equivalent (Note 7): |  |  |
| Continuing operations | $4.12 | $2.05 |
| Discontinued operations | — | .09 |
| Net earnings | $4.12 | $2.14 |
| Earnings per common share assuming full dilution (Note 7): |  |  |
| Continuing operations | $4.05 | $2.04 |
| Discontinued operations | — | .09 |
| Net earnings | $4.05 | $2.13 |

See accompanying notes to consolidated financial statements.

# CONSOLIDATED STATEMENTS OF CHANGES IN FINANCIAL POSITION
## YEARS ENDED JULY 31, 1978 AND 1977

|  | 1978 | 1977 |
|---|---|---|
| **Working Capital Provided:** |  |  |
| Earnings from continuing operations | $11,084,832 | $ 5,355,195 |
| Add expenses not requiring outlay of working capital—depreciation and amortization | 2,466,543 | 2,059,771 |
| Working capital provided from continuing operations | 13,551,375 | 7,414,966 |
| Earnings from discontinued operations | — | 233,733 |
| Other working capital provided from sale of discontinued operations | — | 1,235,286 |
| Additions to long-term debts | 10,000,000 | 6,854,556 |
| Proceeds from sale of shares of stock under stock option and purchase plans | 115,673 | 1,089,370 |
| Reduction of investments and notes receivable | 889,315 | — |
| Property disposals | 188,057 | 171,311 |
| Total working capital provided | 24,744,420 | 16,999,222 |
| **Working capital used for** |  |  |
| Cash dividends on common stock | 2,034,885 | 1,496,698 |
| Expenditures for property, plant, and equipment | 7,527,168 | 3,683,478 |
| Additions to restricted cash | 20,777 | 15,384 |
| Investments and notes receivable | — | 2,222,077 |
| Reduction of long-term debt | 4,450,000 | 5,798,204 |
| Current maturity of long-term debt | — | 300,000 |
| Other | 138,149 | 24,583 |
| Total working capital used | 14,170,979 | 13,540,424 |
| **Increase in working capital** | 10,573,441 | 3,458,798 |
| **Working capital at beginning of period** | 46,593,876 | 43,135,078 |
| **Working capital at end of period** | $57,167,317 | $46,593,876 |

## CONSOLIDATED STATEMENTS OF CHANGES
## IN FINANCIAL POSITION

|  | 1978 | 1977 |
|---|---|---|
| **Summary of changes in the components of** | | |
| **working capital:** | | |
| Cash | $ 3,746,995 | $ 1,394,564 |
| Receivables | 19,169,109 | 5,193,885 |
| Inventories | 9,976,233 | 904,141 |
| Prepaid expenses | 1,062,790 | 23,107 |
| Current portion of long-term debt | 300,000 | 47,458 |
| Trade accounts payable | (5,446,465) | (980,897) |
| Customer advance payments | (5,937,463) | (3,036,855) |
| Other payables and accrued expenses | (6,248,481) | (1,340,674) |
| Accrued income taxes | (6,049,277) | 1,254,069 |
| Increase in working capital | $10,573,441 | $ 3,458,798 |

See accompanying notes to consolidated financial statements.

## NOTES TO CONSOLIDATED FINANCIAL STATEMENTS
### JULY 31, 1978 AND 1977

### 1. Summary of Significant Accounting Policies

#### Basis of Consolidation

The accompanying consolidated financial statements include the accounts of The [        ] Company, its domestic subsidiaries, and two wholly-owned foreign subsidiaries. The accounts of the foreign subsidiaries, which are not material, have been adjusted to conform to U.S. accounting principles and practices and have been translated to appropriate U.S. dollar equivalents. A minor investment in an inactive foreign subsidiary is carried at cost. All material intercompany accounts and transactions have been eliminated in consolidation.

### Inventories

Substantially all inventories are valued at the lower of cost or net realizable market with cost determined by the last-in, first-out method.

Had the first-in, first-out method of cost determination been used, inventories would have been $6,431,000 and $5,033,000 higher than reported at July 31, 1978 and 1977, respectively.

### Property and Depreciation

Property, plant, and equipment are carried at cost. Expenditures for major renewals and betterments which substantially increase the useful lives of existing assets are capitalized, and maintenance and repairs are charged to operating expenses as incurred.

The Company provides for depreciation of plant and equipment utilizing straight-line and accelerated methods over the estimated useful lives of the assets. Buildings, including leasehold improvements, and equipment are generally depreciated over 25 to 45 years and 3 to 20 years, respectively. Tooling costs are generally amortized on units of production basis.

### Amortization of Intangibles

Excess of cost over underlying net assets at date of acquisition attributable to the purchase of the Irrigation Division in 1961, $300,011, is not being amortized in the absence of diminution of value. Other excess cost and intangible assets are being amortized by the straight-line method over periods of 5 to 40 years.

### Product Liability Costs

The Company accrues estimated future product liability costs on current sales. In Fiscal 1978, in addition to accruing for losses based on claims reported during the current year, an additional accrual was made, based on historical data statistically projected for the current year, for estimated losses incurred but not yet reported. The additional accrual did not have a significant effect on the financial statements at July 31, 1978 and 1977 respectively.

### Research and Development

Expenditures for research and development, aggregating $5,831,007 in 1978 and $4,423,889 in 1977, are charged against earnings as incurred.

### Income Taxes

Provisions for federal and state income taxes in the accompanying statements of earnings include deferred taxes representing the tax effects of timing differences between taxable and financial statement income. The principal timing differences relate to the installment method of accounting for selected domestic sales transactions and the taxable portion of earnings of a subsidiary that qualifies as a "Domestic International Sales Corporation" (DISC) for federal income tax purposes. Since the DISC subsidiary's fiscal year ends on August 31, the taxable portion of its current income each year is includable in the Company's tax return in the following year. Timing differences attributable to depreciation of property, plant, and equipment are not significant.

Pursuant to the provisions of the Internal Revenue Code, a portion of the earnings of the Company's DISC subsidiary, which was organized in 1972, is not currently taxable as long as the subsidiary reinvests such earnings in export activities and meets certain other prescribed requirements. No provision has been made for income taxes on such tax-deferred portion of the undistributed earnings of the DISC subsidiary since the Company plans to indefinitely reinvest such earnings and comply with the other qualification requirements.

Investment tax credits are recognized as a reduction of income tax expense in the year the assets are placed in service.

## 2. Compensating Balances and Short-Term Borrowings

The Company has maintained compensating cash balances with various banks under formal and informal arrangements in connection with long-term revolving credit agreements and short-term seasonal lines of credit to assure future credit availability. The terms of the compensating balance arrangements require an average compensating cash balance of 10% of the commitments plus

10% of the average borrowings. Withdrawal by the Company of compensating cash balances is not legally restricted. The Company was required to maintain average compensating cash balances (adjusted for the effect of average float) of $473,000 ($1,986,000 in 1977) during Fiscal 1978.

Maximum short-term borrowings outstanding at any month end during the year ended July 31, 1978, were $35,022,000 ($24,500,000 of short-term banks loans and $10,522,000 of commercial paper). Average outstanding short-term borrowings during the year aggregated approximately $17,848,000 ($19,087,000 in 1977). The weighted average interest rate on short-term borrowings during the year was approximately 7.6% (6.9% in 1977) based on actual interest.expense of $1,319,936 ($1,176,412 in 1977) and average compensating cash balances (adjusted for the effect of average float) of $473,000 ($1,986,000 in 1977), applicable to short-term borrowings. Commercial paper outstanding during the year was supported by unused short-term bank loan commitments and/or unused commitments related to the revolving credit agreement. As of July 31, 1978, there were no short-term borrowings outstanding and the Company had available commitments for $44,000,000 of short-term bank loans.

Under the terms of the revolving credit agreement with banks, the Company may borrow up to $5,000,000 through July 1982; $3,300,000 through July 1983; and $1,600,000 through July 1984, with interest at 109% of prevailing prime rates plus ¼ of 1% through July 1982, and ½ of 1% through July 1984; plus a commitment fee of ½ of 1% per annum on the daily average unused balances; plus a facility fee on the commitment amount at a per annum rate equal to .09 times the prime rate.

The weighted average interest rate on long-term borrowing for 1978 was approximately 8.7% (8.6% in 1977) based on actual interest expense (including commitment fees and facility fees) of $2,315,350 ($1,940,447 in 1977) and average long-term borrowings outstanding of approximately $26,738,000 ($22,590,000 in 1977). There are no compensating balance requirements relating to long-term debt.

The capitalized lease obligation on plant and equipment is financed through the issuance of Industrial Development Revenue Bonds bearing interest at the rates of 6% to 8% over the terms of the lease ending in 1993. Under the terms of the lease agreement, the Company is required to make lease payments sufficient to cover the bond interest and principal amounts as they become due

## 3. Long-Term Debt

A summary of long-term debt is as follows:

|  | 1978 | 1977 |
|---|---|---|
| 8.625% Senior notes, due $1,000,000 annually, August 1984 through 1993 | $10,000,000 | $ — |
| 9.75% Senior notes, due $750,000 annually, August 1982 through 1991 | 7,500,000 | 7,500,000 |
| 8% Senior notes, due $500,000 annually, August 1979 through 1987; balance due August 1987 | 5,500,000 | 6,000,000 |
| Revolving credit notes due August 1982 with interest at 109% of the prime rate plus ¼ of 1% | — | 3,500,000 |
| Unsecured promissory notes payable with interest at 6.6%–8.5% due in amounts varying from $175,000 to $550,000 from 1979 through 1992 | 3,650,000 | 4,000,000 |
| Capitalized lease obligation | 2,000,000 | 2,100,000 |
|  | $28,650,000 | $23,100,000 |

in approximate annual amounts ranging from $116,000 to $312,000.

At July 31, 1978, cash balances of $344,402 are restricted for completion of two production facilities financed by the 6.6% to 8.5% notes payable and the capitalized lease obligation.

Under the terms of the senior notes and revolving credit agreements, the Company must maintain at least $25,000,000 of working capital, limit the amount of long-term debt and deferred taxes to 80% of tangible net worth as defined, and is subject to restrictions, among other things, on payment of cash dividends on common stock. At July 31, 1978, the Company has complied with such requirements and, under the most restrictive agreement, retained earnings of approximately $28,000,000 were free from such restrictions.

Principal payments of long-term debt in each of the next five years ended July 31 are as follows: 1979, -0-; 1980, $900,000; 1981, $850,000; 1982, $825,000; 1983, $1,625,000.

## 4. Income Taxes

The provision for income taxes (including taxes relating to discontinued operations in 1977) consists of the following:

|  | Current | Deferred | Total |
|---|---|---|---|
| 1978: |  |  |  |
| Federal | $7,796,112 | $  203,498 | $7,999,610 |
| State | 1,101,956 | 36,164 | 1,138,120 |
| Total | $8,898,068 | $  239,662 | $9,137,730 |
| 1977: |  |  |  |
| Federal | $1,931,643 | $1,078,379 | $3,010,022 |
| State | 711,396 | 430,654 | 1,142,050 |
| Total | $2,643,039 | $1,509,033 | $4,152,072 |

A reconciliation of the statutory federal income tax provision and rate to the Company's actual provision and rate is summarized as follows:

| | 1978 | | 1977 | |
|---|---|---|---|---|
| | Amount | Rate | Amount | Rate |
| Statutory federal income tax provision | $9,706,830 | 48.0% | $4,675,680 | 48.0% |
| State income taxes net of federal income tax benefits | 573,017 | 2.8% | 369,926 | 3.8% |
| Tax effect of undistributed earnings of the DISC subsidiary not subject to tax | (348,762) | (1.7)% | (333,995) | (3.4)% |
| Investment and other credits | (449,123) | (2.2)% | (249,298) | (2.6)% |
| Long-term capital gains | (6,371) | — | (157,125) | (1.6)% |
| Other, net | (337,861) | (1.7)% | (153,116) | (1.6)% |
| Actual provision for income taxes | $9,137,730 | 45.2% | $4,152,072 | 42.6% |

The cumulative amount of undistributed earnings of the DISC subsidiary for which no federal income taxes have been provided by the Company aggregated approximately $5,200,000 at July 31, 1978. If these earnings were distributed to the Company by the DISC subsidiary, an additional federal income tax provision of approximately $2,500,000 would be required.

## 5. Shareholders' Equity

Changes in common stock and additional paid-in capital during the two years ended July 31, 1978, were as follows:

|  | Common Stock of $1 Par Value | Additional Paid-In Capital |
|---|---|---|
| Balance at July 31, 1976 | $2,508,347 | $2,837,034 |
| Sales of 127,350 shares under stock option and stock purchase plans | 127,350 | 962,020 |
| Additional 793 shares issued for net assets of minor pooled company | 793 | 11,803 |
| Balance at July 31, 1977 | $2,636,490 | $3,810,857 |
| Sales of 12,102 shares under stock option plan | 12,102 | 103,571 |
| Balance at July 31, 1978 | $2,648,592 | $3,914,428 |

At July 31, 1978, shares of authorized but unissued common stock were reserved as follows: 97,498 shares for stock options outstanding, 57,200 shares for granting of future stock options, 250,000 shares for a performance unit award plan, and 175,000 shares for an employee stock purchase plan.

## 6. Stock Option and Stock Purchase Plans

Under the 1976 Stock Option Plan, qualified and nonqualified stock options and stock appreciation rights may be granted to key employees to acquire shares of the Company's common stock. Under terms of this plan, and the 1972 Parallel Stock Option Plan, options may be granted to key employees at prices not less than fair market values at dates of grant. Qualified options are exercisable ratably after one year from date of grant during the following four-year period. Nonqualified options are exercisable over a nine-year period commencing one year from date of grant. Option transactions during the two years ended July 31, 1978, are summarized as follows:

| | Options Outstanding | | Options Currently Exercisable |
|---|---|---|---|
| | Number of Shares | Option Price Per Share | |
| Balance at July 31, 1976 | 94,650 | $ 8.62-16.38 | 9,000 |
| Options granted: | | | |
| 1977 | 10,000 | 12.12-14.63 | — |
| 1978 | 38,800 | 15.38-22.63 | — |
| Options which became exercisable: | | | |
| 1977 | — | — | 83,650 |
| 1978 | — | — | 11,250 |
| Options exercised: | | | |
| 1977 | (27,350) | 8.62-11.38 | (27,350) |
| 1978 | (12,102) | 8.62-14.62 | (12,102) |
| Options cancelled: | | | |
| 1977 | (5,000) | 8.62 | (5,000) |
| 1978 | (1,500) | 8.62-16.38 | (1,500) |
| Balance at July 31, 1978 | 97,498 | $ 8.62-22.63 | 57,948 |

The fair market value of purchased shares at dates of exercise aggregated $255,157 ($15.88–30.88 per share) in 1978. The aggregate option price of options outstanding at July 31, 1978, was $1,164,477.

In November 1976, the Company adopted a stock purchase plan under which employees may be granted rights to purchase up to

175,000 shares of the Company's common stock through payroll deductions. Participants may acquire all or part of the shares to which they are entitled on December 29, 1978, the termination date of the plan, at $14.38 or $19.13 (fair market value of shares on January 3, 1977, or January 2, 1978, respectively) or the fair market value of shares on December 29, 1978, whichever is lower. Under the terms of a similar employee stock purchase plan previously in effect, participants used their accumulated payroll deductions to purchase 100,000 shares as of December 31, 1976, at an average price of $8.48 per share.

Upon exercise of stock options and purchase rights, the portion of the proceeds received equal to the par value of the shares issued is credited to common stock and the excess is credited to additional paid-in capital.

In September 1975, the Board of Directors approved the adoption of a Performance Unit Award Plan to provide additional incentive compensation to key employees over three- and five-year earn-out periods. The amount of compensation earned (to be paid in cash or in a combination of cash and common shares at the end of the earn-out periods) during the earn-out periods will be determined by comparison of the Company's performance to that of a group of other publicly held corporations.

## 7. Earnings per Share

Earnings per common and common stock equivalent shares are computed based on the weighted average number of common shares outstanding during the respective periods. Common stock equivalent shares include potential dilutive stock options, shares issuable under the employee stock purchase plans, and shares issuable under a performance unit award plan. These shares are included under the treasury stock method using the average market price of the Company's shares during each period.

Fully diluted earnings per share are based on primary earnings per share, adjusted to reflect potential additional dilution resulting from the use of end of period market prices when such prices are higher than average market prices.

Shares used in the computations are as follows:

| | 1978 | 1977 |
|---|---|---|
| Weighted average common shares: | | |
| Outstanding | 2,641,785 | 2,575,758 |
| For stock options | 39,698 | 25,236 |
| For employee stock purchase plans | 7,526 | 15,466 |
| For performance unit award plan | 1,058 | — |
| Total for common share and common stock equivalent earnings per share | 2,690,067 | 2,616,460 |
| Additional shares for: | | |
| Stock options | 23,937 | 2,308 |
| Employee stock purchase plans | 23,891 | 1,599 |
| Performance unit award plan | 453 | 239 |
| Total for fully diluted earnings per share | 2,738,348 | 2,620,606 |

## 8. Profit Sharing and Pension Plans

Contributions to employees' profit sharing plans (which cover substantially all employees of the Company and its subsidiaries) were approximately $2,205,000 in 1978 and $1,039,000 in 1977. Such amounts are based on annual earnings before income taxes and contributions under the plans.

In addition, the Company and its subsidiaries have insignificant noncontributory pension plans covering primarily office, sales, and supervisory employees. Pension expense in 1978 and 1977 was not significant.

## 9. Segment Data

The Company classifies its operations into two industry segments: lawn maintenance equipment and center pivot irrigation systems. The center pivot irrigation systems segment is not significant to the Company's total operations.

Export sales were $28,285,000 and $27,577,000 for the years ended July 31, 1978 and 1977, respectively. Sales to any particular geographic area were not significant.

## 10. Lease Commitments

In November 1976, the Financial Accounting Standards Board issued Statement No. 13 "Accounting for Leases." The statement is effective for lease agreements entered into on or after January 1, 1977. The effect of applying Statement No. 13 to leases entered into after that date was not significant to the Company's financial position at July 31, 1978 and 1977, or its results of operations for the years then ended.

Certain leases in effect at December 31, 1976, which are not accounted for by the operating method, would be classified and accounted for as "capital leases" under Statement No. 13. If the Company had accounted for those leases as capital leases, the effect on assets, liabilities, and net income for the years ended July 31, 1978 and 1977, respectively, would not be significant.

Minimum rental commitments in future fiscal years under noncancellable leases are as follows: 1979, $1,384,691; 1980, $876,967; 1981, $529,604; 1982, $291,929; 1983, $119,056; after 1983, $128,902.

Total rental expense for the two years ended July 31 is as follows:

|  | 1978 | 1977 |
|---|---|---|
| Warehouse and office space | $ 648,068 | $ 667,672 |
| Trucks and autos | 1,167,559 | 1,191,889 |
| Equipment | 1,407,914 | 1,072,704 |
|  | $3,223,541 | $2,932,265 |

## 11. Commitments

Certain receivables have been sold to financial institutions. Under one arrangement, the Company may, but is not required to, substitute current accounts for defaulted accounts. Under another arrangement, receivables from insured export sales transactions have been sold and the Company acts as agent for collections under the arrangements.

The Company is contingently liable to repurchase approximately

$8,100,000 of inventory under distributor and dealer floor plan arrangements. The ultimate liability to the Company would be the amount that the repurchase cost of the inventory exceeds its net realizable value. Debts of certain distributors aggregating $950,000 at July 31, 1978, have been guaranteed by the Company.

Litigation is pending between the Company and [          ], involving the Company's claim for damages based upon certain alleged antitrust violations, and [          ] claim of patent infringement. [          ] seeks to obtain an injunction against continued sale by the Company, and damages for past infringement related to the Company's flexible-line trimmers. Management believes the patents in suit are invalid and unenforceable, but at this early stage of the pretrial discovery procedures, is unable to effectively assess the risks involved.

## 12. Discontinued Operations

On November 1, 1976, the Company sold, principally for cash, its [          ] subsidiary. The results of operations prior to such date are included in 1977 consolidated statements of earnings and retained earnings under the caption "Discontinued Operations."

## 13. Quarterly Financial Data (unaudited)

Summarized quarterly financial data (in thousands, except for per share and market price amounts) for Fiscal 1978 and 1977 are as follows:

|  | Three months ended | | | |
|---|---|---|---|---|
| **Fiscal 1978:** | **October** | **January** | **April** | **July** |
| Net sales | $35,911 | $49,889 | $71,770 | $69,833 |
| Gross profit | $12,644 | 17,087 | 23,207 | 23,855 |
| Earnings, continuing operations | $ 1,593 | 2,461 | 3,861 | 3,170 |
| Net earnings | $ 1,593 | 2,461 | 3,861 | 3,170 |
| Earnings per common share and common stock equivalent | $.60 | .92 | 1.44 | 1.17 |
| Earnings per common share assuming full dilution | $.60 | .92 | 1.43 | 1.16 |
| Dividends per common share outstanding | $.16 | .16 | .20 | .25 |
| Market price of common stock: | | | | |
|   High bid | $ 15¾ | 19¼ | 22¼ | 32¼ |
|   Low bid | $ 13 | 13½ | 17¼ | 21¼ |
| **Fiscal 1977:** | | | | |
| Net sales | $22,916 | 38,626 | 48,258 | 51,243 |
| Gross profit | $ 7,920 | 13,016 | 14,281 | 17,600 |
| Earnings, continuing operations | $ 62 | 1,604 | 1,514 | 2,175 |
| Net earnings | $ 89 | 1,474 | 1,851 | 2,175 |
| Earnings per common share and common stock equivalent: | | | | |
|   Continuing operations | $.02 | .62 | .57 | .82 |
|   Net earnings | $.03 | .57 | .70 | .82 |
| Earnings per common share assuming full dilution: | | | | |
|   Continuing operations | $.02 | .62 | .57 | .82 |
|   Net earnings | $.03 | .57 | .70 | .82 |
| Dividends per common share outstanding | $.14 | .14 | .14 | .16 |
| Market price of common stock: | | | | |
|   High bid | $ 13¾ | 14½ | 14½ | 14½ |
|   Low bid | $ 11¾ | 11¼ | 12¼ | 11¾ |

# TEN YEAR REVIEW 1969-1978
## (DOLLARS, EXCEPT PER SHARE AMOUNTS, IN THOUSANDS)

| Operating Data | 1978 | 1977 | 1976 | 1975 | 1974 | 1973 | 1972(a) | 1971(a) | 1970(a) | 1969(a) |
|---|---|---|---|---|---|---|---|---|---|---|
| Net sales | $227,403 | $161,043 | $137,513 | $133,734 | $114,592 | $94,692 | $75,373 | $66,163 | $56,821 | $51,021 |
| Earnings: | | | | | | | | | | |
| Earnings from continuing operations | 11,085 | 5,355 | 3,598 | 1,779 | 4,572 | 3,952 | 2,868 | 3,164 | 3,061 | 2,733 |
| Percent of sales | 4.9% | 3.3% | 2.6% | 1.3% | 4.0% | 4.2% | 3.8% | 4.8% | 5.4% | 5.4% |
| Per common share and common stock equivalent | $4.12 | $2.05 | $1.41 | $.72(b) | $1.84 | $1.60(c) | $1.18(c) | $1.32(c) | $1.28(c) | $1.14(c) |
| Per common share assuming full dilution | $4.05 | $2.04 | $1.41 | $.72(b) | $1.83 | — | — | — | — | — |
| Net earnings | 11,085 | 5,589 | 4,403 | 2,480 | 5,345 | 4,651 | 3,069 | 3,277 | 3,057 | 3,109 |
| Per common share and common stock equivalent | $4.12 | $2.14 | $1.72 | $1.00(b) | $2.15 | $1.88(c) | $1.26(c) | $1.37(c) | $1.28(c) | $1.30(c) |
| Per common share assuming full dilution | $4.05 | $2.13 | $1.72 | $1.00(b) | $2.14 | — | — | — | — | — |
| Dividends | | | | | | | | | | |
| On common stock outstanding | $2,035 | $1,497 | $1,286 | $1,234 | $1,091 | $1,012 | $825 | $736 | $710 | $708 |
| Per common share | $.77 | $.58 | $.515 | $.50 | $.44 | $.41 | $.40 | $.36 | $.35 | $.35 |

**Summary of financial position**

| | | | | | | | | | | |
|---|---|---|---|---|---|---|---|---|---|---|
| Current assets | $107,189 | $73,234 | $65,718 | $74,516 | $61,063 | $44,770 | $38,744 | $34,378 | $23,573 | 21,427 |
| Current liabilities | 50,022 | 26,640 | 22,583 | 35,692 | 20,172 | 13,365 | 10,098 | 9,229 | 6,720 | 5,042 |
| Net working capital | 57,167 | 46,594 | 43,135 | 38,824 | 40,891 | 31,405 | 28,646 | 25,149 | 16,853 | 16,385 |
| Non-current assets | 25,817 | 21,674 | 19,183 | 20,061 | 11,462 | 9,739 | 8,304 | 7,245 | 5,180 | 3,537 |
| Total capitalization | 82,984 | 68,268 | 62,318 | 58,885 | 52,353 | 41,144 | 36,950 | 32,394 | 22,033 | 19,922 |
| Capitalization: | | | | | | | | | | |
| Long-term debt | 28,650 | 23,100 | 22,344 | 22,500 | 17,210 | 10,315 | 10,400 | 9,268 | 1,537 | 1,774 |
| Shareholders' equity | 54,334 | 45,168 | 39,974 | 36,385 | 35,143 | 30,829 | 26,550 | 23,126 | 20,496 | 18,148 |
| Book value per share | $20.51 | $17.13 | $15.94 | $14.74 | $14.24 | $12.43 | $10.84 | $9.62 | $8.55 | $7.57 |
| **Stock data** | | | | | | | | | | |
| Number of common shares outstanding (in thousands) | 2,649 | 2,636 | 2,508 | 2,468 | 2,468 | 2,480 | 2,450 | 2,404 | 1,199 | 1,199 |
| Number of shareholders | 2,659 | 2,679 | 2,188 | 2,127 | 1,921 | 1,834 | 1,566 | 1,387 | 1,290 | 1,218 |
| Low bid price | 16 | 11¾ | 10½ | 8 | 7 | 14¼ | 31½ | 20¼ | 14½ | 18½ |
| High bid price | 32¼ | 14½ | 17¼ | 13 | 16½ | 36¼ | 43¾ | 35¼ | 20¾ | 25½ |

(a) 1972–1969 have been restated for pooling of interests.

(b) Earnings per share were lowered by $.69 in 1975 as a result of the change to the last-in, first-out (LIFO) cost method of accounting for substantially all inventories.

(c) Earnings per share amounts calculated on weighted average shares ousanding, not restated for dilutive effect.

All "per common share" figures have been adjusted to give effect to the 100% stock dividend in July 1971

Stock bid prices listed are on a calendar year basis. The 1978 range represents January through July.

165

# ACCOUNTANTS' UNQUALIFIED OPINION

[                                     ]

CERTIFIED PUBLIC ACCOUNTANTS

The Shareholders and Board of Directors
[                  ]

We have examined the consolidated balance sheets of The
[         ] Company and subsidiaries as of July 31, 1978 and
1977, and the related consolidated statements of earnings and
retained earnings and changes in financial position for the
years then ended. Our examinations were made in accordance
with generally accepted auditing standards and accordingly included such tests of the accounting records and such other
auditing procedures as we considered necessary in the circumstances.

In our opinion, the aforementioned consolidated financial
statements present fairly the financial position of The
[         ] Company and subsidiaries at July 31, 1978 and 1977,
and the results of their operations and the changes in their
financial position for the years then ended, in conformity with
generally accepted accounting principles applied on a consistent basis.

September 26, 1978           [                         ]

# VELVEETA PURCHASE AGREEMENT

THIS AGREEMENT made and entered into in the City of Minneapolis, Minnesota, this _____ day of _____, 19 ___, by and between

> VERNA VELVEETA,
> hereinafter called "Seller,"
>
> and
>
> HARMON HULK,
> hereinafter called "Purchaser"

## RECITALS:

*First:* Purchaser is in the vending machine business and owns and has placed in various locations in Minnesota coin-operated machines that dispense hot drinks, cold drinks, cigarettes, candy, pastry, sandwiches, milk, hot food, and ice cream (hereinafter collectively and individually referred to as "vending machines").

*Second:* Seller is in the coin-operated machine business and owns and has placed in various locations in Minnesota vending machines (as set forth in Exhibit A hereto attached) and other coin-operated machines which provide music or games for the operator.

*Third:* Under the trade name "Velveeta Vending Company" Seller buys such machines, places them in various locations, services the machines, and after paying a commission to the owner or occupant of the "location," Seller keeps the proceeds from the machines' operation.

*Fourth:* Purchaser has agreed to purchase from Seller part of Seller's coin-operated machine business, to-wit: the aforementioned vending machines and certain related assets.

NOW, THEREFORE, in consideration of the mutual covenants herein contained, the parties hereto agree as follows:

1.  Upon and subject to the terms and conditions hereinafter set forth, Seller hereby agrees to sell to Purchaser, and Purchaser hereby agrees to buy from Seller, the following described property:

    (a) All of the property listed and described on Exhibit A, which is hereto attached and hereby made a part hereof, including all spare parts, keys, and duplicate keys to all vending machines.

    (b) All inventory contained in the vending machines described on Exhibit A at the time of closing.

    (c) All vending machine inventory heretofore purchased by Seller which has not been placed in any of Seller's vending machines and which Seller has on hand at date of closing.

    (d) That goodwill attributable to Seller's vending machine business except Seller's trade name "Velveeta Vending Company," which trade name Seller retains the sole right to use.

2.  The purchase price to be paid by Purchaser to Seller for the aforesaid property shall be as follows:

    (a) For the items of property listed in Subparagraph (a) of Paragraph 1 hereof, the sum of Forty Thousand Dollars ($40,000.00).

    (b) For the inventory described in Subparagraph (b) of Paragraph 1 hereof, the net cost to Seller, after deducting all trade or cash discounts, or the wholesale market value thereof, whichever is lower.

    (c) For the inventory described in Subparagraph (c) of Paragraph 1 hereof, the net cost to Seller, after deducting all trade or cash discounts, or the wholesale market value thereof, whichever is lower.

    (d) For the goodwill described in Subparagraph (d) of Paragraph 1 hereof, the sum of Four Thousand Dollars ($4000.00).

    (e) For the covenants hereinafter provided in Paragraphs 3 and 4, the sum of Thirty-eight Thousand Dollars ($38,000.00).

3.  Seller covenants that Seller will not, directly or indirectly, either as owner, manager, employee, agent, shareholder, or in any other manner, continue or enter into the vending

machine business in the Counties of [          ], [          ],
[          ], [          ], [          ], and [          ], for a
period of ten (10) years from and after the date of closing. At
any time during the ten (10) year period referred to above, in
the event that Seller voluntarily transfers all or a substantial
portion of the business she operates and intends to continue to operate after the closing hereof under the trade
name "Velveeta Vending Company," Seller shall, as a condition to such transfer, require that the purchaser, donee or
other transferee agree in writing to be bound by the terms
and covenants contained in this paragraph and to further
agree to bind any subsequent transferees in a similar manner. Purchaser shall be a third-party creditor beneficiary of
such agreement. Acknowledging that damages at law for
breach of his restrictive covenant not to compete would be
difficult of ascertainment, Seller agrees that Purchaser may
have equitable relief by way of restraining order and temporary and permanent injunction, or otherwise, against any
breach or threatened breach of the foregoing restrictive
covenant.

4.  Seller affirmatively covenants that Seller will use her best
efforts for a period of ten (10) years from and after the date
of closing to obtain placement of vending machines owned
by Purchaser in those locations in which Seller has placed
or will place in the future any coin-operated machine. At any
time during the ten- (10) year period referred to above, in the
event that Seller voluntarily transfers all or a substantial
portion of the business she operates and intends to continue to operate after the closing hereof under the trade
name "Velveeta Vending Company," Seller shall, as a condition to such transfer, require that the purchaser, donee, or
other transferee agree in writing to be bound by the terms
and covenants contained in this paragraph and to further
agree to bind any subsequent transferees in a similar manner. Purchaser shall be a third-party creditor beneficiary of
such agreement.

5.  The aggregate purchase price of Eighty-two Thousand
Dollars ($82,000.00) plus the cost of merchandise described
in Subparagraphs (b) and (c) of Paragraph 1 hereof shall be
paid to Seller by Purchaser in the following manner:
(a)  By payment to Seller's attorney, [          ], upon the ex-

ecution of this agreement the sum of Five Thousand Dollars ($5000.00), to be held in trust pursuant to the terms of an escrow agreement hereto attached as Exhibit B.

(b) By payment to Seller at closing a sum equal to twenty-five per cent (25%) of the aggregate purchase price less Five Thousand Dollars ($5000.00).

(c) By payment to Seller on the [XX] day of [          ], 19[XX], the sum of Fifteen Thousand Dollars ($15,000.00) plus accrued interest on the balance of the aggregate purchase price at the rate of six per cent (6%) per annum.

(d) By eleven (11) payments of Two Thousand Three Hundred Dollars ($2300.00) plus interest on the unpaid balance of the aggregate purchase price at six per cent (6%) per annum, the first payment to be made on the [XX] day of [          ], 19[XX], and a like and equal sum on the last day of each succeeding month thereafter until [      XX] 19[XX], when the eleventh payment becomes due and payable; provided, however, that the personal property tax payable in 19[      ] on the personal property which is the subject matter of this purchase agreement shall be paid by Seller and a receipt for such payment furnished to Purchaser immediately thereafter, but if such tax is not paid by Seller before the date such tax becomes due, then such tax may be paid by Purchaser and the amount paid credited to the next monthly installment payable to Seller. Purchaser shall execute and deliver to Seller at the closing a purchase money chattel mortgage securing the balance of the purchase price with a lien upon all of the items of equipment described on Exhibit A.

(e) By payment to Seller on the [XX] day of [          ], 19[XX], the balance of the aggregate purchase price remaining unpaid plus accrued interest at the rate of six per cent (6%) per annum.

(f) At any time after [          XX], 19[XX], Purchaser has the right to prepay the balance due under this agreement without penalty.

6. In order to induce the Purchaser to make said purchase, Seller warrants and represents as follows:

(a) That Seller has good and clear title to all of the items of property listed on Exhibit A, free and clear of all encumbrances except those encumbrances which are specifically set forth on Exhibit C, which encumbrances will be satisfied on or before closing.

(b) That Seller has no business creditors on this date and will have no business creditors as of the date of closing, other than those business creditors who may have individual claims for less than One Hundred Dollars ($100.00) and whose aggregate claims are less than One Thousand Dollars ($1000.00). If Seller has any business creditors at the date of closing, Seller agrees to indemnify Purchaser against and save Purchaser harmless from any expense, loss, or liability resulting from such creditors' claims.

(c) That each of the items of equipment listed on Exhibit A is accurately identified and described therein, is in a state of good repair, and no item of equipment has been in use for more than seven (7) years.

(d) That each of the items of equipment listed on Exhibit A is presently on location at the place therein indicated.

(e) That the agreed commission as to each item of equipment listed on Exhibit A is as therein set forth, and there are no agreements between the owners or occupants of the locations and Seller, other than servicing agreements, not disclosed on Exhibit A.

(f) That as of closing date, all other obligations of Seller arising out of the operation of the business sold hereby will have been paid or satisfied. In this regard, Seller agrees to indemnify Purchaser against and save Purchaser harmless from any expense, loss, or liability arising by reason of breach of this warranty and representation.

7. In order to induce the Purchaser to make said purchase, Seller agrees as follows:

(a) To cooperate with Purchaser or Purchaser's agent in making a complete inspection of the entire route of vending machines, as described on Exhibit A. This inspection shall be accomplished as soon as practicable but in no event later than ten (10) days from the date thereof. During such inspection, Seller and Purchaser's representative shall compile a list of the inventory in each of the machines listed on Exhibit A.

(b) To transfer possession to Purchaser or Purchaser's agent of the key, and all duplicates, to each vending machine immediately after the machine is inspected as provided in Subparagraph (a) hereof. Seller is to simultaneously remove all monies from each machine at the time of such inspection.

(c) To execute and deliver to Purchaser a Bill of Sale with warranties of title to all the property listed on Exhibit A.

8. Seller's vending machine business encompasses many of the same locations as Seller's game and music machine business, and as Purchaser may gain influence with the owners or occupants of the locations as a result of purchasing Seller's vending machine business, which influence could be used to effectuate removal or prevent placement of Seller's game and music machines, Seller desires that Purchaser not compete with Seller in the game and music machine business. Therefore, Purchaser covenants that Purchaser will not, directly or indirectly, either as owner, manager, employee, agent, shareholder, or in any other manner, enter into the business of installing or operating game or music machines in the Counties of [           ], [          ], [           ], [           ], and [           ] for a period of ten (10) years from and after the date of closing.

9. If all of the representations and warranties contained in Paragraph 6 hereof are found to be true and correct by Purchaser, and if Seller promptly and completely performs all of the covenants and conditions contained in Paragraph 7 hereof, then and in that event, the closing shall take place immediately thereafter.

10. All of the provisions hereof are enforceable against each of the persons described herein by the term "Seller" either jointly or severally, and all representations and warranties are the joint and several representations and warranties of Seller, and such representations and warranties shall survive the closing.

IN WITNESS WHEREOF, the parties hereto have hereunto set their hands the day and year first above written.

In the presence of:

_____

As to Seller

Verna Velveeta

**SELLER**

_____

As to Purchaser

By _____

Harmon Hulk

**PURCHASER**

# EXHIBIT A

| Machine | Serial Number | Location | Commission | |
|---|---|---|---|---|
| 800MC NATIONAL CIG. | 1021830 | | Cigarettes | .07 |
| 222 NATIONAL CIG. | 846177 | Omitted—included in actual contract | Cigarettes | .02 |
| 222 NATIONAL CIG. | 846173 | | Cigarettes | .02 |
| 222 NATIONAL CIG. | 846179 | | Cigarettes | .03 |
| ROWE AC-L1020A-COLD | 315-7538 | | Cold Drink | .05 |
| 222 NATIONAL CIG. | 888884 | | Cigarettes | .03½ |
| 510CG NATIONAL CANDY | 10C6366 | | Candy | 10% |
| 222 NATIONAL CIG. | 888883 | | Cigarettes | .02 |
| 800MC NATIONAL CIG. | 1001603 | | Cigarettes | .03½ |
| 510CG NATIONAL CANDY | 10C16258 | | Candy | 10% |
| 510CG NATIONAL CANDY | 10C16257 | | Candy | 10% |
| 10C NATIONAL CANDY | 10C5225 | | Candy | 10% |
| 222 NATIONAL CIG. | 811642 | | Cigarettes | .03 |
| 510CG NATIONAL CANDY | 10C19282 | | Candy | 10% |
| 222 NATIONAL CIG. | 034755 | | Cigarettes | .04½ |
| 222 NATIONAL CIG. | 865786 | | Cigarettes | .03 |
| 800 CROWN NATIONAL CIG. | 1032519 | | Cigarettes | .04½ |
| 222 NATIONAL CIG. | 846176 | | Cigarettes | .02 |
| CC NATIONAL CANDY | CC50359 | | Candy | 10% |
| 222 NATIONAL CIG. | 873764 | | Cigarettes | .02 |
| 222 NATIONAL CIG. | 905388 | | Cigarettes | .03 |
| 222 NATIONAL CIG | 934752 | | Cigarettes | .03 |
| CC NATIONAL CANDY | CC86161 | | Candy | 10% |
| 222 NATIONAL CIG. | 803047 | | Cigarettes | .01 |
| 800 MC NATIONAL CIG. | 929733 | | Cigarettes | .03 |
| 800 CROWN NATIONAL CIG | 1027906 | | Cigarettes | .04½ |
| 222 NATIONAL CIG. | 888882 | | Cigarettes | .03 |
| 222 NATIONAL CIG. | 846178 | | | |
| 222 NATIONAL CIG. | 846174 | | Cigarettes | .02 |
| CC NATIONAL CANDY | CC50079 | | Candy | 10% |
| 222 NATIONAL CIG. | 934751 | | Cigarettes | .02 |
| CC NATIONAL CANDY | CC86162 | | Candy | 10% |
| 222 NATIONAL CIG. | 855057 | | Cigarettes | .02 |
| CC NATIONAL CANDY | CC50963 | | Candy | 10% |

| Machine | Serial Number | Location | Commission |
|---------|---------------|----------|------------|
| 222 NATIONAL CIG. | 846181 | Cigarettes | .02 |
| 222 NATIONAL CANDY | CC86163 | Candy | 10% |
| AC-IJ020 A-COLD | 315-9701 | Cold Drink | 10% |
| AC-1102 HOT | 9131453 | Hot Drink | 10% |
| 800MC NATIONAL CIG | 1021831 | Cigarettes | .04 |
| 222 NATIONAL CIG. | 865787 | Cigarettes | .03 |
| CC NATIONAL CANDY | CC50960 | Candy | 10% |
| 222 NATIONAL CIG. | 865785 | Cigarettes | .02 |
| 222 NATIONAL CIG. | 803049 | Cigarettes | .01 |
| 10C NATIONAL CANDY | 10C5224 | Candy | 10% |
| 800MC NATIONAL CIG. | 929732 | Cigarettes | .03 |
| CC NATIONAL CANDY | 82742 | Candy | 10% |
| 222 NATIONAL CIG. | 846170 | Cigarettes | .03 |
| 222 NATIONAL CIG. | 829523 | Cigarettes | .03 |
| 222 NATIONAL CIG. | 803046 | Cigarettes | -0- |
| 222 NATIONAL CIG. | 865790 | Cigarettes | .01 |
| 800M NATIONAL CIG. | 11133 | Cigarettes | .04 |
| 21CE NATIONAL CANDY | 1974 | Candy | 10% |
| ROWE AC-L1020A-COLD | 315-9230 | Cold Drink | 40% |
| 21CE NATIONAL CANDY | 1973 | Candy | 10% |
| 800 CROWN NATIONAL CIG. | 103257 | Cigarettes | .03 |
| 222 NATIONAL CIG. | 857456 | Cigarettes | .03 |
| CC CROWN NATIONAL CANDY | 96788 | Candy | 10% |
| 222 CROWN NATIONAL CIG. | 953184 | Cigarettes | .02 |
| 222 NATIONAL CIG. | 865788 | Cigarettes | .03 |
| 510CG NATIONAL CANDY | 10C11232 | Candy | 10% |
| 222 NATIONAL CIG. | 846175 | Cigarettes | .02 |
| 222 NATIONAL CIG. | 811644 | Cigarettes | .03 |
| 222 NATIONAL CIG. | 828525 | Cigarettes | .01 |
| CC NATIONAL CANDY | CC50078 | Candy | 10% |
| 800 CROWN NATIONAL CIG. | 1027905 | Cigarettes | .03 |
| 222 CROWN NATIONAL CIG. | 953183 | Cigarettes | .03½ |
| 222 NATIONAL CIG. | 811643 | Cigarettes | .03 |
| 222 NATIONAL CIG. | 809959 | Cigarettes | .02 |
| 222 NATIONAL CIG. | 820479 | Cigarettes | .04 |

| Machine | Serial Number | Location | Commission |
|---|---|---|---|
| 222 NATIONAL CIG | 846171 | Cigarettes | -0- |
| CC NATIONAL CANDY | 82744 | Candy | 10% |
| 222 NATIONAL CIG | 846180 | Cigarettes | .02 |
| CC NATIONAL CANDY | CC50961 | Candy | 10% |
| 800MC NATIONAL CIG. | 1001602 | Cigarettes | .05 |
| 21 CEM CANDY | 21CE-1134 | Candy | 10% |
| 22 M NATIONAL CIG. | 11940 | Cigarettes | .03 |
| ROWE AC-L1020A-COLD | 315-9225 | Cold Drink | 30% |
| ROWE AC-SK9 HOT | 315-51137 | Hot Drink | 30% |
| ROWE AC- PASTERY | 315-01071 | Pastry | -0- |
| 222 NATIONAL CIG. | 846182 | Cigarettes: Regulars, Filters, & Kings | .03 |
| 222 NATIONAL CIG. | 873762 | Cigarettes | .02 |
| 800 CROWN NATIONAL CIG. | 1032518 | Cigarettes | .03 |
| 21 CEM CANDY | 21CE-1135 | Candy | 10% |
| CC CROWN NATIONAL CANDY | 96787 | | |
| 22M CROWN NATIONAL CIG. | 22M-11272 | Cigarettes | .03 |
| ROWE AC-L1020A-COLD | 315-7911 | Cold Drink | 50% |
| 222 NATIONAL CIG. | 865789 | Cigarettes | .02 |
| CC NATIONAL CANDY | CC50962 | Candy | 10% |
| 222 NATIONAL CIG. | 905390 | Cigarettes | .03 |
| 222 NATIONAL CIG. | 829524 | Cigarettes | .03 |
| CC CROWN NATIONAL CANDY | 96789 | Candy | 10% |
| 222 NATIONAL CIG. | 934753 | Cigarettes | .03 |
| CC NATIONAL CANDY | 82743 | Candy | 10% |
| 222 NATIONAL CIG. | 905389 | Cigarettes | .03 |
| 222 NATIONAL CIG. | 803048 | Cigarettes | .03 |
| 222 NATIONAL CIG. | 934754 | Cigarettes | .04½ |
| ROWE AC-20-800 CIG | 40034 | Cigarettes | .02 |
| 222 NATIONAL CIG. | 846172 | Rental | |
| ROWE AC-251-PASTERY | 315-00983 | | -0- |
| 222 NATIONAL CIG. | 803045 | Cigarettes | .05 |

# EXHIBIT B

Velveeta Vending Company
[     ] [          ]
[          ], [          ]
Gentlemen:


The undersigned hereby accepts and agrees to deposit in his trust account the sum of Five Thousand Dollars ($5000.00) tendered by Velveeta Vending Company.

The purpose of this deposit is to insure compliance with the terms of one certain purchase agreement of even date herewith by which [                              ]has agreed to purchase the vending machine business owned by Verna Velveeta.

If the closing is on or before [          XX], 19[XX], I agree to deliver the Five Thousand Dollars ($5000.00) to Verna Velveeta. If there be no closing on or before that date, I agree to hold the Five Thousand Dollars ($5000.00) until there is a determination, by stipulation or by recourse to the courts, as to whom the money should be paid and in what proportions.

                                        Yours very truly,


                                        _____
                                        [          ]

## EXHIBIT C

## Encumbrances

| | |
|---|---|
| First State Bank | $ 3,253.52 |
| Sales & Service Co. | 11,577.26 |
| Twin Towers Bank | 1,875.39 |
| National Candy Company | 5,725.32 |

# SAMPLE STOCK PURCHASE AGREEMENT

This Agreement entered into as [          XX], 19XX, by and between:

---
(Seller)

and

---
(Buyer)

NOW THEREFORE, in consideration of the mutual covenants herein contained, the parties hereto agree as follows:

1. *Sale of Stock.* Seller agrees to and will assign, transfer, convey, and deliver to Buyer free and clear of all liens, charges, and encumbrances 47,150 shares of the common stock of [                    ], a corporation organized under the laws of the State of [     ] (Corporation) which number constitutes one hundred (100%) percent of the oustanding common stock of the Corporation (Corporation Stock).

2. *Seller's Representations.* Seller represents, warrants, and covenants with Buyer that:

   2.1 Corporation is, and on the Closing Date will be, a corporation duly organized and validly existing and in good standing under the laws of the State of [     ]; has, and on the Closing Date will have, the power and authority to conduct all of the activities conducted by it and to own and lease all of the assets owned or leased by it; and is, and on the Closing Date will be, duly licensed or qualified to do business and in good standing as a foreign corporation in all jurisdictions in which the nature of the activities conducted by it or the character of the assets owned and leased by it makes such qualification or license necessary, and all such jurisdictions are listed in Schedule 2.1 hereto attached.

2.2 Schedule 2.2 hereto attached consists of a complete and correct copy of the original and all amendments to the Corporation's (i) Articles of Incorporation; (ii) By-Laws; (iii) stock transfer records; and (iv) all corporate minutes. No changes or additions therein will be made after the date hereof without written notice to Buyer.

2.3 Corporation has heretofore validly issued and has outstanding, and on the Closing Date will have outstanding, 47,150 shares of fully paid and nonassessable common stock. After the date hereof, and before the Closing Date, Corporation will not issue nor will it acquire any shares of its capital stock. Corporation does not have outstanding, and on the Closing Date will not have outstanding, any options to purchase or any rights or warrants to subscribe for or any securities or obligations convertible into, or any contracts or commitments to issue or sell any shares of the capital stock or any such warrants, convertible securities, or obligations.

2.4 Schedule 2.4 hereto attached consists of the audited financial statements of the Corporation for fiscal years ending [        XX], 19XX, 19XX, and 19XX, and monthly statements of profit and loss and monthly balance sheets for [        XX, 19XX]. Said audited financial statements and monthly reports are in accordance with the books and records of the Corporation and fairly present the financial position of the Corporation as of the periods indicated and were prepared in accordance with generally accepted accounting principles applied on a consistent basis with prior periods except as otherwise noted therein.

As of this date the Corporation does not have any liabilities, absolute, contingent, or otherwise, which are not reflected in the [        XX, 19XX] monthly balance sheet (Current Balance Sheet). The inventories reflected on the Current Balance Sheet were, as of the date of said Balance Sheet, current and readily merchantable, containing no material amount of slow moving, obsolete, or damaged goods which have not been written down in conformity with generally accepted accounting principles applied on a consistant basis with prior periods. The Current Balance Sheet contains no material amount of obsolete, damaged or unrepaired machinery or equipment which has not been written down in conformity with generally accepted accounting principles applied on a consistent basis with prior periods. The advances and notes and accounts receivable reflected in the Current Balance Sheet net of reserves therein reflected are, except to the extent heretofore collected, fully collectible and subject to no counterclaims or setoffs and Seller reasonably believes that said receivables will be collected.

2.5   Corporation has filed all tax returns, federal, state, and local, and all related information required to be filed prior to the date hereof, and on the Closing Date will have filed, all tax returns, federal, state, and local, and all related information required to be filed before the Closing Date. Amounts reflected in the Current Balance Sheet for taxes are sufficient for the payment for all accrued and unpaid federal, state, and local taxes of all types payable for or with respect to the respective period reflected in said Current Balance Sheet and for or with respect to all prior periods.

Schedule 2.5 hereto attached consists of copies of the state and federal income tax returns for fiscal years 19XX, 19XX, and 19XX.

2.6   Schedule 2.6 hereto attached consists of the legal description and street address of all real estate owned or occupied by Corporation.

2.7   Except as set forth in Schedule 2.7 hereto attached, Corporation has good and marketable title to the equipment, materials, supplies, and other tangible and intangible property of every kind contained in its offices or facilities and shown as assets on the Current Balance Sheet or in its records and books of account, free and clear of all liens, charges, and encumbrances.

2.8   All of the properties and assets owned or leased by the Corporation and used in its business are substantially in good operating condition and repair and to the best of Seller's knowledge and belief conform in all material respects to all applicable laws, rules, and regulations except as set forth in Schedule 2.8.

2.9 Except as set forth in Schedule 2.9 hereto attached, Corporation is not a party to any license, permit, or other authorization relating to the conduct of its business.

2.10 The consummation of the transactions contemplated by this Agreement will not require the consent or approval of any governmental entity, agency, or third party and will not terminate or adversely affect any listed license, permit, or other authorization.

2.11 No representation or warranty made in this Agreement nor in any document, certificate, or Schedule furnished pursuant to this Agreement, or in connection with the transactions contemplated hereby, contains or will contain any untrue statement of a material fact nor omit to state a material fact necessary to make any statement of fact contained herein or therein in light of the circumstances in which it is made not misleading.

2.12 Except as set forth in Schedule 2.12 hereto attached, Corporation does not have any contract, order, or commitment for the purchase or sale of materials or supplies other than in the usual and ordinary course of business. All outstanding bids or sales proposals by Corporation have been calculated on a basis consistent with its ordinary business practices.

2.13 Except as set forth in Schedule 2.13 hereto attached, Corporation is not a party to or bound by any (i) loan agreement or commitment; (ii) distribution or agency contract; (iii) leases (as lessor or lessee), chattel mortgages, conditional sales agreements, or security agreements; (iv) contract or commitment for capital expenditures exceeding Ten Thousand Dollars ($10,000); (v) contract obligating it on a continuing basis, which contract it may not terminate without premium or penalty on sixty (60) days or less notice; or (vi) contract, agreement, commitment, lease, or instrument (other than for the purchase or sale of materials or supplies) which materially affects the business, properties, or assets of the Corporation or which was entered into other than in the usual and ordinary course of business. There has not been any default under any said contracts, agreements, commitments, leases, or instruments and no party thereto has waived any material rights under or with respect to the same.

2.14 Set forth in Schedule 2.14 hereto attached is a correct and complete list of:

A. All employment, bonus, profit sharing, commission, pension or retirement plans, stock purchase or stock option plans, contracts or agreements with directors, officers, or employees, or consulting agreements to which Corporation is a party or is subject to;

B. The names and current salary rates of all the directors, officers, executives, and other managerial personnel of the Corporation;

C. The names and current salary rates of all the sales personnel of the Corporation, except those listed above;

D. The wage rates for all nonsalaried employees listed by classification;

E. The wage rates listed by classification for all employees of the Corporation not otherwise described above;

F. All group insurance programs in effect and all annual premiums and charges paid in respect thereof;

G. All labor union contracts and collective bargaining agreements to which the Corporation is a party or by which it is bound.

2.15 Set forth in Schedule 2.15 hereto attached is a correct and complete list of each bank and safety deposit facility in which the Corporation has an account or safety deposit box and the names of all persons who may draw thereon or who have access thereto.

2.16 Except as set forth in Schedule 2.16 hereto attached, or otherwise disclosed in writing in this Agreement, the Corporation has no powers of attorney outstanding or any obligation or liability, either actual, accrued, accruing, or contingent, as guarantor, surety, cosigner, endorser, comaker, indemnitor, or otherwise with respect to the obligation of any person, corporation, partnership, joint venture, association, organization, or other entity.

2.17 Since the date of the Current Balance Sheet there have been no changes in the condition, financial or otherwise, of the assets , liabilities, properties, labor relations, or business of the Corporation from that shown therein other than the changes set forth on Schedule 2.17 hereto attached, other than events and conditions generally affecting the economy and changes occurring in the ordinary course of business.

2.18 Other than as set forth herein or in Schedule 2.18 hereto attached, the Corporation has not, and on the Closing Date will not have: (i) discharged or satisfied any lien, charge, or encumbrance or paid any obligation or liability, absolute or contingent, except in the ordinary course of business; (ii) declared or made any payment or distribution to stockholders, purchased or redeemed any shares of its capital stock, or reclassified its stock; (iii) mortgaged, pledged, or subjected to lien, charge, or encumbrance any of its assets except minor liens and encumbrances which in the aggregate are not material; (iv) sold, assigned, or transferred any of its material tangible or intangible assets or cancelled any debts or claims, except in each case in the ordinary course of business; (v) suffered any material casualty loss not adequately covered by insurance or waived any rights of substantial value; (vi) loaned or borrowed any money or guaranteed any indebtedness for money borrowed or of any other type of indebtedness, except in the ordinary course of business; (vii) amended its charter or By-Laws; (viii) made any changes in any principal officer's compensation; or (ix) entered into any material transactions, except in the ordinary course of business.

2.19 Except as set forth in Schedule 2.19 hereto attached, there are no actions, suits, resisted claims, proceedings, or investigations pending or to the knowledge of the Seller threatened against or affecting the Corporation before or by any federal, state, municipal, or other governmental court, department, commission, board, bureau, agency, or instrumentality, domestic or foreign

2.20 Except for wages, bonuses, benefits, or reimbursements in the ordinary course of business or except as otherwise disclosed in the Schedules hereto attached, no officer or director of the Corporation nor the Seller has any material claim or claims against the Corporation nor is the Corporation obligated or liable to any of such persons in any way or for any amounts except as set forth on Schedule 2.20 hereto attached.

2.21 Schedule 2.21 hereto attached accurately lists the policy numbers, insurer's name, annual premiums, and expiration dates for all policies of health, life, fire, liability, and other forms of insurance. The Corporation will maintain, through the Closing Date, said insurance policies.

2.22 Seller has the power and authority to execute and deliver this Agreement and to cause the Corporation to take all required actions and to consummate the transactions hereby contemplated and to take all other actions required to be taken by the Corporation or the Seller pursuant to the provisions hereof, and this Agreement is valid and binding upon Seller. The delivery to Buyer of certificates for shares of the Corporation as contemplated by this Agreement will transfer valid title to Buyer of all issued and outstanding shares of Corporation common stock free and clear of all pledges, liens, encumbrances, equities, voting trusts, security interests, and claims of any kind and character. Neither the execution and the delivery of this Agreement nor the consummation of the transactions hereby contemplated will constitute any violation or breach of the Articles of Incorporation or the By-Laws of the Corporation or any provision of any contract or other instrument to which the Corporation or the Seller is a party or by which any of the assets of the Corporation may be affected or secured or any order, writ, injunction, decree, statute, rule, or regulation or will result in the creation of any lien, charge, or encumbrance on any of the assets of the Corporation or violate any federal or state statutes regulating the transfer of securities.

2.23 Schedule 2.23 hereto attached is a list of all customers who have purchased more than Ten Thousand Dollars ($10,000) in services or supplies from the Corporation in fiscal 19XX, excluding postage.

3. *Purchase Price and Payment.*

3.1 In exchange for the assignment, transfer, conveyance, and delivery to Buyer by Seller of the Corporation Stock, Buyer agrees to pay Seller Two Hundred Fifty Thousand Dollars ($250,000), Five Thousand Dollars ($5000) of which is paid in cash at the time this Agreement is signed and the balance of which is payable according to the terms of a Promissory Note containing the terms set forth in Exhibit 3.1 hereto attached.

4. *Conditions Precedent to Closing.* The obligations of Buyer under this Agreement are subject, at the sole option of Buyer, to the fulfillment before or on the Closing Date of each of the following conditions:

4.1 All of the agreements and covenants contained in this Agreement that are to be complied with, satisfied, and performed by Seller on or before the Closing Date shall in all material respects have been complied with, satisfied, and performed.

4.2 All of the representations and warranties made by the Seller in this Agreement shall be true and accurate in all material respects, both on and as of the date of this Agreement, and as of the Closing Date. It is understood and agreed that all of the representations, warranties, and disclosures contained in this Agreement that are not expressly limited to some other date, shall be deemed to state the fact contained therein as they existed both as of the date of this Agreement and as of the Closing Date.

4.3 All instruments and documents required to carry out this Agreement shall be satisfactory to [                ], counsel for Buyer.

4.4 Buyer shall have established a relationship satisfactory to Buyer with the commercial bank in

[                    ], that has been supplying financing for the Corporation. Buyer will use its best efforts to have Seller removed as a guarantor of the Corporation's debts to said bank.

4.5 Buyer shall have received at the closing a certificate signed by the Seller and dated as of the Closing Date stating that all of the representations and warranties made in this Agreement and in any certificate, Schedule, or document furnished hereunder is true, accurate, and correct in all material respects as of the Closing Date.

4.6 The business and properties of the Corporation shall not have been materially adversely affected whether by fire, casualty, or act of God and there shall have been no other change in the condition, financial or otherwise, of the Corporation which would have a material adverse affect in the aggregate on the value of the Corporation.

4.7 Buyer shall have received at or prior to the closing:

A. All consents required by any party to any agreement with Corporation required as a condition to the continuance of such agreement after the transfer contemplated hereby;

B. Possession at the offices of Corporation of the records, books, corporate seal, and the stock certificate book of Corporation, and all documents, instruments, checkbooks, books of account, and other records of Corporation;

C. Possession at the offices of Corporation of the originals of all written agreements and contracts of Corporation described in this Agreement and the Schedules hereto attached;

D. If requested by Buyer, written instructions to all of Corporation's banks cancelling the right of all or some current signatories to sign checks and transact business with such banks in respect to bank accounts of Corporation maintained thereat;

E. Possession of the certificates representing the Corporation Stock, duly endorsed for transfer to Seller with such verifications or assurances as to the completeness and effectiveness of such endorsements as Buyer may reasonably request.

4.8 Buyer shall have received from _____, counsel for Seller, a favorable opinion dated the Closing Date in form and substance reasonably satisfactory to Buyer to the effect that:

A. Corporation is duly organized, validly existing, and in good standing under the laws of the State of [          ];

B. Corporation is duly qualified and in good standing in the states listed in Schedule 2.1 hereto attached;

C. Corporation has the corporate power and authority to carry on its business as then being conducted;

D. The authorized, issued and outstanding capital stock of Corporation is as represented in this Agreement, and such issued and outstanding shares have been duly and validly authorized and issued and are fully paid and nonassessable, free of any restriction on transfer contained in Corporation's charter or By-Laws or any other instrument of which said counsel has knowledge and the transfer of said shares as contemplated by the Agreement will not violate any federal or state statutes.

4.9 By the closing the Corporation shall have entered into an agreement with Seller substantially in the form set forth in Exhibit 4.9.

4.10 All Schedules required by the terms of this Agreement to be attached are not attached at the time of Buyer's signature. Buyer shall have fifteen (15) days following receipt of the last required Schedule to review the Schedules furnished by Seller and if in Buyer's opinion information is contained in such Schedules which had such information been known to Buyer at the date of this Agreement Buyer would not have entered into this Agreement then Buyer may elect to rescind this Agreement. This fifteen- (15) day period shall begin to run at such time as Seller gives Buyer written notice that all required Schedules have been furnished. If Buyer does not timely exercise this election it shall expire at the end of the aforedescribed fifteen-(15) day period.

If in Buyer's discretion any of the above conditions are not timely performed, Buyer may elect to rescind this Agreement, in which case the purchase money herewith paid shall be returned and neither party shall have further liability to the other. Notwithstanding the foregoing, Buyer may elect to waive its rights to rescind, proceed to close, and pursue such other remedies as may exist in law or equity.

5. *Closing.* The closing shall take place at a location and at such place and time as Buyer determines (Closing Date), but not later than [ XX, 19XX].

6. *Confidentiality.* In the event of the termination of this Agreement, each party will use its best efforts to keep confidential any information (unless readily ascertainable from public or published information or sources) obtained from the other. In the event of termination of this Agreement, promptly after such termination, all documents, work papers, or other written material obtained from one party in connection with this Agreement and not theretofore made public (including all copies thereof) will be returned to the party which provided the material.

7. *Survival of Representations and Warranties.* The representations contained in this Agreement and in any Schedules hereto attached shall be terminated and extinguished on the first anniversary of the Closing Date.

8. *Further Assurances.* The parties hereto agree to take such reasonable steps and to execute such other and further documents as may be necessary or appropriate to cause the terms and conditions contained herein to be carried into effect.

9. *Entire Agreement, Waivers.* This Agreement comprises the entire agreement among the parties hereto at the date hereof and supersedes all prior agreements and understandings among them. Schedules and Exhibits attached to this Agreement are incorporated herein by reference and specifically made a part of this Agreement. Buyer or Seller may extend the time for, or waive the performance of, any of the obligations of the other, waive any inaccuracies in the representations or warranties by the other, or waive conditions contained in this Agreement, but only by an instrument in writing signed by the party granting such extension or waiver.

10. *Notices.* Any notice to any party hereto pursuant to this

Agreement shall be given by registered first-class mail addressed, if to Seller, as follows:

_____

_____

_____

_____

with a copy to _____

_____ and, if to Buyer, as follows:

_____

_____

_____

_____

with a copy to _____.
Any notice shall be deemed delivered when placed in the mail so addressed with postage prepaid. The aforesaid addresses may be changed from time to time by written notice.

11. *Successors and Assigns.* This Agreement shall be transferable and assignable by either of the parties hereto, except assignment or transfer shall not relieve the assigning or transferring party of its obligations for performance hereunder. This Agreement shall inure to the benefit of and be binding upon and enforceable against the respective successors and assigns of the parties hereof.

12. *Corporate Debts.* Buyer is advised of a moral commitment on the part of the Corporation to pay the following two corporate debts as soon as Seller disposes of his interest in the Corporation: (i) approximately Seventeen Thousand Dollars ($17,000) in debentures; and (ii) a Twenty-five Thousand Dollar ($25,000), eight (8%) percent Promissory Note. Seller agrees that at the closing Seller will cause such debts to be paid.

13. *Miscellaneous.*

   A. *Prior Agreements.* Any inconsistent or conflicting provisions of other existing agreements between the parties are superseded and modified hereby.

   B. *Governing Law.* This Agreement shall be construed, and interpreted in accordance with the laws of the State of Connecticut.

   C. *Counterparts.* This Agreement shall be executed in

several counterparts and all so executed shall constitute one Agreement binding on the parties hereto,
notwithstanding that both parties are not signatory to
the original or the same counterpart.

IN WITNESS WHEREOF, the parties hereto have caused this
Agreement to be duly executed.


_____

BUYER


_____

SELLER

# Index of Schedules and Exhibits to
# Sample Stock Purchase Agreement

## Schedules

## Exhibits

# LETTER PURCHASE AGREEMENT

July 1, 19[   ]

<br>_____
<br>_____
<br>_____
<br>_____

Dear [          ]:

This letter sets forth the terms under which [          ] agrees to purchase and you agree to sell all of the outstanding stock of [          ], a corporation organized under the laws of the State of [          ]. If you agree to the terms set forth herein please sign below where indicated.

1. *Stock Purchased.* [          ] hereby purchases and you hereby sell 100 shares of the outstanding common stock of [          ], which 100 shares constitute all of the outstanding capital stock of said corporation. Receipt of the stock certificate evidencing ownership of said stock is herewith delivered to [          ], endorsed in blank. You guarantee that you own this stock, that you have the legal authority to deliver good title free and clear of all liens and encumbrances, and that the stock is fully paid and non-assessable and that the Corporation is validly existing and in good standing.

2. *Additional Representations.* You represent the completeness and accuracy of the following attachments:
   2.1  Corporate Records
       2.11  Articles of Incorporation
       2.12  By-Laws
       2.13  All corporate minutes from formation of Corporation to date
   2.2  Financial Statements
       2.21  Balance sheet, profit and loss statement, and source and use analysis for fiscal years 19XX and 19XX.
       2.22  Monthly profit and loss statements and balance

sheets from the end of the last completed fiscal year to the date of this letter.

2.23 United States and State income tax returns for fiscal years 19XX and 19XX.

2.3 Real Estate—Street address of all real estate occupied by the Corporation.

2.4 Liens and Encumbrances

2.41 With regard to all real and personal property of which ownership is claimed.

2.42 Copies of all loan agreements, chattel mortgages, security agreements, and conditional sales agreements.

2.5 Contracts—Copies of all contracts, agreements, commitments, and leases which have a material impact on the Corporation's business.

2.6 Employees—Names and salaries of all employees of the Corporation.

2.7 Bank Accounts—Name and address of bank and account number for all corporate checking, savings, or other accounts and all safety deposit boxes.

2.8 Guaranties—Copies of all guaranties or sureties given by the Corporation.

2.9 Changes in Condition—Description of all threatened or actual changes in the financial condition of the Corporation not adequately disclosed by the most current financial statements.

2.10 Litigation—Listing of all pending or threatened litigation.

2.11 Insurance—Description of all fire, liability, casualty, and other types of insurance owned by the Corporation, including coverage, premium rate, expiration date, and name of insurer.

3. *Covenant Not to Compete.* For a period of five (5) years from the date of this Agreement, you agree that you will not:

a. Acquire any interest in, accept employment or anything of value from, engage in, or give assistance to any person, business, or enterprise which is or may become engaged in the [          ] business or the monitoring of [          ]

or [         ] or any aspect thereof in the states of
[         ], [         ], [         ], [         ].

b. Hire any employees of [         ] or [         ] or in any way induce or attempt to induce such employees to terminate their employment.

c. Contact any customers with whom you have formerly dealt with on behalf of [         ].

d. Represent to any person or entity that you offer the same services or resources as [         ] or [         ].

4. *Future Services.* You agree to remain as an employee of [         ] for a period five (5) years after the date of this letter for compensation set forth on the Compensation Schedule hereto attached. Your title and duties will be as from time to time agreed to but initially you will function in the capacity of a Vice President and General Manager of [         ], which will operate as the Western Division of [         ]. You will receive the usual and customary fringe benefits, including an automobile, payment of club dues not to exceed Sevety Dollars ($70) per month, reasonable relocation costs in the event of transfer, and the same health and life insurance package provided to [         ]'s senior management personnel. Within this five- (5) year employment period you may be terminated without notice or "cause" but if no "cause" exists you may be terminated within said five- (5) year period only upon payment of one (1) year's severance pay. As used herein, "cause" shall include ony substantial reasons for termination, such as dishonesty, insubordination, incompetence, or inability or failure to perform usual and customary duties. Notwithstanding anything herein to the contrary, if you are terminated, with or without "cause," the covenant not to compete provided in Paragraph No. 3 shall be revised so as not to exceed a point in time six (6) months after the date of your termination. At our option you will become an employee of [         ], in which case your compensation shall be computed in the same manner except bonuses shall be based on [         ]s Western operations. During the time you are employed by [         ] you agree to devote your services and engage exclusively in the business of the Corporation, to use your best efforts for the benefit of the Corporation, and not to engage in other activities which would conflict with the long-

term betterment of the Corporation or impair or restrict your value as a full-time employee of the Corporation and you will faithfully and diligently do and perform the acts and duties reasonably required.

5. *Payment.* In consideration of the sale of stock, employment agreement, and covenant not to compete, [          ] agrees to pay you Thirty Thousand Dollars ($30,000) payable Five Thousand Dollars ($5000) in cash at the time this letter is signed and Twenty-five Thousand Dollars ($25,000) payable _____. This purchase price is allocated as follows: (i) Five Thousand Dollars ($5000), employment agreement; (ii) Ten Thousand Dollars ($10,000), purchase of stock; (iii) Fifteen Thousand Dollars ($15,000), covenant not to compete.

6. *Miscellaneous.*

   a. We are aware that at the time this letter is prepared [          ] owns some of the outstanding capital stock of [          ]. It is our understanding that you will acquire the stock from him before you sign this letter and that you will warrant good title to one hundred (100%) percent of the outstanding capital stock of [          ].

   b. All paragraph headings are intended to facilitate reference in the agreement only and do not constitute a substantive part of this Agreement.

   c. There are no agreements not in writing and this Agreement may not be modified except by a writing signed by both of us.

Very truly yours,                          AGREED TO:


PRESIDENT                          _____

# DELAWARE CERTIFICATE OF INCORPORATION
## OF
## [                    ]

The undersigned, for the purpose of organizing a corporation to conduct business and promote the purposes hereinafter stated under the provisions of and subject to the requirements of the General Corporation Law of the State of Delaware, hereby certifies that:

### First:

The name of the Corporation is [                    ] (the Corporation).

### Second:

The address of the registered office of the Corporation in the State of Delaware is: [          ], County of [          ], City of [          ], Delaware, and the name of the registered agent of the Corporation in the State of Delaware at such address is [                    ].

### Third:

The business and purpose of the Corporation is to engage in any lawful act or activity for which corporations may be organized under the General Corporation Law of the State of Delaware.

### Fourth:

The Corporation shall have authority to issue a total of [          ] shares of common stock without par value. All shares of common stock shall have the same relative rights and voting power and be without any relative preferences or restrictions.

### Fifth:

The name and mailing address of the incorporator is [          ].

### Sixth:

The number of directors of the Corporation shall be fixed from time to time by its by-laws and may be increased or decreased as therein provided.

### Seventh:

The Corporation shall be managed by the Board of Directors which shall exercise all powers conferred under the laws of the State of Delaware including without limitation the power to make, alter, or repeal the by-laws.

IN WITNESS WHEREOF, the undersigned, being the incorporator hereinbefore named, for the purpose of forming a corporation pursuant to the General Corporation Law of the State of Delaware, do make this Certificate, hereby declaring and certifying that this is my act and deed and the fact herein stated are true, and accordingly have hereunto set my hand this XX day of [          ], 19XX.

_____

[                    ]

# SAMPLE PARTNERSHIP AGREEMENT

(1) Name of Partnership

**A Partnership under the Laws
of the
State of Minnesota**

---

## AGREEMENT OF PARTNERSHIP

---

(2) Effective date of Agreement

Dated as of: _____

# INDEX
## PARTNERSHIP AGREEMENT

This Agreement of Partnership entered into as of (4) Effective date of Agreement by and among (5) Partnership Information residents of the State of Minnesota (each hereinafter and sometimes referred to individually and collectively as the "Partners").

## Article 1
## Formation and Name of Partnership

The parties hereto hereby form a partnership named (6) Name of Partnership (hereinafter referred to as the "Partnership") pursuant to the provisions of Chapter 323 of the Minnesota Statutes, known as the Uniform Partnership Act. The rights and liabilities of the parties hereto shall be as provided in the Act unless herein otherwise expressly provided.

### 1.01 Purposes.

The purpose of the Partnership is:

(a)   (7) Nature of Primary Activity of Partnership and to engage in such other business activities as the Partnership shall from time to time determine, including by way of amplification and not by way of limitation, the following purposes:

   (i)    To enter into, perform, and carry out contracts of any kind necessary to, in connection with, or incidental to the accomplishment of the purposes of the Partnership.

   (ii)   To acquire any property, real or personal, in fee or under lease, or any rights therein or appurtenant thereto, necessary or appropriate for the accomplishment of the purposes of the Partnership.

   (iii)  To borrow money, and to issue evidences of indebtedness and to secure the same by mortgage, deed or trust, pledge, or other lien, in furtherance of any or all of the purposes of the Partnership.

   (iv)   To sell or otherwise dispose of all or any portion of the assets of properties of the Partnership.

### 1.02   Location and Principal Place of Business.

The principal business office of the Partnership shall be located at (8) Address of Partnership Office or at such other place as (9) Name of Partnership maintains its principal office, or at such other place as the Partners may from time to time determine.

### 1.03   The Name and Place of Residence of Each Partner.

The name and place of residence of each Partner is set forth in Exhibit A attached hereto.

### 1.04   Term.

The term of the Partnership shall commence as of the date hereof and continue until (10) Termination Date unless the Partnership shall be sooner dissolved and terminated as herein provided or unless said term is extended by the mutual written consent of all the Partners.

## Article 2
## Contributions of Partners and Capital Accounts

### 2.01   Contributions.

Each Partner shall contribute the amount set forth opposite his name on Exhibit B, at such times and upon such conditions as set forth on said Exhibit B.

### 2.02   Additional Contributions.

If the Partners shall unanimously determine that additional capital contributions are required from the Partners for any reason, then each Partner shall make an additional contribution to the capital of the Partnership in an amount of cash to be determined by multiplying the total amount of additional capital required by the percentage interest each Partner has in the Partnership assets, which interest is set forth after each Partner's name on Exhibit A hereto attached.

If any Partner shall fail to timely contribute such additional capital, his interest in the Partnership shall be subject to purchase by the remaining Partners. The Partnership shall promptly give notice thereof to all of the other Partners, stating the Partnership interest which is available for purchase. Within forty-five (45) days after such notice is given, any or all of such other Partners may elect, by notifying the Partnership of such election, to purchase all or any portion of such Partnership interest. If more than one of such Partners elect to purchase such Partnership interest, such Partnership interest and the purchase price therefor shall be allocated among them pro rata, and the Partnership shall promptly notify each such Partner of the amount of Partnership interest to be purchased by him and the purchase price therefor. The purchase price for the Partnership interest subject to purchase shall be an amount equal to (11) Purchase Price in the Event of Default (percentage) of the capital contributions actually made by the defaulting Partner, and shall be payable to him on or prior to the thirtieth (30) day next following the date such Partnership interest became subject to purchase. Any Partner purchasing any Partnership interest pursuant to this Paragraph shall become the owner thereof and shall assume in writing all of the obligations of the defaulting Partner with respect thereto effective as of the date upon which such Partnership interest became subject to purchase, and shall pay to the Partnership at the time or times and subject to the terms and conditions provided for herein, the additional capital contribution or contributions required to be made with respect to such Partnership interest so purchased. The Assignment of any Partnership interest pursuant to this Paragraph shall be effected, as of the date upon which such Partnership interest became subject to purchase, automatically upon payment of the purchase price therefor, without the necessity of any action on the part of the defaulting Partner. Each Partner agrees that if all or any portion of his Partnership interests are purchased pursuant to this Paragraph, he will execute all instruments requested by the Partnership or the purchasing Partner for the purpose of confirming or evidencing the Assignment of such Partnership interests. Notwithstanding that all or a portion of the Partnership interest of a defaulting Partner are purchased pursuant to this Paragraph, the defaulting Partner shall be and remain primarily liable for the full amount of any further additional capital contribution or contributions payable with respect to any of his Partnership interest as required herein, and the Partnership may collect from the defaulting Partner by legal process the entire amount of the unpaid capital contribution or contributions attributable to such Partnership interest provided, however, the defaulting Partner shall be entitled to reimbursement from the purchasing Partner for funds contributed by the defaulting Partner to the Partnership after the date of purchase.

### 2.03 Capital Accounts.

An individual capital account shall be maintained for each Partner to which shall be credited or debited, as the case may be, his contributions to capital or withdrawals or returns of capital and his share of profits, losses, and distributions of the Partnership. The capital account of a Partner shall not be subject to withdrawal by the Partner without the consent of all Partners and shall not bear interest.

## Article 3
## Profits and Losses

### 3.01   Accounting and Fiscal Year.

The fiscal year of the Partnership shall be the calendar year. The net profits and losses of the Partnership shall be determined for each fiscal year, using such methods of accounting as the Partners in their sole and absolute discretion shall determine to use for federal income tax purposes.

### 3.02   Profits and Losses.

The profits and losses of the Partnership for each fiscal year shall be determined as of the end of such fiscal year and allocated to the Partners on the basis of the respective percentages set forth after their names on Exhibit A attached hereto (the individual percentage of each Partner being herein called his "Partnership Percentage"). The profits and losses of the Partnership allocated among the Partners shall be credited or debited, as the case may be, to the individual capital account of each Partner as soon as practicable after the end of each fiscal year during the term of the Partnership.

## Article 4
## Distributions

### 4.01 Distributions of Profits.

The profits of the Partnership, allocated in the manner provided in Section 3.02 hereof, shall be distributed in such amounts and at such times as the Partners may unanimously determine in their discretion.

### 4.02 Distributions of Capital.

The respective amounts of the Partners' capital interests in the Partnership may be returned to them, in whole or in part, in cash, at any time that the Partners may unanimously determine in their discretion. Such returns of capital shall be made pro rata to all Partners in proportion to their respective Partnership Percentage in the Partnership. No Partner shall have the right to demand or receive property other than cash in return for his capital interest. Notwithstanding the foregoing, no part of the capital interest of any Partner shall be returned unless all liabilities of the Partnership have been paid or unless the Partnership has property sufficient to pay them. No Partner shall have a priority over any other Partner either as to the return of contributions or as to distributions of net profits.

### 4.03 Charges to Capital.

All distributions of profits or capital to the Partners shall be charged to their respective capital accounts at the time they are made.

### 4.04 Salaries

Each Partner shall receive such salary for services rendered to the Partnership as the Partners shall unanimously determine and such salaries shall be paid before allocation of the Partnership profits among all the Partners and shall not be charged to such Partner's capital account and shall be considered to be guaranteed payments in accordance with $\S 707(C)$ of the Internal Revenue Code. Such salaries shall be paid at such times and in the same manner as the salaries paid to the other employees of the Partnership.

## Article 5
## Administration and Fiscal Matters

### 5.01 Books and Records

The Partners shall maintain full and accurate books of the Partnership at the Partnership's principal place of business (or such other place as the Partners may unanimously agree), showing all receipts and expenditures, assets and liabilities, profits and losses, and all other records necessary for recording the Partnership's business and affairs, including those sufficient to record the allocations and distributions provided for in Articles 3 and 4. The books of the Partnership shall be kept on such basis as is unanimously determined by the Partners. Each Partner and his duly authorized representatives shall at all times during regular business hours have access to and may inspect and copy any of such books and records.

### 5.02 Reports.

Annual statements showing the income and expenses of the Partnership for the fiscal year and the balance sheets thereof as at the end of such year shall be prepared by the Partners. Each Partner shall be furnished copies of such statements of income and expenses and of such balance sheets.

### 5.03 Bank Accounts and Investment of Funds.

All funds of the Partnership shall be deposited in its name in such checking and savings accounts or time deposits or certificates of deposit as shall be designated by the Partners from time to time. Withdrawals therefrom shall be made upon such signatures as the Partners may designate. The Partnership may invest funds in such short-term obligations as shall be selected by the Partners.

### 5.04 Federal Income Tax Elections.

The Partners shall, as and when they deem appropriate, make and file on behalf of and in the name of the Partnership such elections as are available to the Partnership under the Internal Revenue Code of 1954, as amended, or under applicable state income tax laws.

## Article 6
## Duties and Powers of Partners

### 6.01  Management of Partnership Business.

Except where otherwise expressly provided for in this Agreement all disputes shall be resolved by majority vote with each Partner having the proportional vote represented by his Partnership Percentage as set forth on Exhibit A. Each Partner shall have all necessary powers to carry out the purposes, business, and objectives of the Partnership and shall possess and enjoy all the rights and powers of partners of a partnership except as otherwise provided by Minnesota law or expressly to the contrary in this Agreement.

(a)  No Partner shall on behalf of the Partnership, without the consent of all other Partners:

  (i)   endorse any note, or act as an accommodation party, or otherwise become surety for any person;

  (ii)  borrow or lend money;

  (iii) make, deliver, or accept any commercial paper;

  (iv)  execute any mortgage, security agreement, bond, or lease;

  (v)   purchase or contract to purchase or sell or contract to sell any property for or of the Partnership other than property bought and sold in the regular course of its business.

(b)  The Partners shall devote such of their time as they in their discretion shall deem necessary to the affairs of the Partnership business. In managing the affairs of the Partnership, the Partners shall be free from liability to the Partnership or its Partners for any act or omission to act within the scope of this Agreement, except for bad faith, gross negligence, willful misconduct, or reckless disregard of duties.

(c)  No Partner shall have any duty to make any contributions or loans to or on behalf of the Partnership or assume any obligations of the Partnership not specifically set forth herein.

## Article 7
## Assignment of Interest and Admission of
## Additional Partners

### 7.01 Assignment of Partnership Interests.

(a) Except as otherwise provided herein, no Partner shall sell, transfer, assign, give, or otherwise dispose of his interest in the Partnership or a part thereof to any person, whether voluntarily, by operation of law, or otherwise, without the prior written consent of all Partners. The provisions of this Section 7.01(a) shall not apply however if a Partner receives a bona fide offer from a third part for his interest in the Partnership or a part thereof and such Partner offers in writing to sell such interest or such part thereof to the other Partners at a price and upon terms, specified in such offer, which are no less favorable to such Partners than those upon which such offering Partner certifies he is willing to sell to such third party whose name and address shall be specified in such offer. The other Partners may require evidence that a bona fide offer, at the price and upon the terms specified in such offer, has been made by such third party to such offering Partner. For a period of sixty (60) days after the receipt of such notice the other Partners shall have the exclusive option to purchase such interest in the Partnership in proportion to their respective Partnership Percentages and at the purchase price and on the terms specified in such offer. Promptly after the exercise of such option, the sale of the interest in the Partnership shall be consummated in accordance with the terms of the offer. If such option is not exercised within such sixty- (60) day period, such offering Partner may, for a period of forty-five (45) days after the end of such sixty- (60) day period, dispose of his interest in the Partnership (or part thereof covered by the offer) to the third party named in such offer and at a price and on terms not less favorable to such offering Partner than those upon which his interest or part thereof was offered to the other Partners. If such interest in the Partnership or part thereof is not disposed of within such forty-five- (45) day period, it shall again become subject to the restrictions of this Section 7.01(a).

(b)   Any option contained herein shall be deemed to have been exercised when written notice of exercise by one or more Partners has been given within the period provided herein. In the event more than one Partner exercises any such option, the interest in the Partnership or part thereof to be purchased pursuant to the exercise of such option shall be apportioned among the Partners so accepting in proportion to their respective Partnership Percentages.

(c)   The provisions of Section 7.01(a) shall not apply to:

   (i)   Any assignment (in trust or otherwise), for estate planning purposes, by a Partner of all or part of his interest in the Partnership to or for the benefit of any member of his immediate family.

   (ii)  Any security interest given by a Partner of all or a part of his interest in the Partnership to any other Partner or a bank chartered and doing business under the laws of the United States.

(d)   No assignee of all or part of a Partner's interest in the Partnership, whether or not admitted to the Partnership in accordance with Section 7.02, shall have the right to make any further assignment of such interest in the Partnership except pursuant to the terms and subject to the restrictions of Section 7.01(a).

### 7.02   Substitution of Partners.

The Partnership may, upon the sole discretion of the Partners, admit an assignee or successor in interest as a substituted Partner. Unless admitted as a substituted Partner an assignee or successor shall have only the rights: (1) to receive the profits, losses, and distributions to which his assignor would otherwise be entitled, subject to the restrictions and obligations contained in Section 7.01; and (2) in case of the dissolution of the Partnership, to receive his assignor's interest and to require an accounting from the date only of the last accounting agreed to by all the Partners. Until admitted, the consent of the successor or assignee shall not be required for those actions which this Agreement requires unanimous consent for and such successor or assignee shall not be entitled to a vote in the event of a dispute with the Partners.

### 7.03    Admission of New Partners.

New or additional Partners may be admitted into the Partnership from time to time by the unanimous vote of the Partners, in their sole discretion, upon such terms and conditions as may be agreed to by the Partners and the person being admitted to membership. Such admission shall be evidenced by a written agreement supplemental to and amendatory to this Agreement containing the terms and conditions agreed upon by the parties.

## Article 8
## Dissolution and Termination of Partnership

### 8.01    Dissolution of Partnership.

The Partnership shall be dissolved upon the occurrence of any of the following events:

(a)    the death, bankruptcy, receivership, or withdrawal of any Partner;

(b)    The unanimous written agreement of the General Partners to dissolve the Partnership;

(c)    the sale of all or substantially all of the assets of the Partnership and the distributing of all of such proceeds and any remaining Partnership assets.

### 8.02    Death of Partner.

The death of a Partner shall dissolve the Partnership and in any such event each Partner or his legal representative shall have the right to an accounting or valuation of his interest in the Partnership.

### 8.03    Bankruptcy or Receivership of Partner.

The bankruptcy or receivership of a Partner shall dissolve the Partnership and in any such event each Partner or his legal representative shall have the right to an accounting or valuation of his interest in the Partnership.

### 8.04   Withdrawal of Partner.

A Partner may withdraw from the Partnership at any time for reasonable cause. A refusal to participate in Partnership affairs shall not constitute a withdrawal. The disability of any Partner due to sickness, injury, or other cause shall not constitute a withdrawal unless the disabled Partner specifically elects to withdraw.

### 8.05   Winding Up of Partnership Affairs.

Upon any event provided in Section 8.01:

(a)   No further business shall be done in the Partnership name except the completion of incomplete transactions and the taking such action as may be necessary to wind up the affairs of the Partnership.

(b)   The affairs of the Partnership shall be wound up by the Partners in accordance with the following provisions:

   (i)   A full and general accounting shall be taken by independent accountants retained by the Partnership.

   (ii)   All accounts receivable of the Partnership shall be collected by the Partnership.

   (iii)   All of the Partnership assets shall be sold or otherwise converted to cash. At the request of a majority of the Partners, all of the Partnership assets shall be sold as a unit, enabling the purchaser to carry on the business of the Partnership. At the request of a majority of the Partners, eligible purchasers of the Partnership assets shall be limited to Partners and the sale shall take place by auction according to such rules and under such conditions as may be reasonably imposed by a majority of the Partners.

   (iv)   All debts and liabilities to creditors of the Partnership shall be paid or provided for in order of priority as provided by law.

   (v)   If the Partners or the liquidators deem it reasonably necessary, a reserve shall be set up for any contingent or unforeseen liabilities, or obligations of the Partnership arising out of or in connection with the Partnership business. Such reserve shall be paid over to an escrow agent selected by the Partners or the liquidators for such period of time as it shall reasonably determine, to be held for the purpose of disbursing such reserve in payment of such contingencies. At the expiration of such period the balance of such funds shall be distributed in the manner provided in Section 8.04(c). A reasonable time as determined by the Partners or the liquidators shall be allowed for the orderly winding up of the affairs of the Partnership, including the liquidation or distribution of its assets and the discharge of its liabilities to creditors, so as to enable the Partnership to minimize any losses attendant upon such liquidation. Each Partner shall be furnished with a statement prepared by the independent accountants retained by the Partnership setting forth the assets and liabilities of the Partnership as of the date of dissolution and the manner in which the assets of the Partnership are to be distributed.

(c)  The assets of the Partnership remaining after providing for all liabilities and reserves as above provided shall be divided among the Partners in proportion to their respective capital accounts in the Partnership.

## Article 9
## Responsibilities to Partnership

### 9.01  Other Interest of Partners.

Any Partner may have other business interests and may engage in any other business or trade, profession, or employment whatsoever, whether or not they may be deemed to be competitive with the Partnership; and no Partner shall be required to devote any time and efforts to conducting the Partnership business. Neither the Partnership nor the other Partners shall have any rights in and to such independent ventures or the income or profits derived therefrom. No Partner shall have any duty to present first to the Partnership any business opportunity which it may elect to seek, investigate, or acquire.

## Article 10
## General Provisions

### 10.01   Notices.

Except as otherwise provided in this Agreement, any and all notices, consents, waivers, directions, requests, votes, or other instruments or communications provided for under this Agreement shall be in writing, signed by the party giving the same, and shall be deemed properly given only if sent by registered or certified U.S. mail, postage prepaid, addressed: (a) in the case of the Partnership, to the Partnership, at the principal place of business of the Partnership, or (b) in the case of any Partner individually, to such Partner at his address set forth in Exhibit A hereto. Any notice so given shall be deemed to have been received as of the date on which it was mailed. Each Partner may, by notice to the Partnership, specify any other address for the receipt of such instruments or communications.

### 10.02   Integration.

This Agreement embodies the entire agreement and understanding among the Partners relating to the subject matter hereof, and supersedes all prior agreements and understandings relating to such subject matter.

### 10.03   Applicable Law.

This Agreement and the rights of the Partners shall be governed by and construed and enforced in accordance with the laws of the State of Minnesota.

### 10.04   Counterparts.

This Agreement may be executed in several counterparts and all so executed shall constitute one Agreement binding on all the parties hereto, notwithstanding that all parties are not signatory to the original or the same counterpart, except that no counterpart shall be authentic unless signed by a Partner.

### 10.05 Separability.

In case any one or more of the provisions contained in this Agreement or any application thereof shall be invalid, illegal or unenforceable in any respect, the validity, legality, and enforceability of the remaining provisions contained herein and any other application thereof shall not in any way be affected or impaired thereby.

### 10.06 Binding Effect.

Except as herein otherwise provided to the contrary, this Agreement shall be binding upon, and insure to the benefit of, the Partners and their respective heirs, executors, administrators, successors, and permitted assigns.

IN WITNESS WHEREOF, the undersigned have hereunto signed their respective names as of the date first above written.

PARTNERS

_____

_____

(12) Signature lines for Partners

(13) Name of Partnership

**PARTNERSHIP AGREEMENT**

## Name and Address of Partners                     % of Profits and
Losses of Partnership

(14) Name, Residence Address, and Ownership
     Percentage of Partners

(15) Name of Partnership
**PARTNERSHIP AGREEMENT**

Names of Partners    Amount of Contribution    Date of Contribution

(16) Names of Partners, dollar amount of
contribution, and date of contribution

# SAMPLE CHART OF ACCOUNTS

| Account No. | Schedule | Account Description |
|---|---|---|
| 98 | | BALANCE SHEET |
| 100 | | ASSETS |
| 101 | | CURRENT ASSETS |
| 103 | | CASH IN BANK |
| 104 | | —SAVING |
| 105 | | —REGULAR |
| 106 | | —TRUST |
| 108 | | —PAYROLL |
| 113 | | NOTES RECEIVABLES |
| 114 | | OTHER RECEIVABLES |
| 118 | | DUE FROM [          ] |
| 119 | | DUE FROM [          ] |
| 120 | | DUE FROM [          ] |
| 139 | | TOTAL CURRENT ASSETS |
| 140 | | PROPERTY AND EQUIPMENT |
| 141 | | OFFICE FURN & FIXTURES |
| 142 | | ACCUMULATED DEPRECIATION |
| 143 | | OFFICE EQUIPMENT |
| 144 | | ACCUMULATED DEPRECIATION |
| 145 | | LEASEHOLD IMPROVEMENTS |
| 146 | | ACCUMULATED DEPRECIATION |
| 147 | | VEHICLES |
| 148 | | ACCUMULATED DEPRECIATION |
| 159 | | NET PROPERTY & EQUIPMENT |
| 160 | | OTHER ASSETS |
| 161 | | PREPAID EXPENSES |
| 162 | | RENT |
| 163 | | INTEREST |
| 164 | | OFFICE SUPPLIES |
| 165 | | OTHER EXPENSES |
| 169 | | SMALL EQUIPMENT SUPPLIES |
| 170 | | |
| 171 | | |
| 172 | | ACCUMULATED DEPRECIATION |
| 175 | | GOODWILL |
| 179 | | TOTAL OTHER ASSETS |
| 199 | | TOTAL ASSETS |

| Account No. | Account Description |
|---|---|
| 200 | LIABILITIES AND STOCKHOLDERS |
| 203 | LIABILITIES |
| 204 | CURRENT LIABILITIES |
| 205 | DEPOSITS HELD IN TRUST |
| 206 | INSTALL. NOTE PAY. |
| 207 | LOANS PAYABLE [         ] |
| 208 | LOANS PAYABLE [         ] |
| 209 | LOANS PAYABLE [         ] |
| 211 | PAYROLL TAXES PAYABLE |
| 212 | FICA TAXES |
| 213 | FEDERAL W/H TAXES |
| 214 | MINNESOTA W/H TAXES |
| 220 | ACCOUNTS PAYABLE |
| 225 | ACCRUED INTEREST |
| 230 | DUE TO [         ] |
| 235 | DUE TO [         ] |
| 239 | TOTAL CURRENT LIABILITIES |
| 240 | LONG-TERM DEBT |
| 241 | INSTALLMENT N/P-AUTO |
| 243 | INSTALLMENT NOTES PAY. |
| 244 | LESS CURRENT PORTION |
| 258 | TOTAL LONG-TERM DEBT |
| 259 | TOTAL LIABILITIES |
| 260 | STOCKHOLDERS' EQUITY |
| 261 | COMMON STOCK |
| 262 | PAID IN CAPITAL |
| 263 | INCORPORATION ADJ.—NET |
| 264 | RETAINED EARNINGS |
| 266 | TREASURY STOCK |
| 298 | TOTAL STOCKHOLDERS' EQUITY |
| 299 | TOTAL LIABILITIES AND EQUITY |
| 300 | STATEMENT OF OPERATIONS |
| 301 | REVENUES |
| 302 | FEE INCOME |
| 310 | INTEREST INCOME |
| 312 | MISCELLANEOUS INCOME |
| 399 | TOTAL REVENUE |
| 401 | CLIENT EXPENSES |
| 499 | GROSS PROFIT |
| 500 | OPERATING EXPENSES |

| Account No. | Account Description |
|---|---|
| 501 | ACCOUNTING FEES |
| 503 | ADVERTISING |
| 505 | ASSOCIATION EXPENSE |
| 506 | AUTO EXPENSE—EMPLOYEES |
| 507 | AUTO EXPENSE—[          ] |
| 508 | AUTO EXPENSE—[          ] |
| 509 | AUTO EXPENSE—[          ] |
| 513 | BAD DEBTS |
| 515 | BILLING FEES—A/R |
| 516 | CASUAL LABOR |
| 517 | COFFEE SUPPLIES |
| 520 | CONTRACTURAL SERVICES |
| 521 | CONSULTING FEE |
| 522 | CONTRIBUTIONS |
| 524 | DEPRECIATION—AUTO |
| 525 | DEPRECIATION—OFFICE |
| 526 | EMPLOYEE RELATIONS |
| 527 | ENTERTAINMENT & PROM. |
| 528 | FRINGE BENEFITS—EMPLOYEE |
| 529 | FRINGE BENEFIT—HOSPITAL |
| 530 | HOSP—[          ] |
| 531 | HOSP—[          ] |
| 532 | HOSP—[          ] |
| 536 | FRINGE BENEFIT—SPOUSE LIFE |
| 537 | SPOUSE LIFE—[          ] |
| 538 | SPOUSE LIFE—[          ] |
| 539 | SPOUSE LIFE—[          ] |
| 543 | FRINGE BENEFIT—MED REIMB |
| 544 | MED REIMB—[          ] |
| 545 | MED REIMB—[          ] |
| 546 | MED REIMB—[          ] |
| 549 | GROUP DUES |
| 551 | INSURANCE—GENERAL |
| 554 | LIBRARY MAINTENANCE |
| 559 | MISCELLANEOUS |
| 562 | OFFICE SUPPLIES |
| 565 | PAYROLL TAXES |
| 566 | PETTY CASH |
| 567 | POSTAGE |
| 569 | PROFESSIONAL DEVELOPMENT |
| 572 | PROFESSIONAL DUES |

| Account No. | Account Description |
|---|---|
| 573 | PROF DUES—[          ] |
| 574 | PROF DUES—[          ] |
| 580 | RENT—OFFICE |
| 581 | RENT—OFFICE EQUIPMENT |
| 583 | REPAIRS & MAINTENANCE |
| 585 | SALARIES—OFFICE |
| 586 | SALARIES—PROF STAFF |
| 588 | SALARIES—OFFICERS |
| 589 | SALARIES—[          ] |
| 590 | SALARIES—[          ] |
| 591 | SALARIES—[          ] |
| 594 | SALES TAX ON FIXED ASSET |
| 595 | SECRETARIAL SERVICES |
| 597 | TELEPHONE |
| 599 | TRAVEL EXPENSES |
| 601 | FRINGE BENEFITS—FIRM LIFE |
| 602 | FIRM LIFE—[          ] |
| 603 | FIRM LIFE—[          ] |
| 604 | FIRM LIFE—[          ] |
| 607 | FRINGE BENEFIT—DISABILITY |
| 608 | DISABILITY—[          ] |
| 609 | DISABILITY—[          ] |
| 610 | DISABILITY—[          ] |
| 615 | FRINGE BENE—EMP MED REIMB |
| 616 | MED REIMB—[          ] |
| 617 | MED REIMB—[          ] |
| 618 | MED REIMB—[          ] |
| 619 | MED REIMB—[          ] |
| 620 | MED REIMB—[          ] |
| 621 | MED REIMB—[          ] |
| 622 | MED REIMB—[          ] |
| 623 | MED REIMB—[          ] |
| 624 | MED REIMB—[          ] |
| 669 | TOTAL OPERATING EXPENSES |
| 699 | OPERATING PROFIT (LOSS) |
| 700 | OTHER EXPENSES |
| 701 | INTEREST |
| 707 | PROFIT SHARE CONTRIBUTION |
| 709 | INCOME TAXES |
| 798 | TOTAL OTHER EXPENSES |
| 799 | NET INCOME (LOSS) |

# INDEX